mastery
education

READING | LEVEL | **C**

m^eeasuring Up.
to the
TEXAS ESSENTIAL KNOWLEDGE AND SKILLS

STUDENT EDITION

D1249920

STAAR
EDITION

Copyright © 2013
Mastery Education™ (formerly Peoples Education)
299 Market Street
Saddle Brook, New Jersey 07663

ISBN 978-1-61526-816-0

Printed in the United States of America.

30   29   28   27   26   25

Contents

UNIT 1   Getting Started

Chapter 1   Beginning Reading: Comprehension Skills and Strategies

Chapter 2   Beginning Reading: Phonics

Note: **Eligible standards** are written in **boldface**.   **Ⓡ** = Readiness standard   **Ⓢ** = Supporting standard

UNIT 1 (continued)

Chapter 3 — Reading/Media Literacy

UNIT 2 — Understanding Across Genres

Chapter 1 — Reading/Vocabulary Development

UNIT 3 — Understanding and Analysis of Literary Texts

Chapter 1 — Reading/Comprehension of Literary Text/Sensory Language

UNIT 3 (continued)

Chapter 2

Reading/Comprehension of Literary Text/Theme and Genre

Chapter 3

Reading/Comprehension of Literary Text/Poetry

Chapter 4

Reading/Comprehension of Literary Text/Drama

UNIT 3 (continued)

Chapter 5 — Reading/Comprehension of Literary Text/Fiction

UNIT 4 (continued)

Lesson Correlation to the Grade 3 Texas Essential Knowledge and Skills

This worktext is customized to the *Texas Essential Knowledge and Skills* and will help you prepare for the *State of Texas Assessments of Academic Readiness (STAAR)* in Reading for Grade 3.

Texas Essential Knowledge and Skills	*Measuring Up* Lessons
TEKS 3.1 Reading/Beginning Reading Skills/Phonics. Students use the relationship between letters and sounds, spelling patterns, and morphological analysis to decode written English. Students are expected to:	
(A) Decode multisyllabic words in context and independent of context by applying common letter-sound correspondences including:	7, 12
(i) dropping the final "e" and add endings such as –ing, -ed, or –able (e.g., use, using, used, usable).	7
(ii) doubling final consonants when adding an ending (e.g., hop to hopping).	7
(iii) changing the final "y" to "i" (e.g., baby to babies).	7
(iv) using knowledge of common prefixes and suffixes (e.g., dis-, -ly).	12
(v) using knowledge of derivational affixes (e.g., -de, -ful, -able).	12
(B) use common syllabication patterns to decode words including:	9
(i) closed syllable (CVC) (e.g., mag-net, splen-did).	9
(ii) open syllable (CV) (e.g., ve-to).	9
(iii) final stable syllable (e.g., puz-zle, con-trac-tion).	9
(iv) r-controlled vowels (e.g., fer-ment, car-pool).	9
(v) vowel digraphs and diphthongs (e.g., ei-ther).	9
(C) decode words by applying knowledge of common spelling patterns (e.g., -eigh, -ought).	8
(D) identify and read contractions (e.g., I'd, won't).	10
(E) monitor accuracy of decoding.	7, 8, 9, 10
TEKS 3.2 Readings/Beginning Readings/Strategies. Students comprehend a variety of texts drawing on useful strategies as needed. Students are expected to:	
(A) use ideas (e.g., illustrations, titles, topic sentences, key words, and foreshadowing clues) to make and confirm predictions.	1, 29
(B) ask relevant questions, seek clarification, and locate facts and details about stories and other texts and support answers with evidence from text.	2, 16–24
(C) establish purpose for reading selected texts and monitor comprehension, making corrections and adjustments when that understanding breaks down (e.g., identifying clues, using background knowledge, generating questions, re-reading a portion aloud).	3
TEKS 3.3 Reading/Fluency. Students read grade-level text with fluency and comprehension. Students are expected to	
read aloud grade-level appropriate text with fluency (rate, accuracy, expression, appropriate phrasing) and comprehension.	2, 3, 22
TEKS 3.4 Reading/Vocabulary Development. Students understand new vocabulary and use it when reading and writing. Students are expected to:	
(A) identify the meaning of common prefixes (e.g., in-, dis-) and suffixes (e.g., -full, -less), and know how they change the meaning of roots.	12
(B) use context to determine the relevant meaning of unfamiliar words or distinguish among multiple meaning words and homographs.	13
(C) identify and use antonyms, synonyms, homographs, and homophones.	14

Texas Essential Knowledge and Skills	*Measuring Up* Lessons
(D) identify and apply playful uses of language (e.g., tongue twisters, palindromes, riddles).	14
(E) alphabetize a series of words to the third letter and use a dictionary or a glossary to determine the meanings, syllabication, and pronunciation of unknown words.	15
TEKS 3.5 Reading/Comprehension of Literary Text/Theme and Genre. Students analyze, make inferences and draw conclusions about theme and genre in different cultural, historical, and contemporary contexts and provide evidence from the text to support their understanding. Students are expected to:	
(A) paraphrase the themes and supporting details of fables, legends, myths, or stories.	17
(B) compare and contrast the settings in myths and traditional folktales.	18
TEKS 3.6 Reading/Comprehension of Literary Text/Poetry. Students understand, make inferences and draw conclusions about the structure and elements of poetry and provide evidence from text to support their understandings. Students are expected to	
describe the characteristics of various forms of poetry and how they create imagery (e.g., narrative poetry, lyrical poetry, humorous poetry, free verse).	19
TEKS 3.7 Reading/Comprehension of Literary Text/Drama. Students understand, make inferences and draw conclusions about the structure and elements of drama and provide evidence from text to support their understanding. Students are expected to	
identify the elements of plot and character as presented through dialogue in scripts that are read, viewed, written, or performed.	20
TEKS 3.8 Reading/Comprehension of Literary Text/Fiction. Students understand, make inferences and draw conclusions about the structure and elements of fiction and provide evidence from text to support their understanding. Students are expected to:	
(A) sequence and summarize the plot's main events and explain their influence on future events.	21
(B) describe the interaction of characters including their relationships and the changes they undergo.	22
(C) identify whether the narrator or speaker of a story is first or third person.	23
TEKS 3.9 Reading/Comprehension of Literary Text/Literary Nonfiction. Students understand, make inferences and draw conclusions about the varied structural patterns and features of literary nonfiction and respond by providing evidence from text to support their understanding. Students are expected to	
explain the difference in point of view between a biography and autobiography.	24
TEKS 3.10 Reading/Comprehension of Literary Text/Sensory Language. Students understand, make inferences and draw conclusions about how an author's sensory language creates imagery in literary text and provide evidence from text to support their understanding. Students are expected to	
identify language that creates a graphic visual experience and appeals to the senses.	16
TEKS 3.12 Reading/Comprehension of Informational Text/Culture and History. Students analyze, make inferences and draw conclusions about the author's purpose in cultural, historical, and contemporary contexts and provide evidence from the text to support their understanding. Students are expected to	
identify the topic and explain the author's stated purpose in writing the text.	25
TEKS 3.13 Reading/Comprehension of Informational Text/Expository Text. Students analyze, make inferences and draw conclusions about expository text and provide evidence from text to support their understanding. Students are expected to:	
(A) identify the details or facts that support the main idea.	26
(B) draw conclusions from the facts presented in text and support those assertions with textual evidence.	27
(C) identify explicit cause and effect relationships among ideas in texts.	28

Texas Essential Knowledge and Skills	*Measuring Up* Lessons
(D) use text features (e.g., bold print, captions, key words, italics) to locate information and make and verify predictions about contents of text.	29
TEKS 3.14 Reading/Comprehension of Informational Text/Persuasive Text. Students analyze, make inferences and draw conclusions about persuasive text and provide evidence from text to support their analysis. Students are expected to	
identify what the author is trying to persuade the reader to think or do.	30
TEKS 3.15 Reading/Comprehension of Informational Text/Procedural Texts. Students understand how to glean and use information in procedural texts and documents. Students are expected to:	
(A) follow and explain a set of written multi-step directions.	31
(B) locate and use specific information in graphic features of text.	31
TEKS 3.16 Reading/Media Literacy. Students use comprehension skills to analyze how words, images, graphics, and sounds work together in various forms to impact meaning. Students will continue to apply earlier standards with greater depth in increasingly more complex texts. Students are expected to:	
(A) understand how communication changes when moving from one genre of media to another.	11
(B) explain how various design techniques used in media influence the message (e.g., shape, color, sound).	11
(C) compare various written conventions used for digital media (e.g., language in an informal e-mail vs. language in a web-based news article).	11
Figure 19 Reading/Comprehension Skills. Students use a flexible range of metacognitive reading skills in both assigned and independent reading to understand an author's message. Students will continue to apply earlier standards with greater depth in increasingly more complex texts as they become self-directed, critical readers. The student is expected to:	
(A) establish purposes for reading selected texts based upon own or others' desired outcome to enhance comprehension.	3
(B) ask literal, interpretive, and evaluative questions of text.	2
(C) monitor and adjust comprehension (e.g., using background knowledge, creating sensory images, re-reading a portion aloud, generating questions).	3
(D) make inferences about text using textual evidence to support understanding.	4, 16, 18–25, 27–30
(E) summarize information in text, maintaining meaning and logical order.	5, 21, 25, 26, 28–30
(F) make connections (e.g., thematic links, author analysis) between literary and informational texts with similar ideas and provide textual evidence.	6

Measuring Up

to the
Texas Essential Knowledge and Skills
TEXAS ⭐ STAAR EDITION

Dear Student,

How do you get better at anything you do? Just as with sports or other activities, the key to success in school is practice, practice, practice.

This book will help you review and practice reading strategies and skills. These are the strategies and skills you need to know to measure up to the Texas Essential Knowledge and Skills, or TEKS, for your grade. Practicing these skills and strategies now will help you do better in your work all year.

Throughout this book, you will have the chance to practice the following skills: learning and using new words, reading literary and informational texts, understanding and analyzing what you read, evaluating the impact of media, and applying comprehension skills.

Each lesson consists of three sections:

• **Understand the TEKS** introduces the TEKS skills academic standards covered in the lesson.

• **Guided Instruction** walks you through a reading passage and shows you how to apply your knowledge and skills.

• **On Your Own** gives you the opportunity to read independently, apply what you have learned, and demonstrate your understanding.

There are many chances for you to practice for the STAAR, with STAAR Minitests throughout this book. Each STAAR Minitest has a story for you to read and multiple-choice questions that are like the ones you will see on tests to test your understanding. The questions include a range of difficulties, to truly prepare you for taking the STAAR.

Good luck!

Measuring Up
to the
Texas Essential Knowledge and Skills
TEXAS ★ STAAR EDITION

To Parents and Families,

All students need reading skills to be college and career-ready. The Texas Essential Knowledge and Skills, or TEKS, provide grade-level standards describing what Texas students should know at each grade level for Reading. Students need to meet these standards and must learn to consider, analyze, interpret, and evaluate information instead of just recalling simple facts.

Measuring Up will help your child review the TEKS and prepare for reading tests, including the State of Texas Assessments of Academic Readiness, or STAAR. It contains:

- lessons that focus on practicing the TEKS

- varied reading selections

- **Guided Instruction** with numbered paragraphs and cross-curricular connections that builds student test-taking confidence. Questions prompt students to use critical thinking skills and help them master the TEKS.

- **STAAR Minitests** practice with more difficult multiple-choice questions that require critical thinking. These questions prepare students for the ones they will see on the STAAR.

For success in school and the real world, your child needs good reading skills. Get involved! Your involvement is crucial to your child's success. Here are some suggestions:

- Read aloud to your child. Find a quiet place to read. If the book has pictures, talk about them. As your child listens, ask him or her to anticipate what will happen next. Talk about the characters and what happens to them.

- Treat reading as a pleasure, not a punishment. Give books as presents and show that you like to receive them, too. Respect each other's private reading time.

- Make sure your child has a library card and visit the library together. Also visit bookstores or attend author talks and storytelling sessions.

Work with us to ensure your child's success. Reading is essential for success not only in school but throughout your child's life.

easuring Up

to the
Texas Essential Knowledge and Skills
TEXAS ★ STAAR
EDITION

A los padres y las familias:

Todos los estudiantes necesitan destrezas de lectura para tener éxito en la universidad y en su profesión. El Texas Essential Knowledge and Skills, o TEKS, provee estándares de nivel de grado que describen lo que los estudiantes de Texas deben saber en cada nivel de grado. Los estudiantes deben cumplir estos estándares y aprender a considerar, analizar, interpretar y evaluar en lugar de solo repetir simples hechos.

Measuring Up ayudará a su hijo a repasar los TEKS y a prepararse para los exámenes de lectura, incluyendo el State of Texas Assessments of Academic Readiness, o STAAR. Contiene:

• lecciones que se enfocan en la práctica de los TEKS

• selecciones de lecturas variadas

• **Enseñanza guiada** con párrafos numerados y conexiones intercurriculares que afianzan al estudiante para tomar exámenes. Las preguntas impulsan a los estudiantes a usar el razonamiento crítico y los ayuda a dominar los TEKS.

• **Miniexámenes STAAR** práctica con preguntas más difíciles de opción múltiple que requieren pensamiento crítico. Estas preguntas preparan a los estudiantes para las que verán en el examen STAAR.

Para triunfar en la escuela y en el mundo real, su hijo necesita buenas destrezas de lectura. ¡Participen! Su participación es crucial para el éxito de su hijo. Hay aquí algunas sugerencias:

• Lean en voz alta con su hijo. Busquen un lugar tranquilo para leer. Si el libro tiene ilustraciones, hablen de ellas. A medida que su hijo escucha, pídanle que anticipe lo que va a ocurrir. Hablen de los personajes y de lo que les sucede.

• Traten la lectura como un placer, no como un castigo. Regalen libros y demuestren que les gusta recibirlos también. Respeten los momentos privados de lectura tanto de su hijo como los de ustedes mismos.

• Asegúrese de que su hijo tenga una tarjeta de biblioteca y visitar la biblioteca juntos. También visite las librerías o asistir a charlas autor y sesiones de cuentos.

Trabaje con nosotros para asegurar el éxito de su hijo. La lectura es esencial para el éxito no sólo en la escuela, sino durante toda la vida de su hijo.

mastery
education

What's Ahead in Measuring Up
to the TEKS

Each lesson and Minitest will help you master the TEKS and prepare for the STAAR. It will also help you prepare for other reading exams you take during the school year.

About the TEKS

This book covers the Texas Essential Knowledge and Skills, or TEKS, preparing students for what they should know at each grade level as well as for the STAAR reading exam.

Measuring Up on Multiple-Choice Items

A multiple-choice item has two parts. The first part is called the stem. It has a number in front of it. Sometimes, the stem is in the form of a question. Other times, the stem is in the form of a statement you need to complete. The second part of a multiple-choice item consists of the answer choices.

There are strategies for answering multiple-choice items. Try these:

- Skim all the multiple-choice questions. Start by answering the ones you think are the easiest.
- Cross out the answer choices you know are wrong. Then choose from the choices that are left.
- If an item refers to a paragraph, make sure you reread that paragraph.
- Some items will be more difficult than others. You must connect ideas and information to come up with the right answers.
- Even if you don't know the answer, you can make a good guess based on what you know and get the item right.
- Check and double-check your answers before you turn in the test. Be sure of your answers.

What's Ahead in 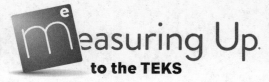easuring Up. to the TEKS

Critical-Thinking Skills

Critical-thinking skills are important. When you use critical-thinking skills, you do more than just recall information. On the test, some questions ask you to make judgments, inferences, or predictions; to form generalizations; and so on. For instance, instead of asking you what a character wore, a question might ask you how what the character wore affected the way she acted. Or, instead of asking you how something happened, a question might ask you why something happened. Rereading parts of the text will help you answer these kinds of questions.

Measuring Up STAAR Minitests

A special feature of *Measuring Up* is the STAAR Minitest. It was created to give you practice and build your confidence for taking hard tests. The more you practice answering hard questions, the more prepared you will be to succeed. Each STAAR Minitest is a review of all the TEKS covered in the lessons and will also give you practice with selections similar to those on the test.

What's Inside: A Lesson Guide

Lessons in this book are divided into three sections in which the Texas Essential Knowledge and Skills are introduced, explained and applied, and independently practiced.

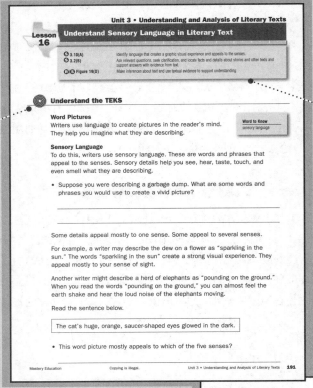

Understand the TEKS
Introduces and explains the reading skill(s) and important terms covered in the lesson.

Words to Know identifies imp ant terms in the lesson, with those words highlighted in context.

Lessons include a list of the Readiness and Supporting TEKS on which the lesson focuses.

Guided Instruction
features a reading selection with Guided Questions that help you interact with the text. The guided reading selection may be followed by additional exercises to challenge you to think about the text in deeper, more complex ways.

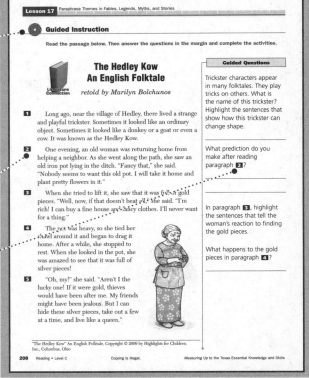

Guided Questions check how well you understand the reading selection and challenge you to think about the passage. Paragraphs are numbered to help you find specific sections.

On Your Own

Read a second passage and answer the items that follow to apply the skills you have learned.

Passages include a wide variety of literature to help you build reading comprehension skills and make connections across texts.

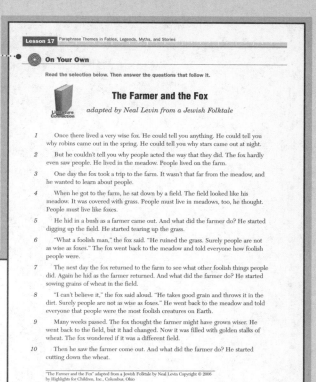

On Your Own

Read the selection below. Then answer the questions that follow it.

The Farmer and the Fox

adapted by Neal Levin from a Jewish Folktale

1   Once there lived a very wise fox. He could tell you anything. He could tell you why robins came out in the spring. He could tell you why stars came out at night.

2   But he couldn't tell you why people acted the way that they did. The fox hardly even saw people. He lived in the meadow. People lived on the farm.

3   One day the fox took a trip to the farm. It wasn't that far from the meadow, and he wanted to learn about people.

4   When he got to the farm, he sat down by a field. The field looked like his meadow. It was covered with grass. People must live in meadows, too, he thought. People must live like foxes.

5   He hid in a bush as a farmer came out. And what did the farmer do? He started digging up the field. He started tearing up the grass.

6   "What a foolish man," the fox said. "He ruined the grass. Surely people are not as wise as foxes." The fox went back to the meadow and told everyone how foolish people were.

7   The next day the fox returned to the farm to see what other foolish things people did. Again he hid as the farmer returned. And what did the farmer do? He started sowing grains of wheat in the field.

8   "I can't believe it," the fox said aloud. "He takes good grain and throws it in the dirt. Surely people are not as wise as foxes." He went back to the meadow and told everyone that people were the most foolish creatures on Earth.

9   Many weeks passed. The fox thought the farmer might have grown wiser. He went back to the field, but it had changed. Now it was filled with golden stalks of wheat. The fox wondered if it was a different field.

10   Then he saw the farmer come out. And what did the farmer do? He started cutting down the wheat.

"The Farmer and the Fox" adapted from a Jewish Folktale by Neal Levin Copyright © 2006 by Highlights for Children, Inc., Columbus, Ohio

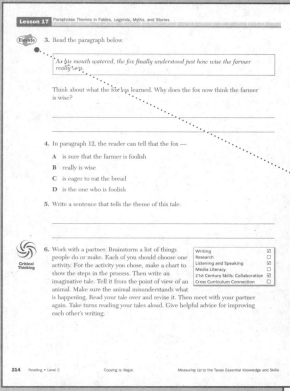

Elevate 3. Read the paragraph below.

> As his mouth watered, the fox finally understood just how wise the farmer really was.

Think about what the fox has learned. Why does the fox now think the farmer is wise?

_____

4. In paragraph 12, the reader can tell that the fox —

A   is sure that the farmer is foolish

B   really is wise

C   is eager to eat the bread

D   is the one who is foolish

5. Write a sentence that tells the theme of this tale.

_____

Critical Thinking 6. Work with a partner. Brainstorm a list of things people do or make. Each of you should choose one activity. For the activity you chose, make a chart to show the steps in the process. Then write an imaginative tale. Tell it from the point of view of an animal. Make sure the animal misunderstands what is happening. Read your tale over and revise it. Then meet with your partner again. Take turns reading your tales aloud. Give helpful advice for improving each other's writing.

Writing	☑
Research	☐
Listening and Speaking	☑
Media Literacy	☐
21st Century Skills: Collaboration	☑
Cross Curriculum Connection	☐

Icons identify Elevate items, which require critical-thinking skills. Icons are also used to call out Critical Thinking exercises and to point out connections to other school subjects and real-world topics.

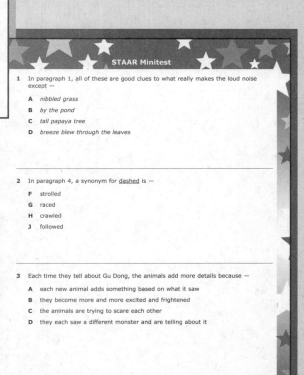

STAAR Minitest

1   In paragraph 1, all of these are good clues to what really makes the loud noise except —

A   *nibbled grass*

B   *by the pond*

C   *tall papaya tree*

D   *breeze blew through the leaves*

2   In paragraph 4, a synonym for <u>dashed</u> is —

F   strolled

G   raced

H   crawled

J   followed

3   Each time they tell about Gu Dong, the animals add more details because —

A   each new animal adds something based on what it saw

B   they become more and more excited and frightened

C   the animals are trying to scare each other

D   they each saw a different monster and are telling about it

STAAR Minitest

Practice what you have learned and show how well you mastered the focus TEKS with questions that match the STAAR. Lessons follow the STAAR multiple choice format and draw upon what you learned in previous lessons.

Lesson 1

Make and Confirm Predictions

3.2(A)   Use ideas (e.g., illustrations, titles, topic sentences, key words, and foreshadowing clues) to make and confirm predictions.

 ## Understand the TEKS

Predictions

A **prediction** is a guess about the future. You make predictions all the time. For example, you see gray clouds forming overhead. The sky darkens. You hear a clap of thunder.

- Based on these details, what do you predict?

> **Words to Know**
> caption
> fiction
> foreshadowing
> nonfiction
> prediction
> title

Fiction and Nonfiction

Fiction is literature that is made up. It comes from the writer's imagination. When a story is made up, the characters are not real people. What happens to them is not real.

Nonfiction tells about real people and events. It contains facts and details about the real world. If it tells a story, then the people are real people and what happens really did happen.

- Write the title of one fiction book or story you have read this year.

- Write the title of one nonfiction book or article you have read this year.

Make predictions when you read fiction and nonfiction. Both have a feature that helps you predict what the selection is about before you start reading. This feature is the title.

- Suppose you read the title "The Tale of Robbie Rabbit's Tail." Do you think this selection will be fiction or nonfiction? Why?

• What do you predict this selection will tell about?

_____

_____

Make Predictions

As you read, pause from time to time. Predict what will happen next. Predict what the rest of the text will tell about. Base your prediction on what you already know from clues and other information in the article.

When you read **fiction**, predict what the characters will do. Think about how the story will turn out.

• The author may plant clues or hints early in the story about what will happen later. This is called **foreshadowing.**

• The author may tell you how the characters are feeling and what they are thinking. This helps you predict how they will act.

• The story may have **illustrations.** Look for important details in the illustrations. The details in the pictures may help you make predictions.

Nonfiction often has special features that help you make predictions.

• **Headings** A heading is a title above a group of paragraphs. A heading helps you predict what information you will find in that section. Glancing at all the headings before you read helps you predict what the selection is about.

• **Topic sentences** A topic sentence tells you the most important idea in a paragraph. It helps you predict what other information you will find in that paragraph.

• **Key or important words** Important words may be set in **boldface** type. Glancing at these boldface words and putting them together helps you predict what the article is about.

• **Illustrations and captions** Nonfiction often contains illustrations that show important information. A **caption** is the title or the sentence below the illustration. Use the information in illustrations and captions to predict.

 Measuring Up to the Texas Essential Knowledge and Skills

Confirm Predictions

After you make a prediction, read on to **confirm** it, or see if your prediction was right. If it was incorrect, you might want to go back and reread a sentence or passage. This way, you can see what information you missed. Then you can **revise** or make a new prediction based on new information.

Comprehension Tip

Use sticky notes as you read. Place them by details you use to make your predictions. Write your predictions on the notes. If you need to revise your predictions, reading over these notes will help you.

Guided Instruction

Read the passage below. Then answer the questions in the margin and complete the activities.

Science Connection

Weaving in My Mango Tree

by Radha H S

1   When I was growing up in India, there was a mango tree in our yard. I spent many hours under the shade of that tree, looking up for the first signs of fruit. Mangoes are sweet and juicy. As soon as I saw a ripe one, I wanted to eat it.

2   One day, I was searching the tree for mangoes when I saw something else. It was big and fuzzy and covered with leaves. Ants were crawling in and out of it. What was in my mango tree? I ran inside and asked my aunt.

Guided Questions

Look at the title and glance at the photographs in the selection. Do you think this selection will tell a true story or a made-up one? Why?

_____

_____

Read paragraph **2**. What do you think the narrator sees in her mango tree? Highlight words in the paragraph that help you make a prediction. (Hint: Glance at the photographs.)

_____

_____

_____

"Weaving in My Mango Tree" by Radha Hemmige Santhanam, Copyright © 2010 by Highlights for Children, Inc., Columbus, Ohio

3   My aunt told me the big fuzzy thing was a cocoon, home to the kenjga, also known as weaver ants. While many insects use silk to spin cocoons for themselves, weaver ants build a home for the whole community.

Weaver Ants Eat Flies

4   Weaver ants are big orange-red insects. If you bother these ants, they may bite you. But if you leave them alone, they could save your mango trees. Weaver ants eat fruit flies and other insects that harm fruit trees.

Weaver ants save mango trees.

5   My aunt told me to leave the weaver ants in the mango tree. Soon, they were living in other trees. Weaver ants can walk on pipes and tree branches to get to new trees. They can even walk on clotheslines. They sewed cocoons in our coconut trees. They made homes in our bitter-lime and lemon trees, too.

6   The weaver ants live in my mango tree to this day. And delicious mangoes still grow. We eat the ones the monkeys leave behind for us!

Weaver ants eat wasps and other insects that come near their cocoon.

Family Business

7   Weaver ants are hard workers. They use teamwork to make their nests. They pull together leaves. Once they have lined up the leaf edges, each adult ant holds a baby (larva) while it releases silk. The larva releases a sticky silk and glues the leaves together. This weaving of silk and leaves is how the weaver ants got their name.

Guided Questions

Look at the heading. Do you think this section will tell about ants working together or individually? Why?

_____

_____

_____

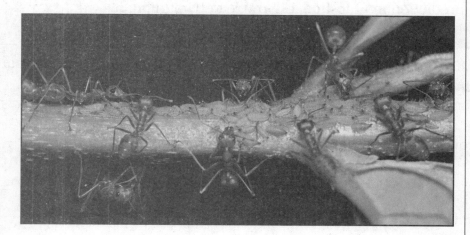

Cocoon

Larva

Answer the following questions based on the passage you just read.

1. Look at the caption for the photograph under paragraph 4. How does this caption help you predict that the narrator will not try to get rid of the weaver ants?

   _____

   _____

2. Keep in mind the prediction in Question 1. Now read paragraph 2.

   > *The weaver ants live in my mango tree to this day. And delicious mangoes still grow. We eat the ones the monkeys leave behind for us!*

   Which sentence confirms the prediction that the narrator will not get rid of the weaver ants?

   _____

3. Read the paragraph below.

   > *Weaver ants are hard workers. They use teamwork to make their nests. They pull together leaves. Once they have lined up the leaf edges, each adult ant holds a baby (larva) while it releases silk. The larva releases a sticky silk and glues the leaves together. This weaving of silk and leaves is how the weaver ants got their name.*

   Complete the sequence chart. Use information from the paragraph above.

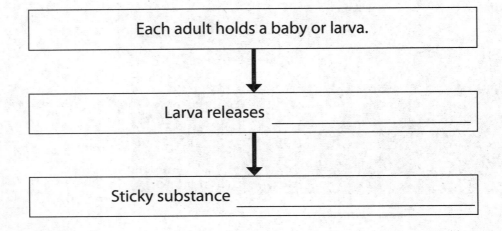

Each adult holds a baby or larva.

Larva releases _____

Sticky substance _____

4. What is the most important way that weaver ants are different from other ants?

5. "Weaving in My Mango Tree" is a magazine article. Imagine it were made into a television movie. Talk to a partner. How would it be different? Make notes about your discussion. Share it with your classmates.

Writing	☐
Research	☐
Listening and Speaking	☑
Media Literacy	☑
21st Century Skills: Collaboration	☑
Cross Curriculum Connection: Science	☑

Critical Thinking

6. Use the Internet or your school media center to find another article about weaver ants.

Media Connection

 On Your Own

Read the selection below. Then answer the questions that follow it.

The Most Beautiful Thing in the World

by Ella Kennen

Literature Connection

1 "I am bored," announced the queen.

2 Her advisor pressed his fingers together. "Some music, your majesty?"

"The Most Beautiful Thing in the World" Copyright © 2012 by Ella Kennen, reprinted with permission of the author.

3   The queen gave a slight nod. But when the court musicians started playing something she had heard a dozen times before, she sent them away.

4   Her advisor tugged at his moustache. "The court acrobats, then?"

5   The queen nodded again. But their flips and turns did not raise her spirits.

6   "What you need," said the advisor, "is a true diversion. A contest, perhaps."

7   The queen sat a little taller. "A contest, you say?" Then she sank back into her throne. "Whatever of?"

8   Her advisor furrowed his brow. "New music, perhaps?"

9   The queen waved her hand.

10   "A baking competition?"

11   The queen frowned.

12   Her advisor started to sweat. "I know! A contest of the best portrait of Her Highness."

13   The queen chortled. "Please. I already know what I look like. Besides, the hall is brimming with portraits."

14   She rose and started pacing. "I am tired of all this," she said, gesturing to the room. "I need a different sort of beauty. Something that can take one's breath away."

15   She gestured to her scribe. "Let everyone know that the Queen is holding a contest for the most beautiful thing in the world. And the prize," she paused, "the prize shall be this crown."

16   Her staff gasped. The queen's crown was pure gold, studded with magnificent gems. There was no treasure like it in the whole country.

17   The announcement was made. Before long, a constant line of hopefuls formed. People showed their poetry, their daughters, even their animals. After several days, the queen had a pounding headache.

18   "This is hopeless," she muttered.

19   "Not quite hopeless, Your Majesty."

20   The queen sat up, wondering who dare contradict her.

21   A bearded man stood behind the palace guards. "I can put an end to this madness, Your Highness." He waved towards the long line of supplicants behind him.

22   The queen raised an eyebrow. "You have brought me the most beautiful thing?"

23   The man laughed. "Not I. Nor anyone here. I have stood in line for two days as your faithful servant to tell you that you seek that which cannot be brought to you. You must go to it." The man gave a deep bow. "That is all."

24   The queen paused, astonished. When she found her voice again she asked, "Whatever do you mean?"

25   But the man was gone.

26   The queen's advisor twisted his hat. "Do not bother yourself with the prattle of a madman, Madam," he said.

27   But the fever of an idea had struck the queen. "Send the rest home," she ordered of the people still waiting in line. "I must prepare for a trip."

28   The advisor nearly dropped his hat. "A trip? Where?"

29   The queen smiled as she had not done since she was a child. "Elsewhere!"

30   A Royal Trip, even one as odd as this, doesn't just happen. Wardrobes and food wagons must be prepared. Soldiers, footmen, and ladies-in-waiting must ready themselves. But after several days of bustle, the royal procession was ready. By now, the Queen was cured of her boredom, and almost delirious to see what awaited.

31   Crowds gathered as the entourage made its way out of the city. The Queen leaned out the carriage window and held her crown high. "To the most beautiful thing in the world!" she cried.

32   "To the most beautiful," the crowds cheered back. The fever had caught, and spread.

33   The queen was not sure what she was seeking, or where to find it. But as her entourage rounded a hill, she looked back to her royal home and felt something stir within her. Between the glow of the setting sun and the gleam of the white towers, the scene looked like something out of a storybook. "Why," she wondered, "have I never seen my home this way before?"

34   The queen spent weeks travelling. She saw beauty in the peasants coaxing life out of the dirt. She saw it in the birds taking one last flight before roosting for the night. In a newly born calf. In the stars twinkling at night. But what was the most beautiful thing?

35   One day, the queen sailed a lake. In the middle of the water, she realized that she was at peace—and that she had been for many days. Suddenly, she understood. With all her might, she tore a piece of her crown off. She tossed the fragment into the lake and watched it slowly sink. "I am ready to return home," she announced.

36   As she journeyed back, the queen left a piece of crown at a small country church. She left a piece at the root of a centuries-old tree. She placed a piece at the bottom of a lush valley and the top of a snow-capped mountain. When her procession stumbled upon a spring, bubbling water from the ground, she added a piece there. She dug a piece into the newly turned dirt in a field. She threaded a piece into the mane a fine filly. Little by little, the queen's crown got smaller until nothing was left.

37   She had found the most beautiful thing. It was the world.

Answer the following questions based on the passage you just read.

1. Before you started reading, what detail helped you predict where this story takes place?

   _____

   Based on the illustration, what did you think the story would be about?

   _____

   _____

 2. Glance at the way this story looks. Which text features helped you predict that this was a fictional story?

   _____

   _____

   _____

 3. Based on the details in paragraphs 1–5, the reader can predict that the queen —

   A will leave the castle

   B will be hard to please

   C will meet a strange man

   D will give away her crown

4. Use the chart below. List some of the places where the queen found beauty. Then write a sentence that tells what the queen learned about finding beauty.

The queen found beauty:	The queen learned that

5. Which sentence from paragraphs 25–27 best helps the reader predict that the queen will try to understand what the bearded man was telling her about finding beauty?

   A *But the man was gone.*

   B *The queen's advisor twisted his hat.*

   C *But the fever of an idea had struck the queen.*

   D *"Send the rest home," she ordered of the people still waiting in line.*

6. Which detail best predicts that the queen will find beauty?

   A The bearded man disappears before explaining himself.

   B The queen looks back at her home and sees it differently.

   C The illustration of the queen standing outside the castle

   D The queen is very unhappy at the beginning of the story.

7. Read the following sentence from the story (paragraph 32).

> *The <u>fever</u> had caught, and spread.*

What does the word *fever* mean?

_____

8. Think about the process of reading. Did you find making predictions as you read helped you better understand the story? Explain.

_____

_____

_____

_____

Critical Thinking

9. Talk with a partner. Evaluate the story that you just read. Do you think it is a good story? Why or why not? What is the message of the story? What does this message mean to you? How are your beliefs about beauty like the queen's? How are they different? After your discussion, write a paragraph or two summarizing your ideas.

Writing	☑
Research	☐
Listening and Speaking	☑
Media Literacy	☐
21st Century Skills: Collaboration	☑
Cross Curriculum Connections	☐

Media Connection

10. Thumb through magazines and books. Find another story that takes place in a castle. You may want to ask a librarian or media specialist to help you. Share it with a partner. Does the story have a lot of dialogue? Is it about a king or queen? Do the characters learn a lesson?

 Measuring Up to the Texas Essential Knowledge and Skills

Ask and Answer Questions

S 3.2(B)   Ask relevant questions, seek clarification, and locate facts and details about stories and other texts and support answers with evidence from text.

3.3   Read aloud grade-level appropriate text with fluency (rate, accuracy, expression, appropriate phrasing) and comprehension.

 ## Understand the TEKS

Ask and Answer Questions

Ask yourself questions about the text as you read. Then find answers to your questions. This will help you better understand the material.

You ask and answer questions when you read both articles that give information and made-up stories.

Make sure your questions are **relevant**. In other words, they have to have a strong connection to what you are reading. For example, you wouldn't ask a question about life on the prairie in the 1800s while reading an article about life in cities today.

To find answers to your questions, you can:

- reread the part of the text you have just finished;
- go back to an earlier part of the text;
- read on to search for the answer;
- look for pictures and other graphics.

Words to Know
clarification
evidence
relevant

Types of Questions

Here are some questions you can ask:

• Is there information that I don't understand?

For example, imagine you are reading about how caterpillars change into butterflies. You do not understand how this happens. You are not clear about what stages the creatures pass through.

Think of a question: *How do caterpillars turn into butterflies?* Then reread the sentence or passage. Look for facts and details that answer your question before you go on.

• Is there something in the passage that I can't picture in my mind?

Look for clues to help you better understand the passage. Clues might be in another sentence. They might be in pictures and other helpful graphics.

For example, imagine you are reading a story about red-tailed hawks that live in a big swamp. You might ask: *What does this hawk look like?* Then you look for the answer to your question. When you glance at the article, you see a picture on the page that shows a red-tailed hawk.

Being able to picture the hawk helps you make sense of the rest of the article, so now you are ready to read on.

Is there something in the text that is confusing?

Imagine you just read about how female sea horses lay eggs. Then you read that the male sea horse carries the eggs. You are confused. Seek **clarification.** Clear up this confusion. Ask a question.

For example, you might ask: *Does the female or the male sea horse have babies?* You reread what you have read so far but can't find an answer to your question. Then you read on with your question in mind.

In the next paragraph, you find out that the female sea horse does lay eggs. So now you know that you got that information straight. But what about the male sea horse? The paragraph tells you that she lays the eggs in a pouch on the male sea horse's belly. The male sea horse carries the eggs and gives birth.

Other Sources for Answers

Sometimes you will not be able to find the answers to your questions in the selection that you are reading. You can then look for answers in other sources. You might look for answers in another book about the same topic, in an encyclopedia, or on the Internet.

Support Your Answers

Use facts and details from the text in your answer. Make sure the facts and details provide enough evidence to support your response.

Comprehension Tip

Use a KWL chart as you read. Write your questions in the first column. Then read the selection to find answers. Sometimes the answers to your questions are right there in the text. Other times, you have to put together the details in the text with what you know to come up with an answer.

 Measuring Up to the Texas Essential Knowledge and Skills

Guided Instruction

Read the passage below. Then answer the questions in the margin and complete the activities.

Science Connection

Follow That Horse

by Shannon Teper

1   Cuddles is on the job! Her owner, Dan Shaw, grips the handle of her harness. He says, "Take a walk." The pair starts off. Because he is blind, Dan can't see the road ahead. He knows he's safe with Cuddles. Cuddles is one of only a few trained guide horses for blind people.

2   Cuddles is a chestnut miniature horse. She stands knee-high next to Dan. At 26 inches tall and 80 pounds, she is the size of a large dog. **A** Since Cuddles is compact, she can go everywhere Dan goes. She rides elevators. She fits under restaurant tables. She flies with Dan on airplanes. Cuddles is also housebroken. A horse that isn't housebroken cannot be a guide horse.

"Follow That Horse" by Shannon Teper, Copyright © 2004 by Highlights for Children, Inc., Columbus, Ohio

---

Guided Questions

Read the title. Ask a question about the title. Then read on to find the answer.

_____

_____

_____

Read paragraph **1**. In your own words, explain who Cuddles is. Then ask a question.

_____

_____

_____

_____

_____

Look at sentence **A** in paragraph **2**. The word *compact* might be unfamiliar. Aside from checking the word in a dictionary, what can you do to try to figure out the meaning of *compact*? What does *compact* mean?

_____

3 **B** Wherever she goes, Cuddles wears four tiny sneakers. At first, the sneakers must have felt strange. Cuddles lifted her hooves high and tried to step out of them. Now she wears sneakers everywhere. They protect her hooves from being hurt by broken glass or hot pavement, and from slipping on polished floors.

4 Cuddles is the first miniature horse to guide a blind owner. Janet and Don Burleson trained Cuddles at the Guide Horse Foundation in Kittrell, North Carolina. The Burlesons wanted to offer another choice to blind people who are allergic to or afraid of dogs.

5 Dan feels more comfortable being guided by a horse. "I've loved horses all my life. I'm proud to walk down the street with a horse," he said.

6 Cuddles learned 23 different commands during her training. Like guide dogs, horses learn commands such as *forward*, *right*, and *left*, as well as requests such as *Find the door*.

7 **C** Cuddles also learned to "spook the place." This means to stand still instead of running away when something frightens her.

8 To keep Dan safe, Cuddles was taught to decide when to disobey. If Dan commands her to cross the street when a car is coming, Cuddles won't cross.

9 Cuddles saved Dan from danger recently when a bike raced into his path. She quickly stepped between him and the bicycle. "She makes sure I'm safe," Dan said.

10 Cuddles has been guiding Dan since May 2001. Now he wouldn't be without her. Dan says, "The best thing about Cuddles is the freedom and independence she's given me. She's brought a lot of happiness to my life."

Read sentence **B** in paragraph **3**. A good question to ask here is "Why does Cuddles wear sneakers?" Read the rest of the paragraph to find the answer.

Read paragraph **4**. At this point, you might ask: "Why did people decide to train a horse as a guide animal?" Read on to find the answer.

Look at sentence **C** in paragraph **7**. What could you do to find out what "spook the place" means? What does it mean?

11 | **Big Facts About Little Horses**

- Miniature horses are cheap to feed. Hay costs $4 per week, and oats cost $.25 cents per day.

- They don't have fleas!

- Most people are not allergic to miniature horses.

- They need room to exercise. A fenced-in yard works best.

- Guide horses need special care. At this time, only people over age 16 are taught to care for and handle guide horses.

- So far, there are only a few trained miniature guide horses.

Look back at the picture on the first page of the article. How does the picture help you understand the article better?

_____

_____

_____

_____

Answer the following questions based on the passage you just read.

1. Sometimes writers include fact sheets. Reread the fact sheet. Did the writer answer all your questions about miniature guide horses? If not, what other questions do you have?

_____

_____

2. Did this article help you better understand what guide animals do? Explain.

_____

_____

_____

3. Dan Shaw says, "The best thing about Cuddles is the freedom and independence she's given me." Why do you think this is important? Explain your answer.

_____

_____

_____

_____

_____

4. How does asking yourself questions help you when you read an article?

_____

_____

_____

Critical Thinking

5. Find out more about guide animals. Good places for information are the books in the library and Web sites on the Internet. You might see if there is an organization for training guide animals in your area. Then write your own fact sheet about guide animals. If you have a computer, use it to create your fact sheet. You might use stock photographs to illustrate it.

Writing	☑
Research	☑
Listening and Speaking	☐
Media Literacy	☐
21st Century Skills: Collaboration	☑
Cross Curriculum Connection: Science	☑

◉ On Your Own

Read the selection below. Then answer the questions that follow it.

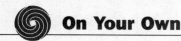

Hector, King of the Barnyard

by Richard Woodard

1   Hector was a proud rooster. He ruled the chicken coop. He was the first to rise. He got the sun out of its bed in the morning. He got the chickens out to look for food. He kept them safe from the fox.

2   "Isn't he handsome?" said the hens. "And what a beautiful voice."

3   "He's so brave and strong."

4   "I always feel safe when Hector is around."

5   Hector strutted around the yard. Nothing missed his gaze. He was everything a chicken king should be.

6   But one day Hector looked out on the farm beyond the hen yard. It bothered him to see the pigs and cows without a leader. He decided to make himself their king, too.

7   Hector flew to the pigpen. Not one pig was digging for worms. They just slept in the shade or wallowed in the mud.

8   "Get up!" he crowed. "I've come to be your king!"

9   The pigs looked up and scratched their heads. Then they went back to sleep.

10   "Lazy loafers!" Hector yelled. "It's time to look for food."

11   One pig got up and walked over to the trough. "Where's the food?" he said. "Bring us a lot of food, and you can be our king."

12   Hector shook his head. "I could never find enough food to feed those lazy pigs," he thought. "They should find their own food, like respectable hens."

13   He looked over at the field where the cows were grazing. "That's more like it," he said. "See how they move around looking for their own food? I'll be their king."

14   He flew over to the cows. "Good, good," he said. "Heads low, eyes open, dig if you must."

15   But as he watched the cows, Hector was amazed to see that they just ate the grass and missed all the bugs. "Faster now," he called out to them. "You eat too slow. They're getting away."

16   Hector flew down to the ground and gobbled up a couple of juicy grasshoppers to show the cows how to do it. "Now you try," he said.

17   One of the cows looked at Hector and said, "We don't eat bugs. We just eat the grass."

18   "The pigs are too lazy, and the cows don't know what's good to eat," Hector complained. "How can I be king to creatures like this?"

19   A horse that was grazing nearby stopped to listen to Hector. "What a silly rooster," thought the horse.

20   Back at the chicken yard the hens were worried. The fox could be around. Where was their king and protector?

21   One hen clucked a worried cluck. Another hen joined in. Pretty soon the yard was full of worried, clucking chickens.

22   "Is that the hens?" the horse asked Hector. "Has the fox gotten into the chicken yard? Too bad they don't have a king."

23   Hector screamed an alarm. He flew past the cows and past the pigpen. He landed in the chicken yard, kicking up dust and scattering hens, looking everywhere for the fox.

24   "Our king is back!" squawked a hen.

25   Hector strutted around the yard as the hens settled down to scratch for bugs. "This is more like it," he said. "The rest of the animals will have to find another king."

Answer the following questions based on the passage you just read.

1. A good question to ask when you start to read any selection is this:

   > *Is this story made up or does it tell about real people and real events?*

   Answer the question above for "Hector, King of the Barnyard."

   _____

   _____

   How do you know?

   _____

   _____

2. Read the first paragraph.

   > *Hector was a proud rooster. He ruled the chicken coop. He was the first to rise. He got the sun out of its bed in the morning. He got the chickens out to look for food. He kept them safe from the fox.*

   What is a good question to ask at this point?

   _____

   _____

3. Based on the information in paragraphs 1–6, what is Hector like? Support
your answer.

_____

_____

_____

_____

4. Why does Hector decide not to be king of the pigs?

   A He doesn't want to look for food for them.

   B He is angry that they won't dig for worms.

   C The pigs are a lot stronger than he is.

   D He doesn't like pigs very much.

5. In paragraph 14, why does Hector expect the cows to dig for bugs?

   A He knows they are frightened of him.

   B He thinks this is what all animals eat since it is what hens eat.

   C The pigs dug for bugs when he told them to.

   D He has seen the cows digging for bugs before.

6. Use the chart below. Jot down a good question to ask after reading each paragraph. Then give the answers to your questions.

Paragraph	Question	Answer
Paragraph 6		
Paragraph 12		
Paragraph 19		

7. What is a good question to ask after reading paragraph 20?

_____

Critical Thinking

8. Practice reading this story aloud with fluency. Work with a partner. Take turns reading the story. Offer helpful advice to give others to make the reading better. Then take turns reading the story aloud.

Writing	☐
Research	☐
Listening and Speaking	☑
Media Literacy	☐
21st Century Skills: Collaboration	☑
Cross Curriculum Connections	☐

Set Purpose and Monitor Comprehension

3.2(C)	Establish purpose for reading selected texts and monitor comprehension, making corrections and adjustments when that understanding breaks down (e.g., identifying clues, using background knowledge, generating questions, re-reading a portion aloud).
3.3	Read aloud grade-level appropriate text with fluency (rate, accuracy, expression, appropriate phrasing) and comprehension.
Figure 19(A)	Establish purposes for reading selected texts based upon own or others' desired outcome to enhance comprehension.
Figure 19(C)	Monitor and adjust comprehension (e.g., using background knowledge, creating sensory images, re-reading a portion aloud, generating questions).

 Understand the TEKS

Set a Purpose

When you read, set a purpose. You can read for several purposes.

> **Words to Know**
> monitor
> purpose
> rate

- You might read a funny story to be **entertained**.
- You might read a science article to **find information about polar bears**.
- You might read instructions to **find out how to do something**, such as put a model together.

Keep your purpose in mind as you read. It affects your **rate**. For example, you probably read quickly when you want to be entertained. You read more slowly when you try to follow directions.

Monitor Your Comprehension

As you read, monitor your comprehension. Keep asking yourself whether you understand what you are reading. If you don't, take time to straighten out the problem.

Adjust Your Rate

If you find you don't understand what you read, you may be reading too quickly. Adjust your rate. Slow down and read more carefully.

- If you are reading a text to study for a test, should you read it slowly and carefully or quickly? Why?

_____

_____

Reread Aloud

Go back and reread a passage that confuses you. Try reading it aloud. You might find that hearing the words helps you better understand the text.

Generate Questions

Ask questions as you read. Then look for answers to your questions.

Identify Clues

Look for clues that will help you comprehend the text better. Important words and terms may be in **boldface** type. Illustrations may provide important information. Headings may help you locate information to clarify the text.

Use Background Knowledge

Think about what you already know. Connect what you know with information in the text. This will help you make inferences.

- Suppose you don't understand some information about how bears hibernate. Should you look under the heading "Bears in Winter" or "Bears in Summer"? How do you know?

_____

_____

Comprehension Tip

Pause every now and then and try putting what you read in your own words. This will help you judge how well you understood it. If you find you can't do this, go back and reread. Then try putting the passage in your own words again.

Guided Instruction

Read the passage below. Then answer the questions in the margin and complete the activities.

Literature Connection

"Michael Spreckle! Where Have You Been?"

by Christopher Tebbetts

1   Michael stumbled out of the jungle and into camp.

2   "Michael Spreckle! Where have you been?" demanded Ms. Venture. She put down her binoculars. "When we set out on safari, we all agreed: The deep, dark jungle is no place to wander off from the rest of the class."

3   Everyone was staring at Michael as he staggered over to them and sat down. He pulled out his jungle journal from inside his shirt and used the battered pages to fan his sweaty face. "Thirsty, thirsty . . . very thirsty," he gasped. **A** Jenny Moosh grabbed a canteen of jungle juice for him.

4   "Hungry, hungry . . . very hungry," Michael whispered weakly. Kevin Blevins gave him a piece of jungle jerky.

5   Ms. Venture's pith helmet bobbed up and down as she tapped her foot.

"Michael Spreckle! Where Have You Been?" by Christopher Tebbetts, Copyright © 2003 by Highlights for Children, Inc., Columbus, Ohio

---

Guided Questions

Read the title and paragraph **1**. Then look at the pictures. What type of selection do you think this is? If you were reading it on summer vacation, what would be your purpose and your reading rate?

_____

_____

_____

_____

Highlight the word *canteen* in sentence **A** in paragraph **3**. Say the word slowly to yourself. What other words in the sentence can help you figure out the meaning? What does *canteen* mean?

_____

_____

_____

_____

_____

6   "Well," Michael said finally. "It's a good thing that herd of white elephants charged right near our camp—and that the one I was riding slowed down. Otherwise I couldn't have jumped off."

7   Everyone began speaking to Michael at once.

8   "A *herd* of white elephants?" said Ethan Smart. "Seeing even one is rare."

9   "You *jumped* off?" said April May, clearly impressed.

10   "How'd you get *on* the elephant?" Bitsy Small asked loudly.

11   Michael waited for everyone to be quiet. "I was swinging on a vine, fifty feet off the ground, and it snapped. I thought I was jungle splat for sure, but she was right there. I landed on her back, and we took off."

12   "So you swung on a vine, landed on an elephant, charged through the jungle, and ended up here?" asked Ms. Venture.

13   "Not *one* vine—lots of vines," corrected Michael. "Tree to tree. I was trying to get away from the baboons."

14   "Baboons?" said Penny Buck.

15   "Dozens of them, screaming like wild animals," said Michael. "I guess that was *their* banana tree I climbed. I would have stayed down on the ground, but there was nothing to eat, and I was starving after all the swimming."

Guided Questions

Pause after reading paragraph **6**. You might think the story is a bit confusing. Reread the paragraph. How do you know this story is going to include some fantastic events?

_____

_____

_____

_____

_____

16   "Ms. Venture always says we're not supposed to go swimming alone," said April May.

17   "Well, you'd swim, too, if you had crocodiles on your tail," said Michael.

18   "CROCODILES?" said everyone.

19   "Yeah. Big bumpy ones, with beady little eyes," said Michael.

20   "So you swam away from the crocodiles, climbed the baboons' banana tree, swung on some vines, landed on an elephant, charged through the jungle, and ended up here?" asked Ms. Venture.

21   "I didn't plan on swimming," said Michael. "I just jumped in the river to wash off, and BAM! Crocodile city."

22   "What do you mean, wash off?" asked Jenny. "You're filthy."

23   "You should've seen me after I pulled myself out of the quicksand," said Michael.

24   "Cool," said Kevin. "How did you land in quicksand?"

25   "I never even saw it coming," said Michael. "But if I had fallen in, I definitely would have been lion lunch. He was closing in on me fast. I could smell the antelope on his breath."

26   Nobody said a word while Michael took another swig of jungle juice.

27   "That lion was pretty mad when he woke up," Michael continued. **B** "He chased me out of the cave faster than you can say *hozziewhatzits*."

Guided Questions

Look at paragraph **17**. What impossible tale does Michael tell now?

_____

_____

_____

Pause at paragraph **20**. This part of the story might also be confusing. Look back at the first paragraph. Where has Michael returned to?

_____

_____

Look at sentence **B** in paragraph **27**. The word *hozziewhatzits* may seem difficult. Sound it out and say it aloud. What do you think it means?

_____

_____

_____

28   "Cave? What cave?" asked Penny.

29   "Just the biggest cave full of bats you've ever seen, that's all," said Michael.

30   Bitsy looked at him skeptically. "Come on Michael," she said. "Where were you really?"

31   "I just told you," said Michael. **C** "Ms. Venture said to work hard on our jungle journals, right? I figured no one else would have stalactite drippings or cave moss. If I knew I was going to stir up some bats, run from a lion, fall in quicksand, jump in a river, swim from crocodiles, climb the baboons' banana tree, swing on vines, land on an elephant, charge through the jungle, and be late getting back, I never would've gone into the jungle in the first place."

32   Everyone was quiet. Somewhere in the distance, a hyena laughed.

33   Michael opened up his journal. "Look! Hair from an elephant's ear."

34   But suddenly no one was paying attention to him. A deep rumbling sound had filled the air.

35   "What is that noise?" asked April.

36   "And this is a quicksand stain!" said Michael, pointing to a page.

37   "It sounds like thunder, sort of," said Penny.

38   "Here's a banana leaf! Anyone?" said Michael, but nobody was listening. Everyone was peering into the jungle. Something was coming closer. The ground began to shake.

39   "What is that?" asked Jenny.

40   "I'm not sure," said Ethan, "but it could be—"

41   The underbrush opened up, and suddenly the camp was filled with enormous, booming, charging—

42   "WHITE ELEPHANTS!"

43   "This way!" yelled Ms. Venture.

Guided Questions

Look at sentence **C** in paragraph **31**. What does this help you understand?

_____

_____

_____

_____

Pause after paragraph **31**. At this point in the story, it might be confusing to figure out which event happened first in Michael's imaginary tale. Reread parts of the story. Then explain in your own words where Michael started out. Why?

_____

_____

_____

_____

Read paragraph **40**. What do you think is happening now?

_____

_____

_____

Guided Questions

44 Everyone dove out of the way just in time. The herd moved through the camp like a fleet of white tanks, then disappeared back into the dense jungle.

45 When the dust settled, Ms. Venture told all of the students to spend the rest of the day in their tents working quietly on their jungle journals.

46 Michael Spreckle's was the best in the class.

Answer the following questions based on the passage you just read.

1. Which parts of the story did you find somewhat confusing? Fill out the chart below. Write what you found confusing in the left-hand column. Write what you found out that helped you clarify this information in the right-hand column.

Confusing Part	What I Found Out

2. Why does the rest of the class keep asking Michael questions?

_____

_____

3. Why is Michael Spreckle's journal the best in the class?

_____

_____

Critical Thinking

4. Work with your class. Choose a narrator and students to read the character parts. Take turns. Read the story aloud. As you read, self-correct any mistakes that you make. Remember to read smoothly and pronounce each word.

Writing	☐
Research	☐
Listening and Speaking	☑
Media Literacy	☐
21st Century Skills: Teamwork	☑
Cross Curriculum Connections	☐

5. Write another adventure for Michael. This time, have the class keep an ocean journal. Read your story aloud to a partner.

 On Your Own

Read the selection below. Then answer the questions that follow it.

Science Connection

An Opossum Named Poppy

by Fay Munier

1   The moon was bright that first night. Still, I couldn't tell—who was that sitting on our tall wooden fence? Perhaps it was a neighbor's cat. I switched on the outdoor light. No, it was not a cat. Our new visitor was a Virginia opossum. He gazed at me while staying on the fence. *How cool*, I thought. We had never seen an opossum in our yard before.

How does Poppy walk along the fence without falling?
His tail helps him balance.

2   I thought I should name him. Thus, he became Poppy. He's mostly gray, but his face is white with a black V on the forehead. He has a pointy nose and a nearly hairless tail. His tail helps him balance while he walks along the fence. It's a prehensile tail, which means that it can grasp and hold objects.

3   The next night, I stood by our sliding glass door. I waited, watched, and wished that Poppy would come again. He did! He stopped at the water bowl that we fill for visiting birds and other animals. He sipped and splashed.

What's for Dinner?

4   Poppy came down from the fence. He waddled about, looking for dinner. Opossums eat almost anything—slugs, insects, garbage, and (Poppy's favorite) snails.

5   Before this little garden helper came along, snails crawled all over our yard. They were eating our plants. We had tried nearly everything to make the snails go away, except Poppy's solution—eating them.

6   Poppy also has a passion for peaches. One night, I caught him on the fence plucking a peach off our tree. Two little hands cuddled one plump peach.

7   Uh-oh—too heavy! Splat. Peach and juice puddled on the concrete patio. Poppy inspected the problem. Then he plucked another peach. This time he held his treasure tightly and ate every sticky bite.

Poppy has a passion
for peaches.

8   After his meal, Poppy licked his paws, rubbed his face, and scrubbed his head and pudgy stomach. This chore took at least 20 minutes. Opossums are serious about cleaning up.

Fifty Teeth!

9   One night I wanted to take a picture of Poppy. With camera in hand, I moved closer and closer . . . until Poppy showed me his teeth. All 50 of them! That's more teeth than any other North American mammal. I decided there would be no picture that night.

10   Back at the window, I watched. Poppy checked out the moon, the stars, and me. I don't think he noticed my smile. But I hope he knows that he will always be welcome in our yard.

Answer the following questions based on the passage you just read.

1. When do you usually give animals names?

_____

When you read the title of this selection, what did you think about the opossum based on the fact that it has a name?

_____

2. Which sentence in paragraph 1 helps the reader know that the narrator will not chase the opossum away?

   A *The moon was bright that first night.*

   B *Perhaps it was a neighbor's cat.*

   C *He gazed at me while staying on the fence.*

   D *How cool, I thought.*

3. Which parts of the article did you find somewhat confusing? Fill out the chart below. Write what you found confusing in the left-hand column. Write what you found out that helped you clarify this information in the right-hand column.

Confusing Part	What I Found Out

4. Look at the first illustration. Read the caption. What does it help you understand?

_____

5. Find the word in paragraph 2 that the picture helps you understand. Write it on the line below. Then write the words from this paragraph that help you define the word.

_____

_____

6. In paragraph 9, why does the narrator decide not to take Poppy's photograph?

_____

7. What is the main point the author makes in paragraph 10?

  A Poppy looks up at the moon and stars.

  B Poppy will always be welcomed in her yard.

  C She watched Poppy from her window.

  D Poppy didn't notice her smiling.

(Elevate) **8.** Look at the second picture. Why did the author include this picture?

_____

How do you think she wants readers to feel about the opossum? Why do you think this?

_____

_____

Critical Thinking

9. Talk to a partner. Tell how monitoring your reading of this selection helped improve your comprehension. Discuss how you will use this strategy in the future. Write a summary of your discussion.

Writing	☑
Research	☐
Listening and Speaking	☑
Media Literacy	☐
21st Century Skills: Collaboration	☑
Cross-Curriculum Connection	☐

Media Connection

10. You can learn more about opossums at http://animals.nationalgeographic.com/ animals/mammals/opossum/.

Lesson 4

Make and Support Inferences

R/S **Figure 19(D)**   Make inferences about text and use textual evidence to support understanding.

Understand the TEKS

An author doesn't tell you absolutely everything. When you read, you have to fill in the blanks for yourself. You read between the lines to make inferences.

Inferences

Making an inference is a thinking skill. An **inference** is a smart guess. Notice the word "smart." You don't pull an inference out of thin air. You use **evidence** to make an inference.

This **evidence** consists of facts and details. You find these facts and details in what you read. Then you connect them to what you know from your life and experience. The more evidence you have, the more likely your inference will be a good one. Evidence backs up, or **supports,** your inference.

Words to Know
evidence
infer
inference
support

Making an inference looks like this.

> Evidence from Text + What I Know = Inference

For example, read the passage below:

> The thing he dreaded happened—the teacher called on him. Kevin felt all his classmates' eyes on him. He just wanted to hide under his desk. He had studied hard last night, and he knew all the answers when his mother had quizzed him. Now, though, his mind went blank. He just stammered out, "I don't know."

Notice the details:

- Felt all his classmates' eyes on him
- Wanted to hide under his desk
- Studied hard last night
- Knew answers last night
- Mind went blank
- Stammered

You probably have seen people act this way. You know that this behavior shows that someone is nervous and shy. So that's the inference you make about Kevin.

Inferences often answer the question, "Why?" Why did Kevin say he didn't know the answer? *Kevin knows the answer, but he is so nervous and shy, he forgot it.*

Read the passage below.

For months Hank had been hoping for a Super Deluxe Transmorp for his birthday. He carefully left hints for his parents. He tore pictures of the Transmorp out of magazines and taped them to the bathroom mirror. He left a store advertisement for one in his mother's purse. He pointed out the Transmorp to his father when they passed the store window.

Finally Hank's birthday arrived. He woke up early and ran down to breakfast. A big package was on the table. He tore open the wrappings and reached in the box. He stared at his prize—twelve matching pairs of socks!

"What do you think?" asked Dad.

Hank stumbled over his words. "It's just fine. Thank you," said Hank as he walked away from the breakfast table with his head hanging low.

"Wait a minute!" said Mom. "We're not done." She pulled another package out from under the table.

"Here's a little something else," said Dad. "Of course, we could always bring it back if you don't like it."

Hank raced back to the table. *Could it be?* he thought. He reached into the package and pulled out—a Transmorp! It was the biggest, greatest, most amazing Transmorp he had ever seen.

A big smile filled his face. "Oh, Mom. Oh, Dad. You shouldn't have. I would have been happy with just the socks."

- Make an inference. How does Hank really feel when he receives the socks?

  _____

- Support your answer with evidence from the text and from what you know.

  _____

  _____

  _____

- Make an inference. How does Hank feel when he receives the Transmorp?

  _____

- Support your answer with evidence from the text and from what you know.

  _____

  _____

  _____

- Make another inference. Do you think Hank would have been happy with just the socks? Why or why not?

  _____

  _____

  _____

Comprehension Tip

Think about what the author doesn't tell you and fill in the blanks. Make a three-column chart. Label the first column "It Says." Label the second column "I Say." Label the third column "And So." Fill in the chart as you read. In the first column, write information from the text that helps you make an inference. In the second column, write what you think about these details. Then add it all together to make an inference.

Guided Instruction

Read the passage below. Then answer the questions in the margin and complete the activities.

Literature Connection

Who Stole Gorgonzola?

by Judith L. Roth

Guided Questions

1   Grandma called the garden gnome Gorgonzola because it was a wacky name. And because she loved cheese.

2   Now Grandma stared at the space where Gorgonzola usually stood in the front yard. There was an imprint of gnome feet in the dirt, but no gnome. "Who took Gorgonzola?" Grandma asked, sounding exasperated. Her hands reached out toward the empty space.

3   "Are there footprints?" I asked. "Maybe we should match them up to the robber's."

What detail in paragraph **1** helps you infer that Grandma has a good sense of humor?

_____

4   Grandma looked at me. "Eliza Ann, Miss Junior Sleuth, why do you sound so happy that Gorgonzola has been taken?"

5   I love a good mystery. She knows that. "I'm not happy. . ."

6   "Well, put your finding skills to use, because I won't be able to sleep until Gorgonzola is back."

7   Gorgonzola was Grandma's guardian gnome. She bought him after Grandpa died. She said she needed a protector in front of the house, but I think maybe the gnome reminded her of Grandpa.

8   She snapped her fingers. "I'll bet it's those kids, the ones who threw eggs at him on Halloween. Do you know where they live?"

9   "I could find out," I said. But I really didn't want to. Those kids were kind of tough. "Let me do some research first."

10   A good detective knows her subject. So I went online to find out more about gnomes. I was shocked to discover there are organizations dedicated to freeing garden gnomes.

11   "Grandma," I yelled, "come see this!"

12   "Grandma looked over my shoulder at the computer monitor. "Well, that's ridiculous. Gorgonzola wasn't here against his will."

13   Grandma was holding something funny on a platter. It looked like a Santa head without the beard. "What's that?" I asked.

14   "Next-door Frank gave this to me a while back. He carved it out of cheese—it's supposed to look like him. I stuck it in the fridge and forgot about it. Want some?"

15   "I don't want to eat Frank's head."

16   "Suit yourself." She sliced off the back of the cheese head and put it on a cracker.

17   I said, "Maybe we can post pictures of Gorgonzola and say when and where he went missing."

18   Grandma chewed. "Hmm. I never thought to take a picture of him."

19   But someone else had.

Guided Questions

Read paragraphs **4** and **5**. Highlight how Eliza says she is feeling. How do you think she is really feeling? Why?

_____

_____

_____

_____

Read paragraph **7**. Highlight the details that support this inference: *The gnome means much more to Grandma than just a garden statue.*

Read paragraph **12**. Highlight the detail that tells you that Grandma thinks of the gnome as almost alive.

20   By the time I stopped at Grandma's the next day, two pictures had arrived in her mailbox. In one, Gorgonzola posed by a huge wheel of cheese at the cheese factory. In another, Gorgonzola posed on a dock, looking out at a lake. On the back of each picture, someone had written *Wish you were here!* as if the cards were from Grandma's gnome.

21   "That's odd," Grandma said. "Has he been kidnapped, or is someone teasing me?"

22   I examined the envelope. "There's no stamp. The perpetrator must have put this in the mailbox himself. He stepped right onto your porch. Did you see anyone?"

23   "Just the mailman and next-door Frank. Frank came by to borrow some spray cheese. The goof sprayed some of it at me before he left."

24   I looked at Grandma. She was oblivious. "Grandma."

25   She was still laughing to herself about the spray cheese. "What?"

26   "It's Frank. Next-door Frank has your garden gnome. He's the one teasing you."

27   "What?"

28   "Wake up and smell the spray cheese. You have an admirer."

29   "You mean, he took my Gorgonzola?" Grandma shook her head.

30   "Maybe Frank wanted company, too." Grandma looked thoughtful. "You think so?"

31   "I can sneak over and find out if Gorgonzola's there," I offered.

32   Grandma cocked her head at me, then said, "No, I think maybe I should go over." Before she left, she stood at the mirror and fussed with her hair.

33   I went out to the porch, and soon I could hear Grandma say, "You know, Frank, I'm going to need that spray cheese back. May I come in?" I could see into Frank's kitchen window. Gorgonzola was on a chair at the table. The other three places were set with plates rimmed with crackers.

Read paragraph **21**. What is the answer to Grandma's question? Why do you think this?

_____

_____

_____

_____

Read paragraph **32**. Why does Grandma go over to Frank's? Highlight a detail that tells you this.

_____

_____

Read paragraph **33**. Highlight the detail that tells you that Frank had planned this outcome all along.

34   A sharp rap on the window startled me. It was Frank, motioning for me to come inside.

35   "I thought the brains of this operation might want to join us for a snack," he said, grinning as I stepped into the house.

36   "I'd love to," I said, then looked at Grandma, who was picking up the spray cheese. She aimed it playfully at Frank. I shook my head and patted Gorgonzola's hat.

37   Mystery solved. Gnome found. Special friend acquired. All in all, a cheeserific day.

Answer the following questions based on the passage you just read.

1. Read the paragraph below.

> *Grandma looked at me. "Eliza Ann, Miss Junior Sleuth, why do you sound so happy that Gorgonzola has been taken?"*

Notice that Grandma calls the girl by both her first and middle name—Eliza Ann—and then adds "Miss Junior Sleuth."

From your experience, how are adults usually feeling when they speak to a child like this?

_____

_____

Make an inference. In what tone of voice does Grandma probably speak to Eliza? Why?

_____

_____

_____

_____

2. Read the paragraphs below.

> *She snapped her fingers. "I'll bet it's those kids, the ones who threw eggs at him on Halloween. Do you know where they live?"*
>
> *"I could find out," I said. But I really didn't want to. Those kids were kind of tough. "Let me do some research first."*

Make an inference about how Eliza feels. Fill in the chart below to answer this question: *Why does Eliza say that she wants to do research first?*

It Says	I Say	And So

 3. Read paragraphs 24–26.

> *I looked at Grandma. She was <u>oblivious</u>. "Grandma."*
>
> *She was still laughing to herself about the spray cheese. "What?"*
>
> *"It's Frank. Next-door Frank has your garden gnome. He's the one teasing you."*

The word *oblivious* means "completely unaware." Unlike Grandma, you, like Eliza, were probably quite aware that the culprit is Frank. What details led to this inference?

_____

_____

_____

 Measuring Up to the Texas Essential Knowledge and Skills

4. Make an inference about the author's purpose. Do you think the author wrote this story to entertain or to teach a serious lesson about life?

_____

Use details from the story to support your response.

_____

_____

_____

_____

_____

Critical Thinking

5. Gnomes are popular figures in cartoons and animated films. Work with a small group of students. Brainstorm ideas for a cartoon series called _Gnome Adventures_. Of course, it stars your favorite gnome, Gorgonzola. Develop a plan for the episodes. Then each student in the group should write a script for one episode.

Writing	☑
Research	☐
Listening and Speaking	☐
Media Literacy	☑
21st Century Skills: Collaboration	☑
Cross-Curriculum Connection: Science	☑

Media Connection

6. Create the illustrations for your episode. You can learn how to draw a gnome at http://www.drawinghowtodraw.com.stepbystepdrawinglessons/2011/07/how-to-draw-cartoon-gnomes-step-by-step-drawing-tutorial or http://www.wikihow.com/Draw-A-Gnome.

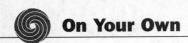

On Your Own

Read the selection below. Then answer the questions that follow it.

Science Connection

Winter's Tail

by Shannon Teper

When dolphins swim, they move their tails up and down. What would happen to a dolphin that lost its tail? Would it be able to survive?

1   In Mosquito Lagoon, a two-month-old dolphin struggled to break free from the rope wrapped around her. Seeing a crab trap in the Florida waters, she had become curious and swum too close. The line attached to the trap coiled around her tail. The harder she pulled to swim away, the tighter the rope became.

2   Luckily, a fisherman saw the injured baby dolphin and called for help. A rescue team brought the dolphin to the Clearwater Marine Aquarium in Florida. There the baby was given the name Winter.

A Struggle to Survive

3   When she arrived, the flat part of Winter's tail was thin and white, like paper. Over the next few weeks, it fell off. All that was left was a rounded stump where her tail had once been. No dolphin had ever survived losing an entire tail before.

4   More than 150 volunteers and veterinarians cared for Winter around the clock. They fed her a special mix of baby formula and mashed-up fish. Winter grew healthier each day. She even learned to swim without a tail.

5   But Winter wasn't swimming like a dolphin. Dolphins move their tails up and down. Since Winter had no tail, she whipped her whole body from side to side and swam like a shark. Veterinarians worried that Winter would injure her spine by twisting it in an unusual way.

A New Tail for Winter

6   That's when Kevin Carroll got involved. He heard Winter's story on the radio and called the aquarium. He told them he made artificial limbs for animals. He had made body parts for dogs, an ostrich, and even a duck. Maybe he could make a tail for Winter.

7   Winter had no tail at all. So Carroll designed a bendable plastic tail that would slip over the end of her body. A gel would be used to hold the artificial tail in place and protect Winter from getting sore when the tail rubbed against her skin.

8   First, trainers helped Winter stretch and bend certain parts of her body, strengthening the muscles she needed to use for swimming. Then they attached her new tail, helping her learn how to move it up and down. Soon, Winter could use her new tail to swim like other dolphins.

9   Now, people from all over the world come to meet Winter. Her determination to swim with an artificial tail inspires visitors who also have disabilities.

10   Bailee Lorg from Knoxville, Tennessee, watched Winter splash and swim. "It's great that she has a fake leg like me," said the four-year-old. "I love her, and I'm so glad that we're both special together.

Answer the following questions based on the passage you just read.

 1. Reread the caption. Then reread paragraphs 1–2. Why do you think the dolphin is taken to the aquarium?

_____

_____

What evidence supports your inference?

_____

_____

2. In paragraph 2, how do the people at the aquarium feel about the baby dolphin? Fill in the chart below to show how you made your inference.

It Says	I Say	And So

 3. What other evidence from paragraph 5 supports the inference you made above?

_____

_____

4. The most important information in paragraph 3 is that –

A Winter's tail was flat

B Winter's tail was thin and white like paper

C no dolphin had ever survived losing a tail

D Winter was left with a round stump where her tail should have been

 5. Reread paragraph 5. The text tells you why the veterinarians were worried about the way Winter swam. Write the reason below.

_____

Now think about what the text doesn't say. Imagine Winter swimming with other dolphins. Make an inference. What is another reason for worry?

_____

_____

6. In paragraph 7, why did Carroll make Winter's artificial tail bendable?

_____

 Measuring Up to the Texas Essential Knowledge and Skills

7. Which detail from the article best shows that Winter inspires people with disabilities?

    A The story of Bailee Lorg

    B The information about Kevin Carroll

    C The story of the fisherman who found the injured dolphin

    D The information about the veterinarians who cared for Winter

 8. How do you think the author wants readers to feel about Winter?

_____

_____

What details from the article support your response?

_____

_____

_____

 9. Winter got caught up in a crab trap. Find out about other dangers dolphins face in the ocean. Use both the library and the Internet. Then work with a group of other students. Pool your information. Prepare an oral report and present it to your classmates.

Critical Thinking

Writing	☐
Research	☑
Listening and Speaking	☑
Media Literacy	☑
21st Century Skills: Collaboration	☑
Cross-Curriculum Connection: Science	☑

 10. You can learn more about Winter at the Clearwater Marine Aquarium website. Visit KidZone at http://www.seewinter.com/winter/dolphin-tale.

Media Connection

Ⓡ/Ⓢ Figure 19(E)   Summarize information in text, maintaining meaning and logical order.

Understand the TEKS

A **summary** is a short form of something. It contains all the important information. In other words, it gives the main points. It leaves out unimportant information.

When you **summarize**, you tell information in order. You don't mix it up. This makes your summary easy to follow.

For example, if you were to summarize what you did today, you wouldn't tell every single thing that happened. You would tell only the important events— meeting friends, acing a test, scoring a winning soccer goal. You would leave out unimportant details—putting on your socks, starting your computer, hanging up your coat. You would tell these events in **chronological**—or time—**order**. This is the order in which they happened.

- Summarize the things you did yesterday before going to school.

_____

_____

Read the beginning of a summary of *Charlotte's Web*.

> In *Charlotte's Web*, a farm spider named Charlotte saves a pig named Wilbur.

- Now read the two sentences in the box below. Circle the one that does not belong in a summary because it is not important.

> Wilbur is the runt of the litter, so the farmer plans to destroy him.
>
> A pig's newborn babies form a litter, and a baby pig is called a piglet.

A summary includes only information from the text. It does not include your thoughts and feelings about what you read.

Words to Know

chronological order

main idea

paraphrase

summarize

summary

- Read the statements below. Circle the one that does not belong in a summary of *Charlotte's Web*.

> It is so sad when Charlotte dies at the fair that I almost cried.
>
> After they hatch, three of Charlotte's babies become Wilbur's friends.

When you summarize, you put information in your own words. This is called paraphrasing. A **paraphrase** is a rewording or restatement of the original information.

For example, read the statement below.

> When a spider reaches adulthood, its physical growth is at an end.

Here is how this statement could be paraphrased.

> Spiders stop growing when they become adults.

Now read the next statement.

> Since a daddy longlegs has eight legs, it may be mistaken for a spider at first glance, but the truth is that it belongs to a different group of animals.

- On the line below, paraphrase the statement above.

_____

When you summarize a narrative, or story, you include important events. You tell these events in the order in which they happen.

When you summarize informational text, you include main ideas and important details. A **main idea** is the most important idea in a paragraph or passage. Important details support, or back up, the main idea.

Comprehension Tip
If the book or magazine is yours, underline or highlight important information as you read. If it is not, use sticky notes to highlight important information. This will help you when you summarize.

Guided Instruction

Read the passage below. Then answer the questions in the margin and complete the activities.

Science Connection

Cloaked in Starlight

by Dan Risch

1   Bobtail squids must taste good. During the day, barracuda try to find and eat them. At night, seals try to gobble them up. So what's a little squirt like a bobtail squid to do?

2   Become invisible!

3   By day, bobtail squids snuggle into the sea floor in the waters off the coast of Hawaii. They use their tentacles to flip sand onto their backs. Their sticky skin holds the sand in place. Not even sharp-eyed barracuda will spot a sand-covered bobtail squid.

4   But what if a bobtail squid is attacked in open water, with no place to hide? Then, the squid disappears a different way. It squirts out ink. The ink hangs in the water in the shape and size of the squid. At the instant the ink shoots out, the bobtail changes color. It becomes almost see-through. The predator bites the inky squid shape. The nearly invisible real squid swims to safety.

Guided Questions

Read paragraphs **1** and **2**. Highlight the two sentences that tell about the bobtail squid's enemies. Then highlight the sentence that tells the main way the bobtail squid protects itself.

Read paragraph **3**. What is one way that the bobtail squid makes itself invisible?

_____

_____

Read paragraph **4**. Highlight the words that tell how this situation is different. Then describe another way the bobtail squid makes itself invisible.

_____

_____

_____

Time to Shine

5   When the sun goes down, the bobtail's cloaking skills really shine.

6   At night, the bobtails swim through the water eating worms and shrimp. The moon and stars light up the water. Predators look up from below to see the dark outlines of prey in the starlit water. But they can't see the bobtail squids.

7   The squids have light-making bacteria living inside their bodies. The bacteria make light much like a firefly does. But the bacteria don't live just anywhere in the squid. The bottom of the squid has many tiny pockets. Inside the pockets, the bacteria eat, grow, and shine brightly.

8   As bobtail squids swim at night, predators don't see their dark outlines. They don't see the bobtail squids at all. With their bottom pockets shining with bacteria, bobtails swim around, safely cloaked in their own starlight.

Light In, Light Out

9   How do bobtail squids stay safe when no starlight or moonlight shines through the water? They turn off their pocket lights!

10   The bobtail squid can let light out. By controlling how much light shines from its pockets, the squid can match its light to the light in the water.

Guided Questions

Read paragraphs **5**–**7**. Highlight the sentence that explains why predators can't see the bobtail squid.

Read the last sentence in paragraph **8**. Put it in your own words.

_____

_____

_____

Answer the following questions based on the passage you just read.

1. Read paragraphs 1 and 2. Write a sentence telling their main idea.

_____

2. Write three ways bobtail squids make themselves invisible to enemies.

A. _____

B. _____

C. _____

3. Now put the information above together to write a summary.

_____

_____

_____

_____

4. Write one sentence that summarizes the information in the box.

_____

_____

Critical Thinking

5. Work with three or four other students. Brainstorm a list of plants and animals that disguise themselves to hide from enemies. Then draw up a list of questions about these disguises. Each student should then choose one animal or plant on the list and research this creature's methods of disguise. Then the group should get back together to discuss each other's findings. Together, create a poster or a presentation called "Masters of Disguise."

Writing	☑
Research	☑
Listening and Speaking	☑
Media Literacy	☐
21st Century Skills: Collaboration	☑
Cross-Curriculum Connection: Science	☑

Media Connection

6. A marine biologist studies the oceans and the creatures living in them. You can find out more about this career and other interesting careers in science at http://www.kids.gov/k_5/k_5_careers.shtml.

On Your Own

Read the selection below. Then answer the questions that follow it.

The Best Story Ever

by Marcie Aboff

1   Meg ran home after school on Friday. She burst into her house and shouted, "Look—A+! Not just an A, an A+!"

2   Meg waved her essay in front of her dad. "Mrs. Miller said I'm an excellent writer," Meg announced. "She said maybe I'll be an author when I grow up!"

3   "Wow, that's great!" said Dad, looking up from his computer.

4   "I'm not going to wait," Meg said. "I'm going to write my first story right now. It'll be the best story ever!"

5   Meg danced up to her bedroom. She made a big sign:

6   She taped the sign to her door.

7   A few minutes later, the door flew open.

8   "Want to play soccer?" asked Nick, her younger brother.

9   "I can't now. I'm busy writing," said Meg.

10   "What are you writing?" asked Nick.

"The Best Story Ever" by Marcie Aboff Copyright © 2006 by Highlights for Children, Inc., Columbus, Ohio

11   "The best story ever!" Meg said. "It's about a beautiful princess. She lives in a giant castle. It's the night of the Palace Ball, but her favorite red dress is missing. So she searches the castle to find out who took it."

12   "And then what happens?" Nick asked.

13   "I'm not sure," Meg said. "But I'll think of something." Meg pointed to the door. "Go now. Authors need quiet."

14   Meg leaned back in her chair. *Where could the dress be?* she wondered. *Did the princess's evil sister steal it? Did the maid put it with the laundry? Did the queen lend it to the princess's younger cousin?* Meg didn't like any of those ideas.

15   "This isn't the best story ever," Meg said. She threw the paper at the wastebasket. "I'll just have to write another one."

16   When Meg's mom came home from work, she knocked on Meg's door. "I hear you're writing a story about a princess," she said.

17   "No, that was before," Meg said. "Now I'm writing about a monster—the most horrible monster ever! He's ten feet tall, with green fangs. He smells like a sewer. He can't make friends with the other monsters because he smells so bad!"

18   "And then what happens?" Mom asked.

19   "I'm not sure," Meg said. "But I'll think of something."

20   "All right," Mom said. "I'll leave and let the author work."

21   But Meg was stuck again. *Who wants to play with a stinky old monster anyway?* she thought. "This isn't the best story either!" Meg cried, and she threw away that story, too.

22   All weekend Meg tried to write stories. She began one about a talking dog and another about a dancing clown. She started a story about a spaceship that landed in her backyard. Meg began lots of stories, but she couldn't finish any of them.

23   On Sunday afternoon, Meg threw another story into the wastebasket. *I must have started one hundred stories!* she thought. She became so angry that she threw her pencil on the floor.

24   "I'll *never* write the best story ever!" Meg cried. She put her head down. Then she noticed a piece of paper lying underneath her dresser. Meg reached for the paper. It was the first story she had written—about the princess who couldn't find her favorite red dress.

25   Meg read the story again. Suddenly, new ideas started popping into her head. She began writing where she had left off. She wrote again after dinner, then again on Monday at recess. In her room on Monday night, Meg wrote the last two words: *The End.*

26   Meg jumped up. "I did it! I finished my story!" she shouted. She didn't know if it was the best story ever, but she knew she liked it. Meg ran downstairs to read it to her family.

27   She started reading the story from the beginning, which hadn't changed. Then she read, "The princess had one hundred dresses lying all over her bedroom floor, but she still couldn't find her favorite red dress. The princess became so angry that she threw her crown on the floor.

28   "'I'll never find my red dress!' the princess cried. She put her head down. Then she noticed one more dress lying underneath her dresser. The princess reached for that dress. It was her favorite red dress—hidden underneath her dresser the whole time! The End."

29   Mom and Dad clapped. Nick cheered.

30   "You really *are* an author!" Dad said.

31   Meg kissed her story. Then she danced upstairs to her bedroom. She emptied her wastebasket. Meg read all her other stories. Some she saved; some she didn't.

32   A little later, Dad came up to say good night. "What are you going to call your princess story?" he asked.

33   Meg knew exactly what she wanted to call it. But then she looked at the stack of other stories that she wanted to finish.

34   Meg grinned. "I'm calling it 'The Best Story . . . So Far!'"

Answer the following questions based on the passage you just read.

1. Read paragraphs 1–6. Write a sentence summarizing what happens.

_____

_____

2. Read paragraphs 7–15. Write a sentence summarizing what happens.

_____

_____

3. Read paragraphs 16–21. Write a sentence summarizing what happens.

_____

4. Summarize paragraphs 22–23.

_____

_____

5. Now read paragraphs 24–26. This is an important point in the story. Think about what Meg does and how this is different from what she did before. Write a sentence summarizing these paragraphs.

_____

6. Summarize paragraphs 27–30.

_____

7. Read paragraphs 31–34. Write a sentence summarizing the ending.

_____

Elevate 8. Tell what Meg has learned.

_____

Elevate 9. Now put all your sentences together to write a summary of "The Best Story Ever."

_____

_____

_____

_____

_____

_____

_____

 Measuring Up to the Texas Essential Knowledge and Skills

Critical Thinking

10. Exchange your summary with a partner. Review each other's work. Keep these questions in mind:

Does the summary:

- Contain only important events?

- Leave out unimportant events and details?

- Tell the events in chronological order?

After you have reviewed each other's summaries, meet to discuss each other's reviews. Based on this discussion, rewrite your summary. This time, see if you can cut down on the number of words you use.

11. Imagine you could interview the author of this story. Jot down questions you would ask her about how she writes.

Writing	☑
Research	☐
Listening and Speaking	☐
Media Literacy	☐
21st Century Skills: Collaboration	☑

Make Connections Between Texts

Figure 19(F)	Make connections (e.g., thematic links, author analysis) between literary and informational texts with similar ideas and provide textual evidence.

Understand the TEKS

Sometimes you read two or more texts that are closely connected. Then you link the information and ideas in one with those in the other.

Texts can have the same:

- author
- topic
- main idea or theme

Words to Know
author
main idea
purpose
theme
topic

Author

The **author** is the person who wrote the selection. You may read two or more texts by the same author. Then you can do an author study. When you do an author study, you connect two or more books or selections. You think about how the characters and events are the same and how they are different. You look at their **theme**, or big idea.

You may also read about the author. Then you can connect events in the text with events in the author's life.

For example, you might:

- read about Laura Ingalls Wilder's life growing up on the prairie
- read two or more books from the *Little House on the Prairie* series
- connect the ideas and information in what you read

Write the name of an author you think would be good for an author study. Tell why.

_____

_____

_____

_____

Purpose

Each type of text has a different purpose.

Informational text may:

- inform
- explain
- tell how something works
- tell how to do something

Literature may:

- entertain
- inspire
- describe
- provide an insight into life

Suppose you are about to adopt a puppy. You might read an article to find out **how to** take care of a puppy. Then you might read a story to understand **what it feels like** to have a puppy.

Topic

The **topic** is what a text is about. You may read two or more texts about the same topic.

- One may be literature. One may be an informational text.
- Both may be literature—for example, a play and a chapter book.
- Both may be informational texts—for example, a magazine article and an encyclopedia entry.

You connect the information and ideas to deepen your understanding.

For example, maybe you remember reading Eric Carle's *The Very Hungry Caterpillar* when you were younger. You could connect this story with an article about how caterpillars grow and change. You can also read and connect a poem describing a caterpillar changing into a butterfly. Then you might study a diagram showing the life cycle of a butterfly. By connecting the texts, you learn more about caterpillars.

- Write a topic you are interested in.

• What are two or more texts you might read to learn more about this topic?

_____

_____

Theme and Main Idea

The big idea about the topic in informational text is called the **main idea**.

The main idea of the article might be:

> Taking care of a puppy is hard work.

The big idea in literature is called the **theme**. It is an insight into life. It tells about life and people in general.

> There is no better friend than a dog.

When you read two or more texts about the same topic, they may have the same big idea or opposite ones. Then you make connections to understand these similarities and differences. You connect your own experience to see what you think.

Comprehension Tip
Create a chart. Make a column for each text. Label the last column "My Thoughts." Write details from the text in each column as you read. Connect the details and write your ideas in the last column.

Guided Instruction

Read the passage below. Then answer the questions in the margin and complete the activities.

Runaway Blue
by Marty Lapointe-Malchik

1   *Ding!*

2   "One big blue-corn pancake for the itty-bitty baby," bellows Betty.

3   "Coming right up," says the cook.

4   *Drip!* The cook forms one eye. *Drop!* Another eye. *Glop!* A nose. *Dribble!* A mouth. But the cook doesn't stop there. "And now for two big feet," he says. *Blob! Blob!* "There's nothing more beautiful than a grill full of grub."

5   *Boing!* Up jumps that blue-corn pancake, and he runs out the door.

6   "Uh-oh," says Itty-Bitty Baby, climbing down from his chair and clutching a pitcher of maple syrup in his itty-bitty hands.

7   Itty-Bitty Baby's mama looks over and screams. "Pedro, put down that paper!" she yells to Papa. "Our baby just took off after his breakfast!"

8   Down the street bolts Runaway Blue with Itty-Bitty Baby toddling after him.

9   Mama spots Itty-Bitty Baby's sitter, Sweet Nina Serena, on the sidewalk. "Sweet Nina Serena, you've got to help us! Baby's breakfast just blew out of town."

10   "Stop! Stop!" yells Sweet Nina Serena to Runaway Blue.

11   "Stop?" the pancake yells back. "For you?" Not Runaway Blue! I've run away from Itty-Bitty Baby. And I'll run away from you, too!"

"Runaway Blue" by Marty Lapointe-Malchik, Copyright © 2010 by Highlights for Children, Inc., Columbus, Ohio

Guided Questions

What is happening in paragraph **4**? What is unusual?

_____

_____

_____

Read paragraph **5**. What is unusual, or fantastic, about what happens?

_____

_____

Now read up to paragraph **11**. What is the purpose of this story? How do you know?

_____

_____

_____

_____

12   On and on runs Runaway Blue, higher and higher to the top of the mesa, into a village, and past some potters. "Pinch him like a pot!" yells Sweet Nina Serena.

13   "Hold it!" holler the potters to Runaway Blue.

14   "Hold it?" the pancake hollers back. "For you? Not Runaway Blue! I've run away from a grill full of grub. I've run away from Sweet Nina Serena. And I'll run away from you, too."

15   Down, down, down the mesa dashes Runaway Blue, faster and faster, all the way to Green Chili Willy's pepper farm on the Rio Grande.

16   "Pick him like a pepper!" shout the potters.

17   "Whoa!" wails Green Chili Willy.

18   "Whoa?" the pancake wails back. "For you? Not Runaway Blue! I've run away from a grill full of grub. I've run away from Itty-Bitty Baby. I've run away from Sweet Nina Serena. I've run away from a village full of potters. And I'll run away from you, too!"

19   On and on races Runaway Blue, faster and faster, but then he stops short on the banks of the Rio Grande. Closer and closer come Itty-Bitty Baby, Sweet Nina Serena, the potters, and Green Chili Willy.

20   Runaway Blue darts onto a log that reaches across the river.

21   "Grab him!" growls Green Chili Willy. "That's Coyote Kit on the other side!"

22   Runaway Blue looks down at the water. Closer and closer comes Coyote Kit.

23   "Yummy!" yips Coyote Kit.

24   "Doggy!" cries Itty-Bitty Baby, dropping the syrup.

25   Runaway Blue thinks fast. He grabs the syrup pitcher. *Drip!* A puddle. *Glop!* A huge puddle oozes toward Coyote Kit. Coyote Kit sniffs at the puddle. He laps at it. He laps and laps. *Swish, swish* goes his tail.

26   Now Runaway Blue thinks even faster than he runs. He jumps onto the tip of Coyote Kit's swishing tail. *Flip!* Up goes that blue-corn pancake high into the air. *Flip. Flap. Flop.* Runaway Blue drops on the other side of the Rio Grande.

Guided Questions

Read paragraphs **12**–**14**. Highlight what Nina Serena wants the potters to do.

Read paragraphs **15**–**18**. Highlight what the potters want Green Chili Willy to do.

Reread paragraphs **11**, **14**, and **18**. Compare what happens each time the pancake speaks. How does this affect the feeling of the story?

_____

_____

_____

_____

Read paragraphs **19**–**26**. What is Runaway Blue's plan for escape?

_____

_____

_____

_____

27 "Don't pat that doggy!" cries Sweet Nina Serena, scooping up Itty-Bitty Baby.

28 Green Chili Willy and the potters push the log off the bank, and Coyote Kit sails down the river.

29 Runaway Blue bolts out of sight.

30 "All gone," says Itty-Bitty Baby.

31 Later that morning, the diner is bustling with business.

32 *DING!*

33 "One big blue-corn pancake for the itty-bitty baby," bellows Betty. "But this time, hold the feet!"

Make Your Own Corn Pancakes
from *Highlights* magazine
Makes 8 big Corn Pancakes
1 cup blue or yellow cornmeal
½ cup flour
1 tablespoon sugar
2 teaspoons baking powder
1 teaspoon baking soda
½ teaspoon salt
2 eggs
½ cup milk
1 cup sour cream
¼ melted butter

Guided Questions

In paragraph **33**, highlight what Betty bellows. Why does she say this?

Read the title of the recipe. How is the purpose of the recipe different from the purpose of the story about a corn pancake?

1. Stir together the cornmeal, flour, sugar, baking powder, baking soda, and salt.

2. In another bowl, beat the eggs. Add the milk, sour cream, and melted butter.

3. Dump the ingredients of one bowl into the other and gently stir together. Let the thick batter sit for 10 minutes.

4. With an adult's help, drop heaping spoonfuls of batter onto a greased griddle over medium heat. Flip the pancakes when bubbles appear in them. Cook until lightly browned. Serve immediately.

5. Top with syrup, powdered sugar, or warm applesauce.

Guided Questions

Look at the numbered steps. How are they arranged?

_____

_____

How were the events in "Runaway Blue" arranged?

_____

_____

_____

_____

Answer the following questions based on the passage you just read.

1. Read the paragraph below from "Runaway Blue."

> Drip! *The cook forms one eye.* Drop! *Another eye.* Glop! *A nose.* Dribble! *A mouth. But the cook doesn't stop there.* "And now for two big feet," *he says.* Blob! Blob! *"There's nothing more beautiful than a grill full of grub."*

What type of language does the author use in this paragraph?

_____

_____

Does the language help the writer accomplish her purpose? Why or why not?

_____

_____

2. Now read the steps in the recipe. What type of language does the author use?

_____

Does the language help the writer accomplish the purpose? Why or why not?

_____

3. Fill in the chart below comparing the two selections.

	Runaway Blue	**Make Your Own Corn Pancakes**
Form		
Purpose		
Organized by		
Language		
Feeling		

 4. Suppose you were editing a magazine. Would you put these selections together? Why or why not?

_____

_____

Critical Thinking

5. Form an editorial team for a magazine. Choose a topic for a monthly issue of the magazine. The team's job is to come up with ideas for topics for selections. Brainstorm ideas, listing as many topics as you can. Then cut your list back to the six that will appear in the issue.

Writing	☐
Research	☐
Listening and Speaking	☑
Media Literacy	☑
21st Century Skills: Collaboration	☑
Cross-Curriculum Connection	☐

Media Connection

6. Choose another author who writes funny stories. (Beverly Cleary would be a good choice.) Use the Internet and your media center to find books and stories. Create your own author study. Choose five texts you recommend for reading. List them on a notecard.

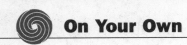

On Your Own

Read the selections below. Then answer the questions that follow them.

Literature
Connection

Little Yin and the Moon

by Jeremy Yoder

1   One hot day, Yin heard her mother weeping in a corner of their hut. In her mother's arms lay Yin's baby brother, Zhou, who was also crying. Yin drew close, placing a hand on her mother's arm. "Mother, why do you cry?"

2   Her mother spoke between sobs. "Little Yin, I cry because the fields are almost empty, and the cow has stopped giving milk. Our family is hungry, and I am frightened."

3   Yin had never seen her mother look so sad or so scared.

4   "Mother, I will find a way to help," Yin said with determination. She put on her wide straw hat and went out to the stable where their red cow stared over the wooden fence. Yin gently stroked the cow's forehead. "Cow, why do you not give milk to feed my family?"

5   The cow blinked her large brown eyes. "Little Yin, the brook has very little water. Without more to drink, I cannot give any milk."

6   Yin crossed the dry rice field to the skinny brook. She knelt down and gently placed her hand in the warm water. "Brook, why do you not give more water so that the cow may drink her fill?"

7   The brook, who usually rushed past, now only trickled. "Little Yin, I cannot give much water because the mountain lake does not offer me more."

8   Yin looked up the mountain. Traveling to the lake would take all day. After taking a tiny bit of food and a blanket for warmth, she kissed her family good-bye and headed out.

9   As darkness fell, Yin reached the small lake halfway up the mountain. She took off a shoe and dipped her toes into the water, creating ripples on the glassy surface. "Lake, why do you not give more water to the brook so that he may laugh again?"

10   The lake brushed a few feeble waves against the shore. "Little Yin, I have grown shallow. If I give more water I will disappear, and then there will be no brook at all."

11   "How can I give you more water?" Yin asked.

12   The lake sighed. "There is nothing you can do. I only grow when it rains. The sun has burned brightly for a long time and will not let rain fall."

13   "There *must* be something I can do," said Yin. "But for now, I must wait for the sun." Yin spread out her blanket and ate the little food she had brought. Still hungry, she lay down and slept.

14   The next morning, the sun peeked over the horizon. Yin wondered how she could talk to the sun, because he was so far away. Gathering her blanket, she looked up the mountain and started to climb.

15   At long last, she reached the top. As the sun rose to the highest point in the sky, Yin squinted against the heat and shouted, "Sun, why do you burn so brightly? Why do you not let rain fall and fill the lake?"

16   Sun gazed down with a stern look. "I burn brightly because I am angry that I cannot help Moon, who has cried for many months."

17   Not knowing what to do next, Yin waited at the top of the mountain. She was very hungry by now and wanted to go home, but the thought of her family gave her strength. Yin wrapped herself in her blanket. Finally night came, and with it, the moon and stars.

18   Moon stared down with such sadness that Yin felt she might cry, too. "Moon, why do you weep and make Sun angry?"

19   Moon sniffled several times. "I cry because I am sad, for I am always cold. Sun is angry because he cannot give me his warmth, for he may only shine during the day, and I at night."

20   Yin was just a poor peasant girl, but she would offer all she had. Draping her blanket over her hands, she held it up to Moon. "Please, take my blanket and stay warm."

21   A soft wind blew the blanket high into the air. Moon accepted the blanket and drew it tight, until only a sliver of Moon could be seen. "Thank you, Little Yin, for your generous gift. I shall now sleep well."

22   Though she was very cold, Yin slept soundly. The next morning, the sky swirled with dark clouds. Yin hurried down the mountain. When she reached the lake, lightning flashed, and rain began to fall.

23   As Yin ran faster, the sky opened and great drops fell into the lake. By the time Yin reached her home, the brook was bubbling with laughter, and the cow was drinking her fill.

24   "Little Yin!" her mother cried happily as Zhou bounced into her arms. "Because of you, our family may eat once again."

25   While Yin's mother milked the cow, Yin gathered what little rice remained in the field, knowing more would grow back soon. After they ate a meal together, Yin wept with joy as Zhou smiled and fell asleep with a full belly.

26   Over the years, as Little Yin grew into an old woman, she would gaze up at Moon and see her blanket. Sometimes only a little bit covered Moon's toes, and other times, the blanket covered Moon entirely. Each time Yin watched, she felt happy, knowing Moon would forever stay warm.

Science Connection

Understanding Our Moon

by Jana Sweeney

1   We have all seen the moon shine brightly in the night sky. But did you know that the moon does not give off, or emit, any light of its own? The moon is not a star. Therefore, it cannot create any light. The moon shines by reflecting sunlight.

2   Only half of the moon faces the sun and reflects sunlight. The other half is always dark. We never see that half of the moon.

Moon Phases

3   Every month, we watch as the moon appears to change slowly from a thin slice to a full circle and then back to a thin slice. These changes in the moon's appearance are called the phases of the moon. But the moon is not really changing size. It only looks that way to us here on Earth. What is really happening is that we are seeing more or less of the side facing the sun.

A Moon in Motion

4   The moon orbits, or goes around, Earth every 29 ½ days. As the moon orbits Earth, we see a little more of the side facing the sun each day until we can see the entire side that is reflecting sunlight. When the moon appears to be getting bigger, it is waxing.

5   Then we see a little less of the sun-facing side each day until the moon seems to disappear. When the moon appears to be getting smaller, it is waning.

"Understanding Our Moon" by Jana Sweeney

 Measuring Up to the Texas Essential Knowledge and Skills

The Different Phases

6   Each phase of the moon has a name. When the moon is between the Earth and the sun, it looks completely dark because Earth blocks the sun's light from reaching the moon. This is called a new moon. After a new moon, as the slice gets bigger, the phase is called waxing crescent. (See the picture.)

7   About one week after the new moon, the moon looks like a half circle. This phase is called first quarter. The moon is one quarter of its way around the Earth.

8   As the moon continues to appear larger, it is the waxing gibbous phase. When the moon looks like a full circle, it is called a full moon.

9   After a full moon, the moon begins to look smaller. This is the waning gibbous phase. When the moon looks like a half circle again, it is called the third quarter. The moon is now three quarters of its way around the Earth.

10   Finally, the moon is not visible. The moon is, again, between the Earth and the sun. This is a new moon, and all of the phases begin again.

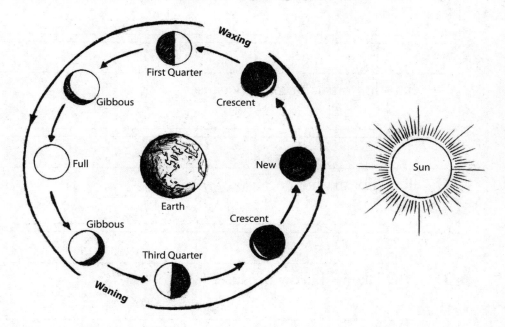

Answer the following questions based on the passage you just read.

1. Both "Little Yin and the Moon" and "Understanding Our Moon" provide an explanation for why the moon looks different at different times of the month. Fill in the chart below comparing the two texts.

	Little Yin and the Moon	Understanding Our Moon
Type of Text		
Type of Explanation		

2. Complete each of these statements showing the chain of causes and effects in "Little Yin and the Moon."

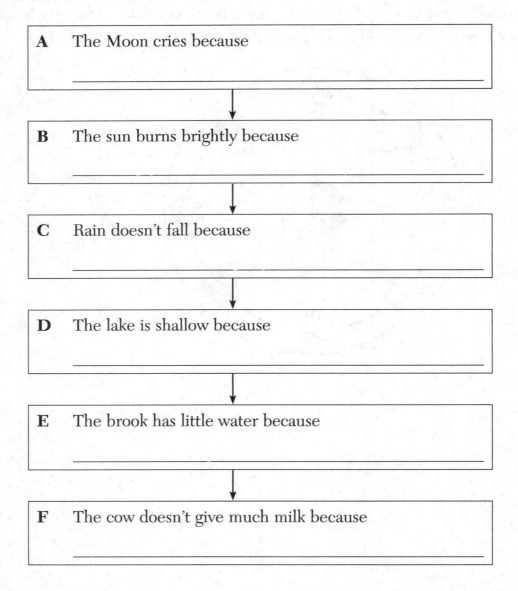

A The Moon cries because

_____

B The sun burns brightly because

_____

C Rain doesn't fall because

_____

D The lake is shallow because

_____

E The brook has little water because

_____

F The cow doesn't give much milk because

_____

 Measuring Up to the Texas Essential Knowledge and Skills

3. Read this paragraph from "Little Yin and the Moon."

> *Moon sniffled several times. "I cry because I am sad, for I am always cold. Sun is angry because he cannot give me his warmth, for he may only shine during the day, and I at night."*

Do we really see the light from the moon at night? Find a statement from "Understanding Our Moon" that supports your answer.

_____

_____

Do you think it is okay for "Little Yin and the Moon" to contain this information, even though it isn't exactly accurate? Explain your thinking.

_____

_____

_____

4. How does "Little Yin and the Moon" explain the phases of the moon?

_____

_____

How does "Understanding Our Moon" explain this?

_____

_____

5. Connect the information in both texts. If Moon started to push her blanket off, she would be in what phase?

A Full

B New moon

C Waxing

D Waning

6. "Understanding Our Moon" uses a diagram as an illustration. Is this a good choice for this text? Why or why not?

_____

_____

Suppose you got to choose an illustration to include in the story "Little Yin and the Moon." How would your illustration be different from the one used in "Understanding Our Moon"? Why?

_____

_____

_____

Critical Thinking

7. Work with a partner. Design a demonstration to explain the phases of the moon. First discuss what you want to show. Make a list of equipment you will need. Then rehearse your demonstration. Finally, present it to your classmates.

Writing	☐
Research	☐
Listening and Speaking	☑
Media Literacy	☐
21st Century Skills: Collaboration	☑
Cross-Curriculum Connection: Science	☑

Media Connection

8. You can watch a video to learn more about the phases of the moon at http://www.youtube.com/watch?v=gHlMReTpJXw.

Read the selection. Then choose the best answer to each question.

A Very Good Story

by Carol Farley
from Spider Magazine

1   When tigers smoked long pipes and told endless stories, an old man and his wife lived in the land of Korea. Their only company was their faithful servant, Hap, because they lived far from any village or city. They were healthy and wealthy, but they were often bored on lonely evenings.

2   "If only we knew a good story!" Mr. Kim would say. "Then we could tell it every evening."

3   Hap was sorry to see that the couple had nothing to amuse themselves. "Perhaps I should go to the nearest city and buy a story for you," he finally suggested.

4   "But do people sell stories?" Mr. Kim's wife asked.

"A Very Good Story" published by SPIDER magazine, November 1999,
Copyright © 1999 by Carol Farley

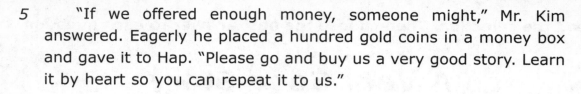

5   "If we offered enough money, someone might," Mr. Kim answered. Eagerly he placed a hundred gold coins in a money box and gave it to Hap. "Please go and buy us a very good story. Learn it by heart so you can repeat it to us."

6   So faithful Hap set out. But his heart was bigger than his brain; he had no idea what would make a good story. After several days of traveling, he came upon a man loitering on the outskirts of a city. "Do you have a story for sale?" Hap asked, jingling the coins in his money box.

7   The man was a cunning and greedy thief who instantly saw that Hap had more money than common sense. "Yes, I have a fine story I might sell," he answered. "How much will you pay?"

8   "One hundred coins," answered Hap.

9   The thief's heart leaped. "One hundred coins?" he cried.

10   "Is that enough?" asked Hap. "My master said that I must buy a *very* good story, but this is all he gave me."

11   Nearly choking with greed, the thief answered, "Oh, have no fear. My story is good, all right. And one hundred coins is sufficient. Give me the money."

12   "No," said Hap. "First I must hear the story so I can repeat it to my master."

13   Other people were nearby, so the thief knew he had to tell some sort of tale. But he could think of nothing. In desperation he looked at a far-off rice field, where a stork had just landed. He simply decided to describe every movement of the bird. Maybe his words would make a good story.

14   "He steps carefully," the thief said. "He comes closer."

15   Hap thought that this was a fine beginning. "He steps carefully," he repeated. "He comes closer."

16   "Now he stops and raises his head," the thief went on.

17   "Now he stops and raises his head," Hap echoed.

18   "He bends down!" the thief said as the bird pecked at the ground. "He creeps closer."

19   Hap could make little sense of the tale, but he dutifully repeated, "He bends down! He creeps closer."

20   Suddenly a fox appeared behind the bird. "There's danger!" cried the thief.

21   "Danger!" Hap repeated.

22   But the stork had seen the danger. Flapping its mighty wings, it flew off to safety. "He's fleeing! All is safe!" the thief shouted.

23   Hap echoed his words, then waited for more. When nothing came, he leaned closer. "Is that the end?"

24   "Of course!" said the thief. "And a very good story it is. Now give me the money."

25   Hap carefully counted out the hundred coins. It was a most peculiar story, he thought, but he knew little of such things.

26   When he returned to Mr. Kim and his wife, they, too, thought the story was very strange, but they were happy finally to have some entertainment. Every night Mr. Kim loudly retold the story, marveling over how little sense it made. His wife and Hap closed their eyes and listened, then begged to hear the tale again.

27   Many moons later, the cunning thief was traveling in their direction. He had long since forgotten about selling Hap his foolish story. He had spent all his money, too. So he joined a band of robbers, who told him that a wealthy old man named Kim, his old wife, and an elderly servant lived alone in the countryside. He decided this was the place he would rob.

28   When the thief reached Mr. Kim's courtyard, it was pitch-dark, and no one was in sight. He tiptoed quietly toward the window.

29   "He steps carefully!" a voice rang out. "He comes closer!"

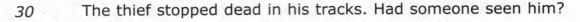

30   The thief stopped dead in his tracks. Had someone seen him?

31   "Now he stops and raises his head!" the voice went on.

32   What magic is this? The thief could scarcely breathe. Someone in that house could see in the dark! Nervously he bent toward the ground, trying to hide himself.

33   "He bends down!" the voice shouted.

34   Frightened out of his wits, the thief heard his heart thumping as loudly as the drum of a monk. Did he dare inch closer to see what manner of person was talking? Perhaps if he crouched on the ground, he could move without being seen. He took a tiny step.

35   "He creeps closer!" the voice rang out.

36   Horrified, the thief leaped to his feet. There was no way to fool this incredible person.

37   "Danger!" cried the voice.

38   The robber waited no longer. This house and this strange person were much too frightening. He whirled around and scurried out of the courtyard.

39   "He's fleeing! All is safe!" the voice shouted after him.

40   The thief did not stop running until he reached the robbers' den. "Never go near the far-off house of Mr. Kim!" he warned them. "There is too much mystery and magic there!"

41   And so Mr. Kim's household remained safe. He and his wife continued to sit with Hap every evening and marvel over the strange story.

42   "Do you think we paid too much for it?" Mr. Kim asked one night.

43   "No," his wife said. "The more I hear the tale, the more it makes me wonder. And wonder is a very valuable thing."

44   So they lived safely and happily ever after, never knowing just how very good their story was.

1 Read the sentence below.

> *When tigers smoked long pipes and told endless stories, an old man and his wife lived in the land of Korea.*

From the details in this sentence, the reader knows that this text is —

A a real-life adventure with real people

B an informational article about Korea

C a how-to article about ways to tell stories

D a made-up story with made-up characters

---

2 All these items describe Hap except —

F kind-hearted, because he wants to help the old man and woman

G crafty, because he tricks the thief

H foolish, because he buys the story

J trusting, because he hears the story and accepts that it must be good

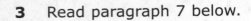

3   Read paragraph 7 below.

> *The man was a cunning and greedy thief who instantly saw that Hap had more money than common sense. "Yes, I have a fine story I might sell," he answered. "How much will you pay?"*

The first sentence supports the inference that the thief —

A   will try to trick Hap

B   wants more money than Hap has

C   is telling the truth

D   will steal Hap's money box

---

4   When the thief hears the story in paragraphs 29–39, he thinks the pronoun *he* refers to —

F   the stork

G   Hap

H   the old man

J   himself

---

5   How does the story turn out to be more valuable than the Kims think?

A   It fills them with wonder.

B   It protects them from thieves.

C   They can hear it over and over again.

D   It entertains them in the evenings.

6 Which of these is the best summary of "A Very Good Story"?

F The Kims are lonely and bored, but they have a lot of money. They think they would be happier if they knew a good story. Mr. Kim gives their servant Hap a box filled with money, and Hap sets off to buy a story. A cunning thief sells Hap a story, and he takes it home to the Kims.

G Hap sets out to buy a story to entertain the old couple he works for. A greedy thief sells Hap a story he makes up by describing a stork. Later, when the thief tries to rob the Kims' house, he hears Mr. Kim tell the story and thinks Mr. Kim is describing him. He runs off, and the Kims go on retelling the story and living in safety.

H A cunning thief makes up a story by describing a stork. Hap buys the story and takes it home to Mr. and Mrs. Kim. Mr. and Mrs. Kim live in Korea, far away from any towns or villages. They are often bored on long evenings and want a story to entertain them.

J In "A Very Good Story," Hap sets out to buy a very good story for Mr. and Mrs. Kim. He buys a story from a thief that describes a robber robbing a person's house. The story is very mysterious, and Mr. and Mrs. Kim like it because it is so peculiar. Mr. Kim retells it every night.

Use Spelling Changes to Decode Words

3.1(Ai), (ii), (iii)	Decode multisyllabic words in context and independent of context by applying common spelling patterns including: (i) dropping the final "e" and add endings such as -ing, -ed, or -able (e.g., use, using, used, usable); (ii) doubling final consonants when adding an ending (e.g., hop to hopping); (iii) changing the final "y" to "i" (e.g., baby to babies).
3.1(E)	Monitor accuracy in decoding.

⟳ Understand the TEKS

Spelling Changes

You know many words. When you read, you may see a word in a form that looks different. You get confused. You think you don't know the word, but you really do.

Words to Know
base word
consonant
vowel

Here are some ways the spelling of a word may change:

Drop Final *e*

Some words end in e. When you add an ending that begins with a vowel, you drop the final e in the original word.

like + ed = liked   move + ed = moved
like + ing = liking   move + ing = moving
like + able = likable   move + able = movable

• Suppose you read the word *lovable*. What is the base word?

_____

Double Final Consonant

Some words follow this pattern:

consonant–vowel–consonant

Words that follow this pattern are called c-v-c words.

When you add the ending *-ed* or *-ing* to c-v-c words, you double the final consonant.

tap + ed = tapped   grin + ed = grinned
tap + ing = tapping   grin + ing = grinning

• Suppose you read the word *snapping*. What is the base word?

_____

Measuring Up to the Texas Essential Knowledge and Skills

c-v-c words that end in *w, x, y,* or *z* do not follow this pattern. You do not double the final consonant.

snow + ed = snowed   box + ed = boxed
snow + ing = snowing   box + ing = boxing

When Does *y* Change to *i*?

Noun Ending in a Consonant and *y* If a noun ends in a consonant and *y*, its plural form looks a little different from its singular form. Change the *y* to *i* and add *es* to form the plural.

baby + es = babies   pony + es = ponies

Nouns Ending in a Vowel and *y* If a noun ends in a vowel and *y*, just add *s*.

monkey + s = monkeys holiday + s = holidays

Verbs Ending in a Consonant and *y* Change the *y* to *i* and add *es* to form the present tense verb that goes with *he, she,* or *it*.

try + es = tries   he tries
deny + es = denies   she denies

Change the *y* to *i* when you add *-ed*.

hurry + ed = hurried   study + ed = studied

The *y* does not change when you add *-ing*.

hurry + ing = hurrying   study + ing = studying

Verbs Ending in a Vowel and *y* Simply add *s* to form the present tense verb that goes with *he, she,* or *it*.

play + s = plays   he plays
destroy + s = destroys it destroys

Do not change the *y* when you add *-ed* or *-ing*.

play + ed = played   destroy + ed = destroyed
play + ing = playing   destroy + ing = destroying

• Suppose you read the word *married*. What is the base word?

Comprehension Tip
Look for the base word when you read a longer word you don't recognize. Use its meaning to determine the meaning of the longer word.

 Guided Instruction

Read the passage below. Then answer the questions in the margin and complete the activities.

Science Connection

Spider's Riddle

by Jan Fields

Guided Questions

1   Chickadee landed on a black cherry twig. **A** She spotted a spider knitting and knitting with soft, white silk.

2   "What are you knitting?" Chickadee asked. "Is it a hat? Everyone should have a stylish hat." Chickadee tilted her head so Spider would be certain to notice her stylish cap.

Look at sentence **A** in paragraph **1**. Highlight the word *knitting*. What is the base word?

_____

3   "It will be warm like a hat," Spider said softly. "But it's not a hat."

4   "Too bad," said Chickadee, snapping up a cherry and flapping away.

Look at paragraph **4**. Find the two c-v-c words in which the consonant was doubled. Highlight them. What are the two base words?

_____

"Spider's Riddle" by Jan Fields, Reprinted by permission of LADYBUG magazine March 2009, text © 2009 by Carus Publishing Company

Guided Questions

5   Butterfly fluttered over to land on the honeysuckle vine twisting through the strong cherry branches. She spotted Spider knitting and knitting

6   "What are you knitting?" Butterfly asked. "Is it a cape?" If you weave flowers in, it might be nearly as pretty as my wings." **B** Butterfly spread her bright wings to show off the pattern.

7   "I do want it to be beautiful," Spider said softly. "But it's not a cape."

8   "Too bad," said Butterfly as she sipped honeysuckle nectar and fluttered away.

9   **C** Chipmunk scrambled up through the branches. He spotted Spider knitting and knitting.

10   "What are you knitting?" he asked. "Is it a food pouch? If you had a pouch, you could carry food. You wouldn't have to sit in this tree all day." **D** Chipmunk shoved a few cherries into his cheek pouches to show how useful they were.

11   "I will fill it with precious things," Spider said softly. "But it is not a food pouch."

12   **E** "Too bad," Chipmunk mumbled, cramming one last cherry into his mouth and scrambling down the tree.

13   Spider knit and knit until she had a dry, snug cradle. She tied it to the silk of her web and filled it with eggs. Then she knit a warm cover and tucked it over them. The breeze blew the web and rocked the babies gently as they slumbered in their eggs.

14   Chickadee, Butterfly, and Chipmunk came to see the tiny cradle.

15   "It isn't stylish," said Chickadee.

16   "It doesn't have colorful patterns," said Butterfly.

17   "You can't carry food in it," said Chipmunk.

18   "But it is very wonderful," Spider said softly.

19   And the others agreed.

Find the word *show* in sentence **B** in paragraph **6**. Highlight it. What consonant does this word end in? Add *-ed* to *show*. Add *-ing* to *show*.

_____

_____

Highlight the word *scrambled* in sentence **C** in paragraph **9**. What is the base word? Add *-ing* to the base word.

_____

Highlight the word *cherries* in sentence **D** in paragraph **10**. What is the base word?

_____

Highlight the word *mumbled* in sentence **E** in paragraph **12**. What is the base word? What did Chipmuck do if he mumbled?

_____

_____

Answer the following questions based on the passage you just read.

1. Read the sentence below. Pay attention to the underlined word.

   > *If you <u>weave</u> flowers in, it might be nearly as pretty as my wings."*

   Add the ending *-ing* to the word *weave*. Write a sentence using the new word.

   _____

   _____

2. Read the sentence below. Pay attention to the underlined word.

   > *Chipmunk <u>shoved</u> a few cherries into his cheek pouches to show how useful they were.*

   What is the base word of *shoved*? What does it mean?

   _____

   Add *-ing* to the base word and write a sentence using the word you formed.

   _____

   _____

3. Complete the chart below.

Base Word	Add *-ed*	Add *-ing*
spot		
knit		
snap		
flap		
sip		
scramble		
carry		

Measuring Up to the Texas Essential Knowledge and Skills

4. Talk to a partner. Brainstorm a list of facts you know about spiders. Then talk about what you learned about spiders from this story.

Critical Thinking

Writing	☐
Research	☐
Listening and Speaking	☑
Media Literacy	☐
21st Century Skills: Collaboration	☑
Cross Curriculum Connection: Science	☑

5. You can find images of spiders at http://www.bing.com/images/search?q=spiders+for+children&qpvt=spiders+for+children&FORM=IGRE. Choose the image to go with this story. Tell your partner the reasons for your choice.

Media Connection

 On Your Own

Read the selection below. Then answer the questions that follow it.

Literature Connection

First Step

by Laurie Alloway

1   "Do you want to stand?" Mom asked my baby sister, Allie.

2   "EEEEahhhh," said Allie, pointing at me.

3   "She wants you to help," said Mom.

4   "She does?" How did Mom get that from EEEEahhhh? I thought.

5   "Here, take her fingers," Mom said to me.

6   "As long as she didn't slobber all over them," I said.

7   "Aaron . . ."

8   "OK, Mom."

9   Allie grabbed my thumb with her wet, pudgy fingers. Yuck. She squeezed my thumb so hard it turned purple. She swayed back and forth like a tree in the wind.

10   "Let go now," said Mom.

11   "Let go?" That didn't sound like a good idea.

"First Step" by Laurie Alloway, Copyright © 2010 by Highlights for Children, Inc., Columbus, Ohio

12   Allie's knees <u>wobbled</u>.

13   "EEEEEaaaaaahhhh," she said.

14   "Come on, you can walk," said Mom.

15   Allie put one foot forward and, plop, sat down on the carpet.

16   "Waaaaaaa," she cried.

17   "It's OK. Try again," said Mom.

18   Allie reached for my hand. This time, her fingers weren't slobbery. I guess the slobber had already rubbed off. Allie wiggled and wobbled from side to side. When I let go, she put her arms out to balance. She put one foot forward. Then another. She stood still for a second. Then <u>plop</u>.

19   Mom clapped. "Did you see that, Aaron? Allie took her first step. Allie's walking. Hip, hip, hooray for Allie!"

20   I rolled my eyes. That was walking? But by the time we bundled up and headed for the ice-skating rink the next week, Allie could take six steps without falling.

21   It was my first ice-skating lesson. Mom helped me lace up my skates. She held my hand as I wobbled like Allie toward the rink. My teacher grabbed my other hand and helped me onto the ice. I swayed, almost falling backward. Mom waved. Allie pointed. *How can I take my first step without falling?* I thought. I looked down at the ice and remembered Allie's pudgy fingers.

22   "You can do it," yelled Mom.

23   The teacher held my hand as I put one foot in front of the other, trying to balance. The teacher let go. Plop. I landed on the ice.

24   "Keep trying. You can do it!" yelled Mom. Allie screeched.

25   *I'm not giving up*, I thought, reaching for the teacher's hand. I stood and put one shaky foot forward. The teacher let go. I put another foot forward, my arms free. I was moving on my own!

26   "Way to go, Aaron. You're ice-skating," cheered Mom, clapping. "Did you see that, Allie? Your brother's ice-skating."

27   "EEEEahhhh." Allie squealed and clapped.

28   *I'm ice-skating*, I thought. *I'm really ice-skating*. I put another foot forward. It felt good to be <u>sliding</u> on the ice.

29   *Hip, hip, hooray for Allie and me.*

Answer the following questions based on the passage you just read.

1. Read the sentence below.

   > *Allie <u>grabbed</u> my thumb with her wet, pudgy fingers.*

   The *-ing* form of a verb has a helping verb that goes with it (*is, are, was, were, has, have*). Rewrite the sentence above. Use the *-ing* form of the underlined verb and the helping verb *is*.

   _____

   _____

2. Read the sentence below. Pay attention to the underlined word.

   > *The teacher held my hand as I put one foot in front of the other, <u>trying</u> to balance.*

   What is the base word in *trying*? Write a sentence using the *-ed* form of this verb.

   _____

   _____

3. What does <u>wobbled</u> mean in paragraph 12?

   A Moved in an unsteady way

   B Fell over suddenly

   C Started to cry

   D Walked well

4. Which item below is the correct form of <u>plop</u> in paragraph 18 when you add *-ed*?

   A Ploped

   B Ploied

   C Plopied

   D Plopped

5. Complete the chart below. Add the plural form of each noun.

Singular	Plural
baby	
boy	
story	
tray	
berry	
cry	

6. What is the base word for <u>sliding</u> in paragraph 28?

A Slid

B Slidi

C Slide

D Sled

7. Suppose you are reading a story set in the past. Why is it important to understanding the spelling pattern for dropping final *e*?

_____

_____

Critical Thinking

8. Write about a time you learned to do something new. Tell how you felt. Draw an illustration to go with it. Read over your writing to make sure you have spelled all the words correctly. Then read your passage aloud to a partner.

Writing	☑
Research	☐
Listening and Speaking	☑
Media Literacy	☐
21st Century Skills: Adaptability	☑
Cross Curriculum Connection	☐

9. With a partner, look toward magazines and newspapers. Find examples of words that follow the spelling patterns you have learned. Create a chart showing your findings. Then present the chart to your classmates.

Use Spelling Patterns to Decode Words

| 3.1(C) | Decode words by applying knowledge of common spelling patterns (e.g., -eigh, -ought). |
| 3.1(E) | Monitor accuracy in decoding. |

Understand the TEKS

Patterns

Words follow patterns. A **pattern** is a group of letters that often appear together.

If you know how to read one word in a pattern, you can decode other words with the same pattern.

Words to Know
homophone
long vowel
short vowel
spelling pattern

c-v-c Words

Words that follow the pattern consonant-vowel-consonant have a short vowel sound.

    mat   rip   hop

c-v-c and *e* Words

Words that end in an *e* after the c-v-c have a long vowel sound.

    mate   ripe   hope

-eigh

The letters *-eigh* spell the long /a/ sound you hear in *say*.

    neigh   sleigh   weigh

-eight

The letters *-eight* spell the sound of long /a/ followed by *t*. It's the sound that you hear in *late*.

    eight   freight   weight

-ought and -aught

The letters *-ought* and *-aught* form the sound you hear in *bought*.

    brought   ought   caught

• What is another word that follows this spelling pattern?

-ough

The letters -ough can spell two different sounds. Sometimes, they spell the sound you hear in *cuff*.

      rough   tough   enough

Sometimes they spell the sound you hear in *cow*.

      bough   plough

-ight

The letters -ight spell the sound you hear in *kite*.

      fight   light   might

• What is another word that follows this spelling pattern?

_____

-ouse

The letters -ouse spell the sound you hear in *mouse.*

      house   louse   douse

-ooth

The letters -ooth spell the /oo/ you hear in *food* followed by *th*.

      booth   tooth

-ack

The letters -ack have a short /a/ sound.

      back   pack   tack

Homophones

Homophones are two words that sound alike but are spelled differently and have different meanings. Often, they follow different spelling patterns.

      tail – tale   eight – ate   right – write

• What is a homophone for *sale*?

_____

Comprehension Tip

Look for spelling patterns as you read. They may help you decode words you do not know.

Guided Instruction

Read the passage below. Then answer the questions in the margin and complete the activities.

Literature
Connection

The Fifth Reason

by Debbie Levy

1   I thought I liked Cora, who moved to my neighborhood last summer.

2   I thought we'd be friends, so I invited her to my house.

3   We played Crazy Eights. I won every time.

4   I love winning.

5   We rode our bikes up and down the street.

6   I love riding my bike.

7   We talked and talked and talked.

8   I love talking about myself.

9   I waited for Cora to invite me to her house.

10   I waited and waited.

11   And waited.

"The Fifth Reason" by Debbie Levy, Copyright © 2009 by Highlights for Children, Inc., Columbus, Ohio

Guided Questions

Highlight the word *thought* in paragraph **1**. What is a word that rhymes with *thought*?

_____

Highlight the name of the game in paragraph **3**. What is a homophone for *eight*?

_____

Highlight the word *house* in paragraph **9**. What is a word that rhymes with *house*?

_____

12   She never invited me.

13   And so I decided I had four good reasons not to like Cora after all.

14   **Reason Number One:** She knew only one card game.

15   Cora didn't know Slapjack, Go Fish, or Concentration. Just Crazy Eights. We played Crazy Eights over and over.

16   **Reason Number Two:** She didn't want to ride her bike fast.

17   I like to have races to see who can ride the fastest. Cora was too afraid she'd fall. I told her I had bike races all the time, and no one ever fell.

18   **Reason Number Three:** She didn't tell me her secrets.

19   When we talked and talked and talked, I told her important secrets about myself.

20   I told her the worst thing that ever happened to me, which is that my dog died. We have a new dog, but I still miss the old one.

21   Cora didn't tell me a single secret about herself.

22   **And Reason Number Four:** She never invited me to her house.

23   I didn't ask Cora to my house again.

24   Sometimes I saw Cora looking at me from her yard. She looked like she wanted something. But I had four very good reasons not to listen.

25   One day, I was walking my dog when I saw cars parked on the street outside Cora's house.

26   People from the cars walked to Cora's front door. Some carried presents.

27   Presents meant there was a party. There was a party at Cora's house, and I wasn't invited. So now I had Reason Number Five for not liking Cora.

28   "Let's go home, Jeepers," I said to my dog. "We weren't invited."

Guided Questions

Highlight the word *four.* What is a homophone for *four*?

_____

What does *four* mean in paragraph **13**?

_____

_____

Read paragraph **17**. Highlight the words *like, ride, bike,* and *time*. How do you know that the vowel *i* is long?

_____

29   Just then, I heard Cora call after me. "Freda," she said. "Wait." She walked down to the sidewalk.

30   "My little brother is very sick," she said. "Kevin's been sick for a long time."

31   I knew Cora had a brother. But I didn't know he was sick.

32   "I'm sorry," I said.

33   "Today he came home from the hospital," Cora said. "Some of my parents' friends brought dinner for us and presents for him."

34   So there was no Reason Number Five.

35   I asked, "Is Kevin getting better?"

36   "Sometimes he gets better," Cora said. "Sometimes he gets worse. That's when he has to go to the hospital."

37   We stood quietly on the sidewalk.

38   Cora took a deep breath. She said, "The thing that I'm most afraid of is that one day Kevin will go to the hospital and won't come back."

39   "I hope that never happens," I said.

40   "Kevin needs a lot of rest, so our house has to be quiet," Cora said. "That's why I didn't invite you over. But would you like to come over tomorrow after school?"

41   "Yes, I would," I said.

42   "If my brother's not resting, we'll play Crazy Eights. It's his favorite."

43   "I would love to play Crazy Eights," I said.

44   "I'm going a little crazy from all the Crazy Eights we play," Cora said. "But Kevin says it's his lucky game. So I don't really mind."

45   "We'll go crazy from Crazy Eights together," I said. I thought I liked Cora, and I thought we'd be friends. It turned out I was right. I don't need to count the reasons why.

Guided Questions

Highlight the word *wait* in paragraph **29**. What is a homophone for *wait*?

_____

Highlight the word *brought* in paragraph **33**. What is another word that follows this pattern?

_____

Highlight the word *right* in paragraph **45**. What is a word that rhymes with *right* and follows the same spelling pattern?

_____

Complete the sentences below by filling in the correct letters. Use your knowledge of spelling patterns to help you.

1. I th _____ we were friends, but I was wrong.

2. She never invited me to play at her h _____

3. I b _____ a new game for her brother.

4. Did he lose w _____ in the hospital?

5. Complete the chart below. Write a homophone for each word.

Word	Homophone
weigh	
right	
sight	
sleigh	
night	

6. What is the real reason why Freda decides she doesn't like Cora? What should she have done before she decided this?

_____

_____

Critical Thinking

7. Talk to a partner. Discuss what this story tells you about friendship. Then tell your partner about another story you have read dealing with friendship. You can also tell about a movie you have seen.

Writing	☐
Research	☐
Listening and Speaking	☑
Media Literacy	☐
21st Century Skills: Collaboration	☑
Cross Curriculum Connection	☐

 **On Your Own**

Read the selection below. Then answer the questions that follow it.

Literature
Connection

The Carnival

by Beth Cavner

1   The fish were beautiful, swimming around in their little bowls—orange, even though the name said they were gold. There were so many things to see at the school carnival, and yet Annie couldn't stop looking at the fish. All she had to do was toss a ping-pong ball into one of the bowls, and a fish would be hers. For a quarter she would get three ping-pong balls—three tries. Surely three tries would be enough.

2   But before Annie could step up and pay her quarter, Becky grabbed her hand.

3   "Come on. I've been looking all over for you," Becky said. "Let's get something to eat. I'm hungry."

4   Becky led the way to the hot dog <u>booth</u>. Twenty-five cents for a hot dog. Twenty-five cents for a lemonade. Annie still had two quarters left, and she only needed one for three tries. Surely three tries would be enough.

5   "Come on," said Becky when they had finished their snack. "Let's look around."

6   At the face-painting booth, Becky had a butterfly painted on her face for a quarter. Annie decided not to, just in case.

7   At the hair-braiding booth, Becky had a bright orange ribbon braided into her hair for a quarter. Annie decided not to, just in case.

8   Finally, at the whirligig ride outside, Becky said, "Come on, Annie. I don't want to go on alone. It's just a quarter."

9   Just a quarter, and Annie still had two quarters left. She only needed one for three tries. Surely, three tries would be enough.

10   "O.K.," said Annie. "Let's go."

"The Carnival" by Beth Cavner, Reprinted by permission of LADYBUG magazine
September 2003, text © 2003 by Beth Cavner

11   Paying their quarters, they hopped on the ride and fastened their seat belts. The whirligig whirled them around in circles, faster and faster. Finally it stopped.

12   Hopping off the ride, Annie <u>thought</u>, Now it's time for the fish booth. But Becky grabbed her hand.

13   "Annie, I feel sick," she said. "I need to call my mom. I need to go home." So together they went back inside to the pay phone.

14   "Oh, Annie," Becky wailed. "I spent too much money. I only have a dime left. It's not enough to make a phone call!"

15   Annie felt in her pocket. One quarter left. One quarter that she had carefully saved so she could win a fish.

16   Annie looked at her friend. Their mothers were coming to pick them up later, but Annie could tell that Becky needed to go home now. Her face was very pale. Annie handed Becky her last quarter.

17   "Here, now you have enough," she said.

18   Becky's mother arrived within minutes of the phone call, and Annie waved good-bye to her friend. She looked at her watch. Thirty minutes until her own mother was coming.

19   Annie wandered over to the fish booth so she could at least watch the fish while she waited. She saw a bigger boy pay a quarter for three ping-pongs—three tries. Surely three tries would be enough. He did it in one. With a happy grin on his face, he looked around. Seeing Annie, he handed her his remaining two balls.

20   "Here," he said. "I don't need these. Good luck!" And taking his fish, he walked away.

21   Annie stared at the balls in her hand. Two tries. Surely two tries would be enough.

22   She only needed one.

23   Annie handed the last ball to a little boy who was watching her with a wistful look. "Good luck!" she told him. Then, holding the small bowl <u>tightly</u> to her body, she looked down at her orange fish. One try was all it had taken.

Answer the following questions based on the passage you just read.

1. Read the sentence below. Pay attention to the underlined word.

   > *The fish were beautiful, swimming around in their little bowls—orange, even though the <u>name</u> said they were gold.*

   Does the vowel sound you hear in *name* have the same sound as the *a* in *made* or in *mad*? How do you know?

   _____

   _____

   What are three other words that follow the same spelling pattern?

   _____

2. What word below has the same vowel sound you hear in <u>booth</u> in paragraph 4?

   A Pool   **C** Full

   B Book   **D** Good

3. Read the sentence below. Pay attention to the underlined word.

   > *Becky led the <u>way</u> to the hot dog booth.*

   What is a homophone for *way*?

   _____

   Write a sentence using this word.

   _____

   _____

4. Which word from paragraph 1 rhymes with *stuff*?

 A *bowls*   **C** *carnival*

 B *ping-pong*   **D** *enough*

5. Read the sentence below. Pay attention to the underlined word.

> *At the hair-braiding booth, Becky had a <u>bright</u> orange ribbon braided into her hair for a quarter.*

Complete the word web. In the ovals, write as many words as you can think of that follow the same spelling pattern as in *bright*. You may add ovals to the web.

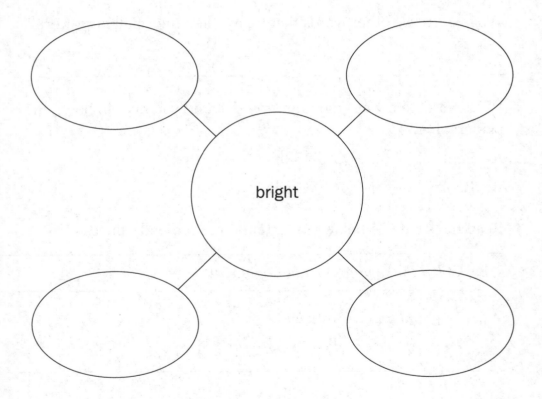

6. Which word below does not rhyme with <u>thought</u> in paragraph 12?

 A Caught   **C** Taught

 B Straight   **D** Fought

7. Which word below does not have the same spelling pattern as <u>tightly</u> in paragraph 23?

   A Delight   **C** Fight

   B Frighten   **D** Site

8. Homophones can cause confusion when you are reading. How can you make sure you choose the meaning of the correct homophone?

_____

Critical Thinking

9. Work with a partner. Connect the ideas you learned about friendship in the first story with the ideas you learned in this story. Then share your own ideas about what makes a friend. After your discussion, write a poem about friendship.

Writing	☑
Research	☐
Listening and Speaking	☑
Media Literacy	☐
21st Century Skills: Collaboration	☑
Cross-Curriculum Connection	☐

Media Connection

10. You can find poems about friendship at http://www.mydearvalentine.com/friendship/poems/for-kids.html and http://www.tooter4kids.com/Friendship/poems.htm.

Use Syllable Patterns to Decode Words

3.1(Bi), (Bii), (Biii), (Biv), (Bv)	Use common syllabication patterns to decode words including: (i) closed syllable (CVC) (e.g., mag-net), splen-did); (ii) open syllable (CV) (e.g., ve-to); (iii) final stable syllable (e.g., puz-zle, con-trac-tion); (iv) r-controlled vowels (e.g., fer-ment, car-pool); (v) vowel digraphs and diphthongs (e.g., ei-ther).
3.1(E)	Monitor accuracy in decoding.

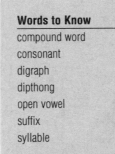 Understand the TEKS

Syllables

A **syllable** is part of a word that can be pronounced by itself. Every syllable has a vowel sound. You can divide words that have more than one vowel sound into syllables. This makes them easier to decode.

c-v-c Patterns

If two syllables both follow the c-v-c pattern, divide the syllables between this pattern.

	c-v-c	c-v-c
magnet	mag	net
signal	sig	nal

- How would you divide the word *runner* into syllables?

_____

Words to Know
compound word
consonant
digraph
dipthong
open vowel
suffix
syllable

c-v

The end of a word may have an open vowel sound. It does not have a consonant sound after the vowel sound. Usually, this sound is the long sound of the vowel. Divide these words before the consonant that appears in front of the second vowel.

		c-v
veto	ve	to
ditto	dit	to

Final Stable Syllable

A **suffix** is a group of letters added to the end of a word or root. It forms a new word. Always keep the letters that make up the suffix together. Divide the word before the suffix.

		Suffix
fighter	fight	er
mission	mis	sion

Copying is illegal. *Measuring Up* to the Texas Essential Knowledge and Skills

Some words end in a consonant plus -*le*. Keep these letters together when you divide the word.

puzzle	puz	zle
circle	cir	cle

r-Controlled Vowels

When the letter *r* appears after a vowel, it controls the sound of the vowel. Always keep the vowel and the letter *r* together.

gerbil	ger	bil
mirror	mir	ror

Vowel Digraphs and Diphthongs

A **digraph** is a pair of letters that spells one sound. For example, the letters *ea* spell the long /a/ sound.

A **diphthong** is a vowel sound produced by gliding the sound of one vowel into another. For example, notice the sound spelled by the letters *oy* in *toy*.

Keep the letters that form a digraph or diphthong together when you divide a word into syllables.

leopard	leo	pard
poison	poi	son

- How would you divide the word *either* into syllables?

Two Consonants

When two consonants appear in the middle of the word, divide the word between the consonants. The consonants can be the same letters or different letters.

happy	hap	py
canvas	can	vas

Compound Words

Some words are made up of two or more other words. They are called **compound words**. Break a compound word between the original words.

showboat	show	boat
uptown	up	town

- How would you divide the word *notebook* into syllables?

Comprehension Tip
When you read a long word you do not recognize, divide it into syllables.
Then sound out each syllable.

 Guided Instruction

Read the passage below. Then answer the questions in the margin and complete the activities.

Science Connection

Putting Their Best Foot Forward

by Daryl-Lynne Gottier

1   **A** Tiny footprints in the wet sand lead to the water's edge. There, they disappear. Those small marks tell us that a bird has been here.

2   **B** Those tracks give important clues about how the bird lives and eats. Each kind of bird has special feet that are suited to its way of life.

3   Most birds around your home perch in trees. **C** They stay in the branches or line up on telephone wires. They have three toes in front and a stronger one that points back. The middle toe is about as long as the back one, helping the birds hang on to their perch.

4   Gulls and ducks live and eat around the water. They need to swim and dive for food and safety. Their feet are built like flippers, with three toes in front that are webbed together by a thin layer of skin.

"Putting Their Best Foot Forward" by Daryl-Lynne Gottier Copyright © 2009 by Highlights for Children, Inc., Columbus, Ohio

---

Guided Questions

Underline the word *footprints* in sentence **A** in paragraph **1**. Draw a line between the two syllables.

Look at sentence **B** in paragraph **2**. Say the word *important* aloud. How many syllables do you hear? Draw lines between the syllables.

_____

Underline the word *telephone* in sentence **C** in paragraph **3**. Draw lines to divide the syllables. What do the birds do on the telephone wires? Why?

_____

_____

_____

5 **D** Other birds, such as wild turkeys and grouse, spend most of their time on the ground. They run through tall grass and bushes. They have three toes that go forward and one little toe in back. Like chickens, they scratch the ground for food, so having strong nails is a must.

6 **E** A grouse's feet also work like snowshoes. In winter, tooth-like growths appear around its toes and let it walk on top of the snow with ease.

7 Woodpeckers walk up and down the trunks of trees. Their feet have two forward toes and two that face backward. Sharp, pointy claws help them hang on, allowing them to scale trees. They use their eyes, ears, and beak to find places in the bark where bugs are hiding.

8 **F** Birds of prey, such as hawks and eagles, have powerful feet. They catch their prey in water, on land, or in the sky, and then fly away with it. Their feet have long, sharp claws called talons. The bottoms of their feet have a rough surface. Ospreys' feet even have little spines to help them hold slippery fish.

9 The toes on birds' feet are arranged in many ways to do many different jobs. The next time you see prints in the sand or wet tracks across the pavement, look for clues about that bird's life. What kind of tracks might disappear at the edge of the water?

Guided Questions

Underline the word *grouse* in sentence **D** in paragraph **5**. Say the word aloud. How many syllables do you hear in *grouse*? What is a word that rhymes with *grouse*?

Underline the word *snowshoes* in sentence **E** in paragraph **6**. What two words make up this word?

Underline the word *powerful* in sentence **F** in paragraph **8**. Draw lines between the syllables. Which syllable is a suffix?

Answer the following questions based on the passage you just read.

1. Read the sentence below. Pay attention to the underlined words.

> *Their feet are built like <u>flippers</u>, with three toes in front that are <u>webbed</u> <u>together</u> by a thin <u>layer</u> of skin.*

Use the chart below to show how to divide the underlined words into syllables.

Word	Syllables
flippers	
webbed	
together	
layer	

2. Read the paragraph below.

> *Other birds, such as wild turkeys and grouse, spend most of their time on the ground. They run through tall grass and bushes. They have three toes that go forward and one little toe in back. Like chickens, they scratch the ground for food, so having strong nails is a must.*

In the chart below, list all the two-syllable words. Then divide these words into syllables.

Word	Syllables

3. Read the paragraph below.

> *The toes on birds' feet are arranged in many ways to do many different jobs. The next time you see prints in the sand or wet tracks across the pavement, look for clues about that bird's life. What kind of tracks might disappear at the edge of the water?*

In the chart below, list all the three-syllable words. Then divide these words into syllables.

Word	Syllables

Critical Thinking

4. Do some research to find out more about animal footprints. Then work with a small group of students. Compile your research. Work as a team to create a chart showing different types of animal footprints.

Writing	☐
Research	☑
Listening and Speaking	☑
Media Literacy	☐
21st Century Skills: Collaboration	☑
Cross Curriculum Connection: Science	☑

Media Connection

5. You can see diffierent charts for identifying animal tracks at http://www.bing.com/images/search?q=Printable+Animal+Tracks&FORM=RESTAB.

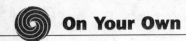

🌀 **On Your Own**

Read the selection below. Then answer the questions that follow it.

Literature Connection

Bert and Mert at the Zoo

by James Rhodes

1   "Let's do something special today, Bert," Mert said.

2   Bert was standing on his head, eating a slice of upside-down cake.

3   "Let's go to the zoo," Mert said.

4   Bert stood upright. "Good idea, Mert. I like to watch the monkeys."

5   They got out their <u>bicycle</u> built for two and pedaled over to the zoo. Bert pedaled one mile, and Mert pedaled the next mile. When they rode down a hill, nobody pedaled.

6   They came to a traffic light. Bert put on the brakes.

7   "What are we waiting for?" Mert asked.

8   "For the light to change," Bert said.

9   "What's it going to change into?" Mert wondered.

10   Officer Teetlebaum waved Bert and Mert over to him, so they pulled up to the curb.

11   "Are you two on a case?" Officer Teetlebaum asked. (Bert and Mert were always finding lost things and solving mysteries.)

12   "No, we're on our bicycle," Mert said.

13   "We're going to the zoo," Bert said. "We're taking the day off."

14   "Keep an eye out for Wily Willie," Officer Teetlebaum said. "He's up to no good. That guy's always playing tricks on people."

15   "We'll keep four eyes out for him," Bert said.

16   At the zoo, Bert and Mert met the zookeeper. "What's new?" they asked her.

17   "The gnu's new," said the keeper, pointing to a baby gnu who had just arrived at the zoo.

18   "New gnus are good news," Bert said.

19   "But we have a problem," the keeper said. "Maybe you two can help out."

20   Bert put on his Sherlock Holmes hat, and Mert got out his giant magnifying glass. "What's the problem?" Bert asked.

21   "Come, I'll show you," the keeper said.

22   Bert and Mert followed the keeper to where the zebra was kept. Instead of a zebra, though, there was a white horse.

23   "See? The zebra's gone. And this horse was left in its place."

24   "Hmm," said Bert.

25   "We'll look around for some clues," said Mert.

26   The keeper had other things to do, so she left them alone.

27   Bert and Mert snooped around the zoo. They looked everywhere and at everything. When they came to the elephants, Mert said, "The elephants might have heard something. They're always traveling."

28   "How do you know?" Bert asked.

29   "Because they carry their trunks with them."

30   Soon Bert and Mert came upon a schoolteacher surrounded by students.

31   The teacher sighed and said to Bert and Mert, "I had to bring them on a field trip because somebody took all of the chalk from my classroom. Can you believe that?"

32   Bert and Mert said they could.

33   Then Bert stumbled over a bucket that was tipped on its side. Mert helped Bert to his feet. "Are you all right?"

34   "I had a nice trip," Bert said.

35   "Look, Bert!" Mert said. "See what's in the bucket!"

36   "It looks like ground-up chalk," Bert said.

37   "And have a look at these," Mert said, taking out his magnifying glass. Someone had stepped in chalk and left footprints on the ground.

38   "Let's follow them," Bert said. "Do you think we'll find the zebra?"

39   "Who knows?" Mert said.

40   Then they came upon a pair of shoes sticking out under a fence. Bert cried, "We've found the thief!"

41   Together they opened the fence gate. There stood Wily Willie!

42   "Just as we thought," Mert said.

43   "Wily Willie, you're the one who did this!"

44   The zookeeper came running over, and with her was Officer Teetlebaum.

45   "What's going on here?" asked Officer Teetlebaum. "Why, Wily Willie! I should have known you would be mixed up in all of this."

46   "Where's the missing zebra?" the keeper demanded. "Does this man know?"

47   "He should," Bert said. "He was the one who did it."

48   "Did what?" Officer Teetlebaum asked.

49   "Grab a bucket of water and follow us," Mert said.

50   They all went back to where the zebra was kept.

51   "Now?" Bert asked.

52   Mert nodded.

53   Bert poured water on the horse, and most of the white came off. Now the horse was striped with black.

54   "There's your zebra," Mert said.

55   "Wily Willie turned the zebra white with chalk. Chalk he stole from the teacher," Bert said.

       Measuring Up to the Texas Essential Knowledge and Skills

56   "Come along, Wily Willie," Officer Teetlebaum said as he led Wily Willie away.

57   Bert and Mert had solved the case. The zookeeper gave them all the popcorn they could eat.

58   Then they hopped on their bicycle. Mert pedaled one mile, and Bert pedaled the next mile. When they rode down a hill, nobody pedaled. Soon they were home.

Answer the following questions based on the passage you just read.

1. Which of the words below has the same number of syllables as <u>bicycle</u> in paragraph 5?

   A Napkin   **C** Direction

   B Impossible   **D** Parade

2. Break the words below into syllables. Write your answers in the second column.

traffic	
officer	
mysteries	

3. Read the sentence below.

> *At the zoo, Bert and Mert met the zookeeper. "What's new?" they asked her.*

Which word in this paragraph is a compound word? Divide it into syllables.

_____

4. Which of these words from the story has four syllables?

   A *followed*   **C** *magnifying*

   B *zebra*   **D** *traveling*

5. Read the paragraphs below.

> *Soon Bert and Mert came upon a schoolteacher surrounded by students.*
>
> *The teacher sighed and said to Bert and Mert, "I had to bring them on a field trip because somebody took all of the chalk from my classroom. Can you believe that?"*

Which two words in these paragraphs are compound words? Divide them into syllables.

_____

Write a sentence using both words above.

_____

_____

6. Make a list of animals mentioned in this story. Then sort your list, using the chart below. You may add other animals you would find in a zoo to the list.

One-Syllable	Two-Syllable	Three-Syllable
horse	monkeys	elephants
	zebra	

7. Think about what you have learned. How will it help you decode long words in the future?

_____

_____

Critical Thinking

8. A pun is a humorous use of words that are homophones or that have more than one meaning. Talk to a partner about the use of puns in this story. Tell whether or not they helped make the story funny. Then share jokes you know that are based on the use of puns. (If you need to, read some jokes in a magazine or joke book or search for them on the Internet.)

Writing	☐
Research	☐
Listening and Speaking	☑
Media Literacy	☐
21st Century Skills: Collaboration	☑
Cross Curriculum Connection	☐

Identify and Read Contractions

3.1(D)   Identify and read contractions (e.g., I'd, won't).
3.1(E)   Monitor accuracy in decoding.

 Understand the TEKS

Contractions

A **contraction** is made up of two words that are joined together and then shortened. When they are shortened, one or more letters are dropped. A punctuation mark called an apostrophe (') takes the place of the dropped letter or letters.

Words to Know
apostrophe
contraction
dialogue
possessive

do + not = don't	*o* is dropped.
we + are = we're	*a* is dropped.
I + will = I'll	*w* and *i* are dropped.
I + would = I'd	The letters *woul* are dropped.
it + is = it's	*i* is dropped.
let + us = let's	*u* is dropped.

Many contractions combine and shorten a verb and the word *not*. In these contractions, the *o* in *not* is dropped.

do + not = don't

would + not = wouldn't

could + not = couldn't

should + not = shouldn't

The contraction for *can + not* is *can't*. One *n* and the *o* are dropped.

The contraction *won't* is a little different, too. It combines and shortens the words *will* and *not*. However, the new word isn't *willn't*. It's *won't*.

will + not = won't

Dialogue and Quotations

People often use contractions when they speak. As a result, when you read dialogue—words characters say in stories—you often see contractions. Contractions also show up in quotations.

"I'd like to go to the amusement park," said Tomas.

• What word is a contraction?

_____

• What two words were combined and shortened to make this contraction?

_____

Anita shouted, "I won't do it—not now, not tomorrow, not ever!"

• What word is a contraction?

_____

• What two words were shortened to form this contraction?

_____

Possessives

Be careful. Sometimes an apostrophe indicates a possessive, not a contraction. A **possessive** tells who or what something belongs to. It shows ownership.

The kitten's claws need to be cut.

• What does *kitten's* mean in this sentence?

_____

It's and its When you combine and shorten *it* and *is,* you get the contraction *it's.*

The weather announcer said that *it's* going to rain tomorrow.

 Measuring Up to the Texas Essential Knowledge and Skills

When you form the possessive of *it*, you do not use the apostrophe. This makes it easier to tell the two words apart.

> The kitten licked *its* coat.

Comprehension Tip

When you read a contraction, try to figure out which words were joined. This will help you determine the meaning of the contraction.

Guided Instruction

Read the passage below. Then answer the questions in the margin and complete the activities.

Literature Connection

The Owl's Breakfast

by Susan Yoder Ackerman

Guided Questions

Look at the title. Is *owl's* a contraction or does it show possession or ownership? What does it mean?

_____

_____

_____

1   One morning a tiny tabby kitten was curled up in a pot of petunias on our front porch. It was plain to see that she had chosen to be a house-and-garden cat, not a barn cat like all the others on the Yoder Dairy Farm. She purred when I picked her up. She rubbed her chin on my hand.

2   We named her Sophie.

3   Good thing she came to live with us. **A** I don't think she would have made it out in the barn. Sure, Dad put out bowls of milk at milking time, but the cats understood that in exchange, they kept the mice out of the grain. That meant some serious hunting.

4   Sophie sighed and turned away when I dangled a toy mouse in front of her. Why should she even play with it? **B** She wasn't a hunter. She turned up her pretty pink nose at anything but dry cat food. She ignored any treats offered of chicken scraps or the ham out of my sandwich.

5   As for the birds in the garden, she seemed to think they were adorable. She stretched out in the window to watch them. When summer came, she lay among the strawberry plants, washing her dainty paws as a robin tugged worms in the row beside her.

6   One day Dad came home with a wounded bird—a beautiful snowy barn owl with a broken wing.

7   Mom had sunflower seeds for the cardinals and cracked corn for the doves, but she had no idea what to feed an owl. "Oh dear," she said. "What do they eat?"

8   As she was getting out her bird book, Dad said, "Look at the cat!"

9   Sophie had tiptoed over and was staring into the owl's wire cage.

10   I knew the cage was tight and the owl was safe, but the cat made me nervous.

11   Sophie stood there, staring with big green eyes into the unblinking dark eyes of the owl.

12   "Mice! That's what owls eat," said Mom, looking up from her book. "There are plenty of those out in the barn. Let's see if we can catch one."

13   I don't know how the mice could resist the peanut butter we put into the mousetraps, but they did. The next morning and again the day after that, the traps were empty.

Look at sentence **A** in paragraph **3**. Highlight the contraction. What two words were combined?

_____

Highlight the word *wasn't* in sentence **B** in paragraph **4**. What does this contraction mean?

_____

Highlight the two contractions in paragraph **12**. What do they mean?

_____

 Measuring Up to the Texas Essential Knowledge and Skills

14 "I guess we're not any better at catching mice than Sophie is," said Mom.

15 "How long can an owl go without eating?" I asked.

16 Mom didn't know. "We could try a meatball," she said. **C** "I'll save one or two out of the spaghetti sauce."

Highlight *I'll* in sentence **C** in paragraph **16**. What two words were combined? What letters were dropped?

_____

_____

17 Well, meatballs were not the answer. The owl didn't even look at them.

18 "We could try making a mouse," said Mom, getting desperate.

19 She took a piece of fuzzy gray cloth. Into it she bundled a handful of hamburger shaped like a mouse. She tacked on a thin black ribbon for a tail. Then she laid it before the silent bird.

20 "It's a nice mouse!" she said. "Don't you want to eat it?"

21 The owl didn't turn its head even the slightest.

22 **D** Was I imagining it, or did its eyes look a little less bright? It had been four days since Dad brought it home, and who knew how long it had been without food before that? I wondered if the owl might have been better off in the barn with a hurt wing instead of facing cat's claws and starvation here with us.

Highlight the word *its* in sentence **D** in paragraph **22**. Is this word a contraction or a possessive? What does it mean in this sentence?

_____

_____

23 "Sophie!" I said. "Leave the poor owl alone!" She was pacing in front of the owl's cage again. I picked her up to take her to sleep in her usual place on my comforter. I had taken only two steps when she leaped out of my arms and back to her spot by the owl's cage.

24 It was hard to sleep that night. I had a tight feeling in my stomach. The beautiful owl might not make it, and there was nothing I could do about it.

25 The sun wasn't up yet when a loud cry awakened me. I jumped out of bed. The owl? The cat? The cry came again. I ran into the family room and turned on the light.

26 There was Sophie crouching in front of the owl. She howled again, her whiskers pressed against the cage.

27   Then I saw it. Between her paws lay a small dark field mouse. A mouse for the hungry owl!

28   "Mom! Dad!" I yelled. "Come see what Sophie caught!"

29   We petted and praised the cat while the owl gulped its breakfast. Later I even tried to reward Sophie with a strip of bacon. But she sniffed it and backed away. No meat for her, thank you.

30   Not long after Sophie fed the owl, the bird seemed stronger, and Dad took it back to the barn where it could catch its own mice.

31   As for Sophie, she's back to sunning herself in the window and watching Mom feed the chickadees. And she's never caught another mouse.

Guided Questions

Paragraph **31** uses the same contraction twice. Highlight the contraction. Tell what it means.

Answer the following questions based on the passage you just read.

1. Read the sentence below.

> "I guess <u>we're</u> not any better at catching mice than Sophie is," said Mom.

Rewrite this sentence. Replace the contraction with the two words that were joined.

_____

_____

 2. Read the sentences below.

> "<u>It's</u> a nice mouse!" she said. "<u>Don't</u> you want to eat it?"

Rewrite these sentences. Replace the contractions with the two words that were joined.

_____

Why are these sentences better with contractions?

_____

3. Complete the chart below.

Words	Contraction
do + not	
would + not	
can + not	
will + not	
was + not	
have + not	
has + not	
did + not	
does + not	

Critical Thinking

4. Talk with a partner. Discuss whether using contractions makes writing sound formal or informal. In what types of writing would you use contractions? In what types would you use fewer contractions?

Writing	☑
Research	☐
Listening and Speaking	☑
Media Literacy	☑
21st Century Skills: Collaboration	☑
Cross-Curriculum Connection	☐

On Your Own

Read the selection below. Then answer the questions that follow it.

Literature Connection

The Private I's and the Case of the Mixed-Up Message

by Wendi Silvano

1 Izzy, Inez, and Ivy were reading in the living room. The phone rang.

2 "I'll get it," said Izzy.

3 It was Mom, calling from work. "I really need your help," she said.

4 "What's wrong?" asked Izzy.

5 "Grandma called," said Mom.

6 "She's having a hard time seeing after her eye operation. She wants to come stay with us until she can see better. She said she would catch the first flight out."

7 "Great!" said Izzy.

8 "There's only one problem," said Mom. "She said she would e-mail me what time her flight gets in. My computer is down at work. I tried to call her, but the line's busy. I'm afraid I'll miss her flight."

9 "How can we help?" asked Izzy.

10 "You can check our family e-mail account," said Mom. "Find Grandma's message and call me."

11 "We're on it," said Izzy.

12 "What's up?" asked Inez.

13 "Grandma's coming!" said Izzy.

14 "Fantastic!" said Ivy. "When?"

15 "That's what we need to find out. Come on."

16 They went to the computer. Izzy clicked into the family's e-mail.

17 "There's Grandma's message!" said Ivy.

18   Izzy opened the message.

Hi, rbrtyonr,

My plsnr lsnfd sy gibr o'vlovk.

I vsn'y esiy yo drr you sll.

Lobr,

Htsnfms

19   "This message is all mixed up," said Inez. "I can't read it."

20   "We need to figure this out fast," said Izzy.

21   "This looks like a case for the Private I's," said Inez. She got her notebook. She wrote: **The Case of the Mixed-Up Message.**

22   "<u>Let's</u> think," said Izzy. "Why would the letters be mixed up?"

23   "Grandma wrote in code?" said Ivy.

24   "I don't think she would," said Inez. "She can barely even see."

25   "That's an important clue," said Izzy.

26   Inez wrote: **Grandma can barely see to write.**

27   "Maybe she couldn't see to type very well," said Ivy.

28   "That's it!" said Izzy. "We need to look at the keyboard."

29   Inez wrote: **Plan: Check the keyboard.**

30   Izzy looked at Grandma's note. Then she looked at the keyboard. "We need to figure out *how* Grandma mixed up the letters."

31   "I'm sure the end is supposed to say *Love, Grandma*," said Inez.

32   "Brilliant!" said Izzy. She put her fingers on the keyboard. She looked at the last word of the message.

33   "If *H* should be *G* . . . and *t* should be *r* . . . I see what happened! Grandma's left hand shifted over one key by mistake."

34   "Try the rest of the note," said Inez. "See if it makes real words."

35   Izzy moved her fingers on the keyboard. Inez wrote down each letter in her notebook.

Hi, everyone,

My plane lands at five o'clock. I <u>can't</u> wait to see you all.

Love,

Grandma

36   "We did it!" cried Inez.

37   "Way to go!" said Izzy. "I'll call Mom."

38   "And I'll go find Grandma's favorite blanket," said Ivy.

39   Inez wrote: **The Case of the Mixed-Up Message: Solved.**

Answer the following questions based on the passage you just read.

1. Read paragraph below.

> *"There's only one problem," said Mom. "She said she would e-mail me what time her flight gets in. My computer is down at work. I tried to call her, but the line's busy. I'm afraid I'll miss her flight."*

Then fill in the chart. In the left-hand column, write each contraction in this paragraph. In the right-hand column, write its meaning.

Contraction	Meaning

 2. Reread the two lines of dialogue below.

> *"What's up?" asked Inez.*
> *"Grandma's coming!" said Izzy.*

Rewrite this dialogue without using contractions.

_____

_____

•   How did not using contractions change the way the dialogue sounds?

_____

_____

3. In paragraph 11, what is the meaning of the contraction <u>We're</u>?

    A We will   **C** We are

    B We should   **D** We would not

4. Read the sentences below.

> At first, the girls <u>could not</u> solve the puzzle.
>
> "<u>We would</u> like to help," they said, "but <u>we are</u> stumped."

Rewrite these sentences. Use contractions in place of the underlined words.

_____

_____

5. What two words form the contraction <u>let's</u> in paragraph 22?

    A Let is   **C** Let us

    B Let has   **D** Let me

6. Which item below shows what was dropped from the contraction <u>can't</u> in Grandma's letter in paragraph 35?

    A no   **C** o

    B n   **D** not

Critical Thinking

7. Jot down questions you would like to ask the author about this story. Then meet with a partner. Share your questions.

Writing	☐
Research	☐
Listening and Speaking	☑
Media Literacy	☐
21st Century Skills: Collaboration	☑
Cross Curriculum Connection	☐

S 3.16	Use comprehension skills to analyze how words, images, graphics, and sounds work together in various forms to impact meaning. Continue to apply earlier standards with greater depth in increasingly more complex texts.
3.16(A)	Understand how communication changes when moving from one genre of media to another.
3.16(B)	Explain how various design techniques used in media influence the message (e.g., space, color, sound).
3.16(C)	Compare various written conventions used for digital media (e.g., language in an informal e-mail vs. language in a web-based news article)

 Understand the TEKS

What is meant by the word *media*? **Media** refers to the various ways of communicating with a large number of people.

- When you watch television, you are watching a form of media.
- When you read a newspaper, you are reading a form of media.
- When you see a commercial or advertisement, you are viewing media.

Print and Electronic Media
Some media are print.

newspapers	books	magazines
posters	brochures	advertisements

Some media are electronic.

television	e-mails	Web sites	text messages
commercials	podcasts	music downloads	radio

The different types of electronic media keep growing.

- Name three types of electronic media you use that people didn't have twenty years ago.

_____

Purposes

Media have different purposes. For example, the purpose may be:

- to inform
- to entertain
- to explain
- to persuade

> **Words to Know**
> design
> formal language
> graphics
> image
> informal language
> media

- What is a form of media whose purpose is to persuade?

_____

- What is a form of media whose purpose is to inform?

_____

Moving from One Form to Another

Communication changes when it moves from one form to another. For example, suppose you have read a chapter book. The book is so popular, it is made into a movie.

How is a movie different from the novel? Unlike the novel, a movie includes actors, sound, lighting, movement, special effects, costumes, and sets, for example.

Design Techniques

Design techniques help media achieve their purpose.

Type Some forms of media include type. The designer must choose the typeface. Some typefaces make the message seem formal or serious.

This message looks serious.

Some make the message seem modern.

This message looks modern.

Some make the message seem casual.

This message looks casual.

Designers also decide when to use all capital letters LIKE THIS. They decide when to use boldface type **like this** and italic type *like this*.

Size The designer must decide how large to make something. It could be an image. It could be the type on the page. The larger the size, the more you notice it.

Space The designer must decide how much empty space to leave around something. This empty space is called "white space."

Your attention is pulled to an image that has a lot of white space around it. On a crowded page, an image gets lost.

Color Color draws attention and creates a mood. Yellow seems cheerful. Red says "Look at me." Blue is more peaceful.

• What color would you use for a poster alerting people to danger?

_____

Sound Media may also include sound.

- **Volume** Volume is how loud or low the sound is. You might raise the volume to draw attention. You might keep the volume low to create a more comforting effect.

- **Music** Media may use music to create a mood. Music can build excitement. It can keep you interested. It can create a peaceful effect.

- **Sound Effects** Media may use special effects such as thunder bursts, footsteps, and floorboards groaning.

• Suppose you are producing a radio show. Someone is entering a house. What sound effects might you use to help listeners picture this?

_____

_____

Written Conventions
Language is like clothing. You choose the form that fits the occasion.

Informal Language
When you have a conversation with a friend, you may use informal language. It sounds casual. You may use only parts of sentences. You may use a lot of contractions. Your language may include a few mistakes. You may even use some slang.

Formal
There are times when you use formal language. It sounds proper and correct. You make sure you speak in complete sentences and use correct grammar.

Use formal language when you communicate with people you don't know well or with a large group of people.

Language and Media
An e-mail or text message from a friend is like a friendly letter or a note you dash off. It is an informal form of communication. Blogs may also be informal. If the form is informal, the language may be informal, too. Perhaps you have read

or taken part in a threaded conversation on the Web. Threaded conversations are another form of casual writing.

Some forms of writing on The Web are formal. When you read a news article on the Web, you expect the language to be formal. When you visit a museum Web site and read different articles, you expect to see formal language, too.

Suppose you and your classmates carry on a threaded conversation about movies you see. After about a month, you decide to set up a school Web site with movie recommendations. It would be based on comments made during the threaded conversation.

• Should your Web site use formal language or informal language? Why?

_____

_____

Comprehension Tip
Use your ears as well as your eyes when you "read" electronic media with sound. Put together the sounds and the images to understand the message.

Guided Instruction

Read the passage below. Then answer the questions in the margin and complete the activities.

Dragon Fire Studios wants to turn the story "The Mystery of the Stolen Painting" into a movie. Here is a storyboard the production team created to show what would happen in each scene.

Title Screen: Mysterious music in background. It starts off low and gets louder and louder.

Camera zooms in on art museum. Police sirens in the background.

Inside the museum. Police are talking to a woman. She points to empty space between two paintings.

| **Guided Questions** |

Look at frame **1**. How does the music affect the way you feel about the movie?

_____

_____

In frame **2**, what sound effect suggests that a burglary has occurred?

_____

_____

In frame **3**, when should the camera zoom in on the empty space on the wall? Why?

_____

_____

_____

_____

_____

Police woman on phone with man. He is giving her a tip.

Basement of mansion. Very rich man is sitting in chair staring at wall filled with paintings.

Police arrive at mansion. Capture rich man.

Return to museum. Missing painting now hangs on wall.

Guided Questions

In frame **4**, why don't you see the second man's face clearly?

_____

_____

Look at frame **6**. What type of sound effects might you use in this scene?

_____

_____

_____

_____

Suppose you add background music for frame **7**. What mood, or feeling, would the music create?

_____

_____

Answer the following questions based on the passage you just read.

1. When should the camera focus on the group of people in frame 3? Why?

_____

_____

Write the words the woman might say.

_____

_____

(Elevate) **2.** Look at the fifth frame. Imagine you are the director. How would you have the camera move?

_____

_____

Why?

_____

_____

3. In a book, the last scene might start a new chapter. How would you show the change of scenes in a movie?

_____

_____

4. The production team wants to send this storyboard to the head of the studio. They asked their new assistant, Derek, to write a memo to go with it.

To: Jasmina Sousa
     President, Dragon Fire Studios
Fr: Production Team
Re: Storyboard

Here it is, dude—our absolutely fab storyboard for the film of *The Mystery of the Stolen Painting*. It shows each of the big scenes, and they look awesome, don't you think?

We'd like to grab you to gab about our ideas and pick your brain. And boss, let us know the where and when, alright?

When the production team read over the memo, they saw that the language was too informal. After all, it was going to the head of the studio. Help Derek out. Rewrite each sentence in formal language.

A. Here it is, dude—our absolutely fab storyboard for the film of *The Mystery of the Stolen Painting*.

_____

_____

B. It shows each of the big scenes, and they look awesome, don't you think?

_____

C. We'd like to grab you to gab about our ideas and pick your brain.

_____

D. And boss, let us know the where and when, alright?

_____

Critical Thinking

5. Work in a team. Select a story you all have read. It is your team's job to turn this story into a movie. Talk about the changes you will make. Discuss sound, lighting, sets, and dialogue. Then collaborate to create a storyboard. Use the storyboard on pp. 00–00 as a model.

Writing	☑
Research	☐
Listening and Speaking	☑
21st Century Skills: Media Literacy	☑
Cross-Curriculum Connection	☐

Media Connection

6. With your family's permission and help, watch a movie or television show of a story you have read. Tell the class how the movie was different from the book. Which did you like better? Why?

On Your Own

Read the advertisement below. Then answer the questions that follow it.

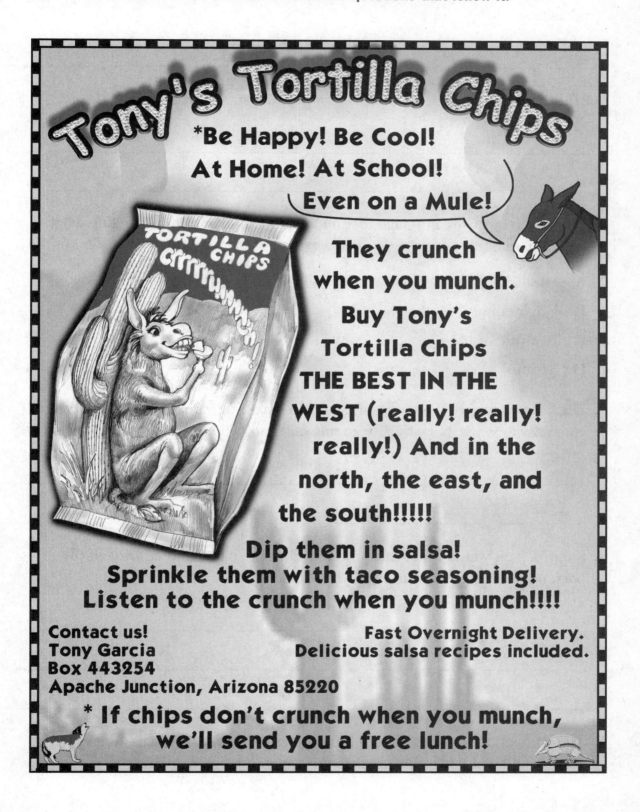

Answer the following questions based on the advertisement you just read.

1. The purpose of an ad is to get readers to buy something. What product is this ad selling?

   _____

   How could you make the name of the product stand out more?

   _____

   _____

2. The advertiser uses an image of a mule eating a tortilla chip to create what type of feeling?

   A Humorous

   B Frightening

   C Realistic or life-like

   D Serious

(Elevate) 3. Does the picture of the mule eating a chip make you want to buy the product? If your answer is yes, tell why. If your answer is no, tell how you would change it.

   _____

   _____

4. Suppose you want to buy this product. Find the name and address of the person to contact. Write it on the lines below.

   _____

   _____

   _____

(Elevate) 5. The contact information should be very easy to find, but in this ad it isn't. How would you make this important information easier to find?

   _____

6. This ad is so cluttered, nothing stands out. What would you remove so that the important details pop? Why?

_____

_____

7. The advertiser uses all these methods to stress that the chips are crunchy except —

A stretching out the word *crrrrrunnnnch*

B using exclamation marks

C placing the word *crrrrrunnnnch* in bold type

D creating a rhyme

Critical Thinking

8. Work as part of an advertising team. Brainstorm ideas for a new product to sell. Then get to work. Decide who is responsible for the words, for the images, and for the design. Then create an ad for your new product.

Writing	☑
Research	☐
Listening and Speaking	☑
21st Century Skills: Media Literacy	☑
Cross Curriculum Connection	☐

Media Connection

9. Not all advertising is good or fair. Sometimes, it is meant to trick you. Learn more about advertising tricks at http://pbskids.org/dontbuyit/advertisingtricks/. Tell your class about your findings.

Read the selection. Then choose the best answer to each question.

Vernon's Questions

by Dan Crawford
from Spider Magazine

1   It was time for *Moose Maurice's Cartoon Roundup*. I sat on the couch to watch TV, and Vernon sat in the chair by the window. Vernon's my little brother. He watches TV, but he doesn't really pay attention because he's not very old yet.

2   The show was just getting exciting, when all of a sudden he asked me, "What's gray?"

3   "It's a color, Vernon," I said.

4   "No," he said. "I mean what things are gray?"

5   I didn't look at him—I already know what he looks like. "Clouds are gray. Streets are gray. Oh, lots of things are gray."

6   "Are there any gray animals?"

---

7   I hate the way Vernon always has to talk when I'm watching something interesting. But if I tell him to be quiet, he just talks more—and louder.

8   "Yes, there are gray animals," I said. I tried to think of one. "A rhinoceros is gray."

9   "What's a rhinoceros?"

10   "A gray animal," I said. "With a horn on its nose."

11   "Oh." Vernon was quiet for almost one whole second. "Not that one. Another one."

12   "An elephant is gray," I said.

13   "Is an elephant big?"

14   "Oh yes," I told him. "It's big and gray and has huge ears. And it has a long thin nose that looks like a hose to pick up food."

15   "Does it eat leaves?"

16   "Peanuts, I think," I said. "And hay."

17   "It has to eat leaves, too," Vernon told me.

18   "O.K., it eats leaves," I said.

19   "Good."

20   By that time the commercial was over, so I looked at Vernon. He wasn't even facing the TV; he was leaning against the window.

21   "What's outside?" I asked.

22   "Nothing now." He turned around in the chair to watch TV. I got up and went over to the window.

23   Footprints like great big holes were all over our front yard, and something had pulled lots of branches and leaves off our trees. Six police cars and a big truck were sitting out in the street. The neighbors were standing around talking and laughing and pointing at the truck.

24   I was going to ask Vernon what he knew about all this, but he was watching the cartoon. I'm old enough to know I shouldn't bother somebody who's busy.

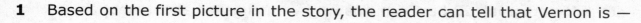

1 Based on the first picture in the story, the reader can tell that Vernon is —

   A sad

   B worried

   C curious

   D bored

2 Which sentence below does not support the idea that the boy finds his little brother Vernon annoying?

   F *The show was just getting exciting, when all of a sudden he asked me, "What's gray?"*

   G *He watches TV, but he doesn't really pay attention because he's not very old yet.*

   H *I didn't look at him—I already know what he looks like.*

   J *I hate the way Vernon always has to talk when I'm watching something interesting.*

3 From Vernon's questions, the reader can conclude that he —

   A sees an elephant outside the window

   B is trying to annoy his brother

   C thinks an elephant has a horn on its head

   D is watching a circus parade

4 Which detail in paragraph 23 best explains why Vernon asked about what an elephant eats?

   F   There are footprints like great big holes.

   G   The branches and leaves are pulled off the trees.

   H   There are six police cars in the street.

   J   The neighbors are talking and laughing.

5 Look at the second picture in the story. What is the main reason why the designer placed this picture at the end?

   A   To show that the creature caused a lot of damage

   B   To not give away the ending

   C   Because there is more space for it on the page

   D   To show that the story is made up

6 Which word best describes the feeling the second picture in the story creates?

   F   Frightening

   G   Angry

   H   Calm

   J   Comical

Lesson 12

Use Prefixes and Suffixes to Find Word Meaning

| 3.1(Aiv), (Av) | Decode multisyllabic words in context and independent of context by applying common spelling patterns including: (iv) using knowledge of common prefixes and suffixes (e.g., dis-, -ly); (v) using knowledge of derivational affixes (e.g., -de, -ful, -able). |
| **Ⓡ 3.4(A)** | Identify the meaning of common prefixes (e.g., in-, dis-) and suffixes (e.g., -ful, -less), and how they change the meaning of roots. |

 ## Understand the TEKS

Word Parts

Many longer words are made up of parts.

| Prefix
dis | + | Word
agree | + | Suffix
able | = | New Word
disagreeable |

Each word part has a meaning. Often, you can find the meaning of these words by adding together the meanings of the word parts.

Words to Know
prefix
suffix

Prefixes

A **prefix** is a letter or group of letters. It is added to the beginning of a word or root.

Here are some prefixes and their meanings. You will see words with these prefixes when you read the selections in this lesson.

Prefix	Meaning	Example
dis-	apart, away from, reverse of	**dis**appear
il-, im-, in-, ir-	not	**im**possible
pre-	before, ahead of time	**pre**make
re-	again	**re**make
un-	not, reverse of	**un**lock

• Add the prefix *un-* to the word *lock*. What does *unlock* mean?

Suffix

A **suffix** is a letter or group of letters added to the end of a word or root. A suffix adds a meaning and also shows a part of speech.

Here are some suffixes and their meanings. The chart also shows the part of speech the suffix forms. You will see words with these suffixes when you read the selections in this lesson.

Suffix	Meaning	Part of Speech	Example
-able, -ible	able to	adjective	mov**able**
-ful	full of	adjective	wonder**ful**
-less	less, without	adjective	sense**less**
-ly	like something, in a certain way	adjective adverb	love**ly** quick**ly**
-ous	full of	adjective	joy**ous**

Find Meaning

If you see a word you don't know, break the word into parts. Look for a prefix or a suffix. It may help you figure out the word's meaning.

For example, suppose you don't know the word *slowly*. You can break it into parts—*slow* and *ly*. You know that *-ly* means "like something, or in a certain way." You know that *slow* means "not fast."

• What does *slowly* mean?

Two Special Suffixes

Take a look at two special suffixes— *-er* and *-est*. They help you compare people or things.

Use *-er* to compare two people or things.

   Miguel is <u>taller</u> than Jake.

Use *-est* to compare three or more things.

   Miguel is the <u>tallest</u> boy in the class.

Spelling Changes

Sometimes there is a spelling change when you add a suffix. For example, look what happens in the words below.

beauty + ful = beautiful   *y* changed to *i*
love + able = lovable   *e* dropped

Comprehension Tip

When you use word parts, check the meaning you come up with against the context. Read the sentence aloud. Replace the unfamiliar word with the meaning. Make sure the sentence still makes sense.

Guided Instruction

Read the passage below. Then answer the questions in the margin and complete the activities.

Literature
Connection

The Magic Needle

by Betty X. Davis

 Long ago, in the land of the Far North, Meqak could cut a hole in the ice to fish for trout. She could set a trap and catch a fox. She could drive a dogsled. **A** But for Meqak, sewing was impossible.

2 **B** With dainty fingers, other nine-year-old Inuit girls worked their ivory needles and made beautiful bearskin trousers, fox-fur coats, and kamiks. Their thread of caribou sinew never tangled. Their stitches held strong and even. But Meqak's did not.

3 Her mother guided Meqak's right hand with her own, in and out. But when alone, Meqak's fingers would not obey. If only I could use . . . but no . . . she thought. **C** It was unthinkable to switch and use her left hand. Bad magic would surely happen.

4 One day, in frustration, she threw her needle out into the snow. Her parents made her search for it, but she never found it. Good, she thought. Now I won't have to sew!

5 She begged her father to let her handle the dogs she loved or fish for the food her family needed.

Guided Questions

Find the word *impossible* in sentence **A** in paragraph **1** and underline it. Circle the prefix and the suffix. Was Meqak able to sew or not?

_____

_____

Find the word *beautiful* in sentence **B** in paragraph **2**. Underline it. Circle the suffix. What is another word that means the same as *beautiful*?

_____

Find the word with both a prefix and a suffix in sentence **C** in paragraph **3**. Underline it. Circle the prefix and the suffix. What does this word mean?

_____

_____

"The Magic Needle" by Betty X. Davis, Reprinted by permission of SPIDER magazine December 2005, text © 2005 by Carus Publishing Company

6   "No, Meqak," he said firmly. "First you learn to sew. All girls must sew."

7   With a bowed head, she asked her mother for another needle.

8   "I do not have an extra needle, Meqak, and you cannot use mine. Needles are too valuable. I must save mine to make a blanket for the baby and rabbit-skin mittens for your brothers. You may go once to the house of Samik, the carver. Take the fox fur that was to be your parka and take also some choice seal meat. Respectfully ask him for a needle."

Read paragraph **8**. Find the word that tells how Meqak's mother wants her to speak to Samik. Underline it. Circle the two suffixes. What does it mean?

_____

_____

9   Meqak trudged through deep snow to the far side of the village to see Samik, a man respected for carving needles and knifes and animal figures but forbidden to hunt bear or caribou.

10   The village elders thought that an unwelcome spirit shadowed Samik. Although he could throw a spear straight and true, he was not allowed to hunt because he threw with his left hand. The elders feared that this unnaturalness could offend the spirits and drive animals from their land.

In paragraph **10**, underline the two words that have a prefix that means "not." Remove the prefix to form their opposites. Write the words.

_____

_____

11   Meqak was not afraid of the elders or of Samik. She was only afraid of sewing.

12   At the tunnel entrance of the sod house, she met Samik's wife. "Good day," Meqak said, looking down. "I wish to see Samik." In the custom of humility, she added, "I have a poor fox skin and scraps of inferior seal meat. I would like one of his excellent ivory needles."

13   A short, burly man with sad eyes but a warm smile joined his wife. They praised the fur and the meat, and he said, "My needles are badly made. I may have one to spare."

14   Silently his wife returned to her task of guarding the drying meat from hungry birds.

15   Samik looked into Meqak's dark eyes and read the trouble that lay heavy on her heart. "Tell me, Meqak, why do you need a needle?"

16   With downcast eyes, she whispered, "I lost my own. My fingers cannot learn to sew."

17   "Are they quick enough to catch a rabbit?" he asked.

18   To her surprise, he tossed her a small rabbit he had carved from walrus tusk. **D** She caught it easily. "I cannot catch a real rabbit. But I caught this with one hand!"

19   "You are clever," he said. "And, little Meqak, you have fine hands. I saw you catch my rabbit. I can teach you to sew perfectly, but only with a magic needle."

20   She knew about magic. **E** Magic was in the sun that climbed the mountain and disappeared when the bears slept, in the stars that peeked out in winter darkness, and in the whale that ruled the world under the sea. But in a needle? "You have a magic needle, Samik?" she asked.

21   He nodded his shaggy head. "But a magic needle loses its power if anyone sees you sew. Can you promise no one will look when you use this needle?"

22   "Yes, I promise! My family would hide their eyes so as not to spoil the magic."

23   For many hours he taught her, leading her fingers until the needle glided like a slender fish and the stitches ran along like little ants. She felt the magic seep through her whole body. She knew it was real magic and that Samik must be obeyed.

24   Then, with joy in her heart, Meqak hurried home to show off the needle and proclaim its magic to her family. But when she sewed, she sat alone by a soapstone lamp.

25   With seams as straight as the flight of an arrow, she pierced tough sealskin to make sturdy kamiks for her feet. She embroidered a beautiful caribou-skin shirt with feathers and shells. The stitches never failed. The magic needle never faltered. And only the soapstone lamp saw Meqak as she sewed.

26   Others begged the carver for magic needles. "I had only one," he always said, "and that one I gave to Meqak."

27   Her father was so pleased that he let her take time from sewing to run with the boys and the dogs, fish for trout, and chase rabbits.

Look at sentence **D** in paragraph **18**. Underline the word that tells you how Meqak caught the rabbit. Circle the suffix. What is the base word, or the word without the suffix?

Read sentence **E** in paragraph **20**. Underline the word that tells that the sun went away. Remove the prefix to form the word that means the opposite.

28   And the magic? It stayed forever. Her family knew that the needle would lose its power if others saw her sew. They respected magic and never challenged it.

29   Only Meqak and Samik understood that the real magic was not in the needle. The "magic" was in the little left hand that held it.

Answer the following questions based on the passage you just read.

1. Read the paragraph below. Look at the underlined words.

> *With dainty fingers, other nine-year-old Inuit girls worked their ivory needles and* <u>*made*</u> *beautiful bearskin trousers, fox-fur coats, and kamiks. Their thread of caribou sinew never tangled. Their stitches held strong and* <u>*even*</u>*. But Meqak's did not.*

Add a prefix to the word *made* to form a word that means that they made it again.

_____

Add a prefix to the word *even* to form its opposite.

_____

2. Read the paragraph below. Pay attention to the underlined word.

> *And the magic? It stayed forever. Her family knew that the needle would lose its* <u>*power*</u> *if others saw her sew. They respected magic and never challenged it.*

Add the suffix *-ful* to *power* to form the word that means "full of power." Write a sentence using it.

_____

_____

Add the suffix *-less* to *power* to form the word that means "without power." Write a sentence using it.

_____

_____

3. Complete the chart below.

dis- + obey =
dis- + please =
joy + -ful =
heavy + -ly =
joy + -ful + -ly =
joy + -less =
joy + -less + ly =
perfect + -ly =
im- + perfect =
im- + perfect + -ly =

4. Suppose you wanted to create a list of words and their antonyms, or their opposites. Explain how you could use prefixes and suffixes to do this.

_____

_____

Critical Thinking

5. Reread the last paragraph of this story. Meet with one or two other students. Talk about what big idea this paragraph tells. Discuss other stories you have read or movies you have seen that have a similar message.

Writing	☐
Research	☐
Listening and Speaking	☑
Media Literacy	☐
21st Century Skills: Collaboration	☑
Cross Curriculum Connections	☐

On Your Own

Read the selection below. Then answer the questions that follow it.

Literature Connection

Thump Time and the Seed-Spitting Contest

by Isabella Garcia Lopez

> Every year in Texas, the Annual Watermelon Thump takes place in late June. People come from all over the world for this event.

1   It's June, so it must be thump time in Texas. That's right. It's time again for the Annual Watermelon Thump. Every year, it starts on the last Thursday in June and runs through the last Sunday. The biggest feature of the Watermelon Thump is the Seed-Spitting Contest. It is a remarkable event.

2   For weeks, Jackson prepared for the event. He saved the largest and blackest seeds. Then Jackson invited his friends over to practice. He set up a cool spit way in the driveway, and put down a thick piece of tape for the starting line. He also set up the boundaries. He and his dad moved the picnic table to the front lawn, so they'd have a place to sit. They would remove the table and return it to the backyard when the contest was over.

3   Jackson looked around. Everything looked okay so he went inside.

4   "Mom, did you put the watermelon on ice?" asked Jackson nervously. "You know how much Luis, Jenny, and Max like VERY cold watermelon."

"Thump Time and the Seed-Spitting Contest" by Isabella Garcia Lopez

5   Jackson's mom laughed and said, "Sure I did! And I made plenty of food. I <u>premade</u> some barbeque sauce so that we can have barbeque ribs. I even made some cabbage and radish slaw. I know that Max *really* likes slaw!"

6   "Mom, you're the best!" laughed Jackson whole-heartedly. "Oh, and we need a pitcher of water. You know that it's easier to spit the seed if your mouth is moist."

7   "The pitcher of water is already in the refrigerator, Jackson!" said his mom.

8   Jackson went back outside and saw Luis coming down the street on his bike.

9   "Hey, Luis! Have you been practicing?" asked Jackson.

10   "Yes, I've been practicing every day before school. I think that I might win!" said Luis confidently.

11   "Really, why do you say that?" asked Jackson. Now he was a bit worried because Luis was good, REALLY good! Although Luis was his friend, Jackson would be a little unhappy if Luis won and he didn't.

12   "Well, yesterday I spit a seed 15 feet 2½ inches," said Luis.

13   "Wow! Fantastic! I haven't spit a seed farther than about 12 feet," Jackson replied. He didn't tell his friend, but he felt a little <u>discouraged</u>.

14   Just then, Jenny and Max rode up on their bikes.

15   "Hi! Ready?" asked Jackson.

16   "Ready," said Jenny.

17   "Not ready!" laughed Max.

18   "Why not?" asked Luis.

19   "I'm not sure why, but I just can't seem to spit a seed very far these days," Max replied. "It just seems impossible. And whenever I think about the record that Gillian set last year, I lose my confidence. She spit that watermelon seed 16 feet 8¼ inches! It's hopeless."

20   "C'mon, Max. We can beat her!" said Jenny encouragingly. Let's get started. Max, you go first. Luis can go second. Jackson will go third, and I'll go last, and remember, we each get to spit two watermelon seeds each time."

21   Max took a seed out of the jar and stood at the starting line. Jackson held the measuring stick. On the table, there was a chart to show how far everyone spit the watermelon seeds. Max spit the first watermelon seed 11 feet 2 inches. He tried again. He spit the second 10 feet 3 inches.

22   Luis went next. He spit the seed 14 feet 6 inches. Then he spit it 15 feet 7 inches!

23   "Wow, Luis!" Everyone yelled excitedly. "You beat your own record." Secretly, Max, Jenny, and Jackson thought he'd win this year.

24   Jackson stood at the starting line. He spit the seed 10 feet 5½ inches. *Not good,* he thought to himself sadly. He spit another seed: 14 feet 11 inches! Everyone yelled. "Go Jackson!"

25   Jenny went next. First, she picked the biggest seed she could find in the jar. Then she took a gulp of water, ran up to the starting line, and spit the seed. It flew through the air. Max measured. Jenny had spit the seed 16 feet 4 inches!

26   *Unbelievable,* thought Jackson. *Jenny has never spit a seed that far.*

27   "Okay," said Max. "Let's take a break. I want some ribs and slaw! We can practice some more in a while."

28   "Hey, everyone," said Luis. "Let's have one more practice and invite Gillian. Maybe we can get some good pointers from her."

29   "Good idea!" Max said, "but I think we just got some GREAT ideas from Jenny!"

Answer the following questions based on the passage you just read.

1. Read the sentence below. Look for the spelling change in *biggest*.

> *The* <u>biggest</u> *feature of the Watermelon Thump is the Seed-Spitting Contest.*

You use the suffix *-est* to compare three or more things. What is the base word in *biggest*?

_____

What spelling change was made when the suffix *-est* was added?

_____

Add the suffix *-er* to the base word. Write a sentence using the new word.

_____

2. Read the sentence below.

> *They would remove the table and return it to the backyard when the contest was over.*

Which two words have the same prefix?

_____

What do these words mean?

_____

_____

3. Read the sentence below.

> *"Mom, did you put the watermelon on ice?" asked Jackson <u>nervously</u>.*

If Jackson asks the question *nervously*, how is he feeling?

_____

Write a sentence telling about something you do nervously.

_____

_____

4. In paragraph 5, if Jackson's mother <u>premade</u> the barbeque sauce, she made it —

A ahead of time

B carefully

C late in the day

D quickly

5. What does <u>discouraged</u> mean in paragraph 13?

   A Being very brave

   B Not feeling confident

   C Full of joy

   D In an excited way

 6. Read the sentence below.

> *"Mom, you're the best!" laughed Jackson* <u>*whole-heartedly*</u>.

When you read dialogue—words characters say—you often see adverbs ending in *-ly*. They tell you how a character said something. In the sentence above, Jackson laughed sincerely, or with his whole heart.

Fill in the web below. In the ovals, write other *-ly* words you find in this story telling how characters speak.

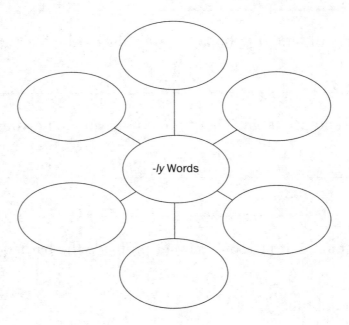

With a partner, act out the meaning of each adverb.

Critical Thinking

7. Look through your favorite book or story. Search for *-ly* adverbs that tell how people speak. Jot them down in a notebook. Then write a short story about a contest. Use at least five of the adverbs you found.

Writing	☑
Research	☑
Listening and Speaking	☐
Media Literacy	☐
21st Century Skills	☐
Cross Curriculum Connections	☐

8. Talk to people in your community. Do some research on the Web or in the library. Find out more about the Texas Watermelon Thump.

Use Context Clues to Find the Meaning of Words

® 3.4(B)   Use context to determine the relevant meaning of unfamiliar words or distinguish among multiple meaning words and homographs.

 Understand the TEKS

Context Clues

When you read a word and you don't know what it means, look for **context** clues. These are clues that help you figure out the meaning of words you don't know. You can find context clues in the surrounding words or sentences.

> **Words to Know**
> context
> context clue
> homograph
> multiple-meaning word

For example, read these sentences.

> Neal walked <u>briskly</u> toward the lookout tree. He moved quickly because he could see the bear getting closer and closer.

Suppose you do not know the meaning of *briskly*. The context clue that helps you is the word *quickly*. It helps you figure out that *briskly* means "at a fast pace."

Now read this paragraph.

> Luisa was very happy. Her class had been chosen to <u>participate</u> at the opening of the new museum. It was a big event. Her class was going to dance. What a big honor it was to be part of this celebration!

Suppose you do not know the meaning of the word *participate*. The context clues that help you are the words "big event" and "part of this celebration."

- What do you think *participate* means?

_____

Multiple-Meaning Words

Some words can have more than one meaning. They are called **multiple-meaning** words.

The word *brilliant* can mean "sparkling; shining brightly." For example: *a brilliant diamond*. It can also mean "having great ability; very smart."

For example: *a brilliant scientist.* Another meaning is "excellent; perfect; terrific." For example: *a brilliant* plan.

If you come across the word *brilliant* when you read, you can figure out which meaning is intended from the context. Read the context carefully. Determine how the word is being used. Look for context clues in the sentence or in surrounding sentences.

Read the paragraph below.

> No one could solve the mystery until Inspector Cassandra Hudson came on the case. It took this <u>brilliant</u> detective only a day to come up with a solution that others couldn't come up with after months on the job.

Look at the clues. No one else is able to solve the case. Others have tried for months. Hudson comes up with a solution in a day.

• What is the meaning of *brilliant* in this context?

_____

Homographs

Homographs look alike but they have different meanings. Usually, they have two different entries in the dictionary.

For example, the words *arm* and *arm* are homographs. Look at the sentences below.

> During the American Revolution, the farmers wanted to <u>arm</u> themselves against the British.
>
> My right <u>arm</u> is stronger than my left.

• Circle the sentence in which <u>*arm*</u> means "to give or hold weapons."

• What does <u>*arm*</u> mean in the other sentence?

_____

Comprehension Tip

Look for words in *italic* or **bold** type when you read. Usually, these are words the author defines or explains.

 Guided Instruction

Read the passage below. Then answer the questions in the margin and complete the activities.

Science Connection

Ask a Pirate About Treasure
An Interview Between Ask Magazine and a Pirate

1 **Ask:** Tell me about gems!

2 **Pirate Pete:** Gems are those big colored things in sparkly jewelry.

3 **Ask:** Where can I get some?

4 **Pete:** I used to steal them from treasure ships. But people shoot at you! It's really dangerous!

5 Then I thought, why go to all that trouble when you can get them right out of the earth? So I became a geologist.

6 **Ask:** Do you have a treasure map?

7 **Pete**: The best kind! It's made of rocks! Gems form deep down under the earth, where it's hot and crushing enough to melt minerals (the different ingredients of rocks) into lovely hard gems. **A** Then Earth's plates move around and scrunch up magma, and bring the gems up to where I—I mean we—can get at them. So I always start by looking for well-baked rocks that have the right mix of minerals for gem-making. Of course, when you find gems in the wild, they don't look anything like the ones in crowns. They are not sparkly at all—they just look like rocks. Maybe because they *are* rocks. So the real trick is to tell which rocks are the good ones.

| **Guided Questions** |

Look at paragraph **2**. Circle the word *gems*. Underline the words Pete uses to explain what gems are.

Underline the word *geologist* in paragraph **5**. Circle the context clue that tells you what a geologist studies.

Look at the word *magma* in sentence **A** in paragraph **7**. Underline it. Magma is molten, or melted, rock deep within the earth. Circle the words in the surrounding sentences that show that magma is extremely hot.

"Ask a Pirate About Treasure" Reprinted by permission of ASK magazine July/August 2009, text © 2009 by Carus Publishing Company

8   **Ask:** How do you tell which rocks are the good ones?

9   **Pete:** Well, if I try to steal them from you, that's a clue. Or you can give them the geologist's personality test for rocks. And of course, if it runs away, it's probably a turtle.

Personality Test for Rocks

How hard is it?

10   Geologists rank the toughness of rocks from 1 to 10, with 10 the hardest. **B** Each rank can scratch any rock below it. Diamond is at the top, at 10—nothing can scratch it but another diamond. Next hardest are sapphire and ruby. At the bottom is wimpy talc, so soft they make baby powder out of it.

What color is it, really?

11   Rub your stone on rough porcelain to see what color streak it leaves. The streak is not always the same color as the stone! Or try shining different colored light through it.

What shape are its crystals?

12   **C** Gems (like most rocks) are made up of crystals, repeating shapes that fit together like blocks. Every mineral has its own shape of crystal (gems are especially large ones). Every kind of rock also breaks in its own special way. Some crumble, some break in curves, some split in spikes. Looking at crystal shape and how the rock breaks can tell you what kind of rock you have.

How shiny is it?

13   Geologists have lots of fancy ways to say how shiny a rock is. **D** You might say a glass and a spoon are both shiny, but to a geologist the spoon is "metallic," while the glass is "vitreous," or glassy. And how transparent is your rock? Or is it sort of milky? Does it have streaks or cracks inside?

How heavy is it?

14   How much does your rock weigh compared to water? Diamonds are heavy, so a pea-sized diamond weighs a lot more than a pea. This is one way you can tell them apart; also, the pea is green.

Guided Questions

Underline the word *rank* in sentence **B** in paragraph **10**. In this context, does *rank* mean "an official job level and title" or "a position or level on a list"?

_____

_____

Underline the word *crystals* in sentence **C** in paragraph **12**. Circle the words that tell you what crystals are.

Underline the word *vitreous* in sentence **D** in paragraph **13**. Circle the word that tells you what it means. What is something that is vitreous?

_____

Rank Your Rock		
Hardness	**Can Be Scratched by**	**Example**
1	finger	talc
2	fingernail	school chalk (gypsum)
3	penny	calcite
4	nail	fluorite
5	glass	turquoise
6	pocket-knife	opal, jade
7	steel file	quartz, garnet
8	sandpaper	emerald, topaz
9	diamond	sapphire, ruby
10	another diamond	diamond

Guided Questions

Read the chart. Circle something that can be scratched by glass. What hardness is it?

_____

Answer the following questions based on the passage you just read.

1. Read the sentence below. Pay attention to the underlined word.

> *Of course, when you find gems in the <u>wild</u>, they don't look anything like the ones in crowns.*

Wild can mean "an area that has been left in a natural state." It can also mean "unruly, or not showing discipline." What does it mean in the sentence above?

_____

Write a sentence using it with the other meaning.

_____

2. Read the paragraph below.

> *Geologists rank the toughness of rocks from 1 to 10, with 10 the hardest. Each rank can scratch any rock below it. Diamond is at the top, at 10—nothing can scratch it but another diamond. Next hardest are sapphire and ruby. At the bottom is wimpy talc, so soft they make baby powder out of it.*

What two words in the first sentence have almost the same meaning?

_____

What word in the last sentence shows that talc does not have the quality you just named?

_____

 3. Complete the chart below for the word *gem*.

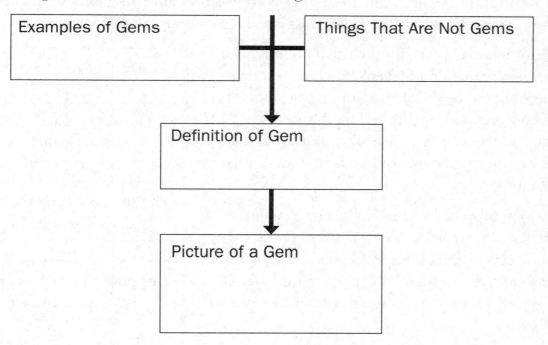

Examples of Gems	Things That Are Not Gems

Definition of Gem

Picture of a Gem

 4. Jot down other questions you would like to ask Pirate Pete about gems. Then work with a partner. Exchange your lists of questions. Do some research to answer each other's questions. Then work with your partner to compile a list of questions and answers. Use them to dramatize an interview with a pirate.

Writing	☐
Research	☑
Listening and Speaking	☑
Media Literacy	☐
21st Century Skills: Collaboration	☑
Cross Curriculum Connections: Science	☑

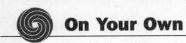

On Your Own

Read the selection below. Then answer the questions that follow it.

**Social Studies
Connection**

Who's Been Working
on the Railroad?

by Lucy Brown

1   When you look around today, you see many kinds of vehicles. There are cars and trucks. There are huge, <u>gigantic</u> airplanes and long, long trains. There are buses and boats. There are even space ships that fly to the moon! It wasn't always like this. Long ago, travel in America was very hard. Native Americans and pioneers traveled on foot or on horseback. When pioneers moved to the west, they traveled in wagon trains.

2   People couldn't get anywhere fast. It could take more than one month for a letter to travel from Pennsylvania to California. It was the same for goods. Many items were moved by boats. The boats traveled along coastal waters, rivers and canals.

3   All this changed with the dream of one man. His name was John Stevens. He believed that there should be railroads. Here is the story of how one person changed the history of transportation in America. Transportation is a way of moving people or goods from one place to another.

4   John Stevens lived in Hoboken, New Jersey. He was an engineer. An *engineer* is a person who designs and builds machines and vehicles. Stevens liked to spend his time building steam engines. This is why he is also called "the genius of steam."

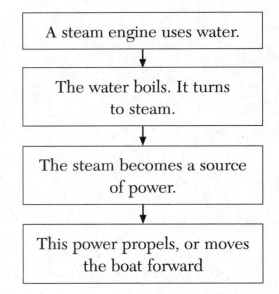

A steam engine uses water.

↓

The water boils. It turns to steam.

↓

The steam becomes a source of power.

↓

This power propels, or moves the boat forward

"Who's Been Working on the Railroad?" by Lucy Brown

5   In 1804, he built a **steamboat** (a boat that moves using power from steam). The boat was 86 feet long. He built another steamboat in 1807. This time he built it with his sons. It was called the *Phoenix*. They operated the boat between Trenton, New Jersey and Philadelphia, Pennsylvania. They couldn't use the boat on New York waterways. Robert Fulton had a monopoly. A **monopoly** is when a company controls something. Fulton had built the first steamboat in America. His company had all the rights to run steamboats between New York City and Albany, New York. No one else could run boats. The monopoly was finally stopped. The Stevens family then operated their steamboats on the Hudson River.

6   Like Fulton, they used the steamboats for commerce. **Commerce** is the buying and selling of goods in order to make money. Stevens made a lot of money. Over time, the way that steamboats were built was a direct result of the inventions of the Stevens family. They greatly improved what Fulton had done. After awhile, John Stevens turned his business over to his sons. This gave him more time to try to figure out how to use steam on land.

7   One day in 1823, Colonel Stevens went to Strasbourg, PA. He traveled by horse-drawn coach. He was there for a reason. Pennsylvania had given him the first railroad charter. A **charter** is a written grant. It is often given by a government. It gave Stevens permission to build a railroad. The rail line would be between Philadelphia and Columbia. He wanted to make a survey (a detailed plan or study of a piece of land). This plan was to show a route for a railroad. It was the first time a person looked into the possibility of a railroad route in America. For this reason, Stevens became known as the "father of the railroad."

8   But, no one would give him money. He had already shown how a locomotive, an
engine used to pull railway cars, could climb a hill. But it still took some more time.
He really believed in railroads. He spent a lot of his own money. He really pushed
hard. He never gave up. In 1846, the Pennsylvania Railroad was born. It became a
huge railroad company. Railroads were the biggest business in the 1800s. It made
fortunes for people. With a lot of hard work, Stevens' dream came true.

9   About three years later, there was more than 9,000 miles of track. New towns
were built near the tracks. Just about each town had its own depot (railroad station).
People got mail faster. They got supplies faster. They got information more quickly.
The railroad changed America. This was all because of a man named John Stevens!
He was the man who really worked on the railroad. And, he was the man who never
gave up his dream!

Answer the following questions based on the passage you just read.

1. Read the paragraph below. Pay attention to the underlined word.

> *When you look around today, you see many kinds of <u>vehicles</u>. There are cars and
> trucks. There are huge, gigantic airplanes and long, long trains. There are buses
> and boats. There are even space ships that fly to the moon! It wasn't always like
> this. Long ago, travel in America was very hard. Native Americans and pioneers
> traveled on foot or on horseback. When pioneers moved to the west, they traveled
> in wagon trains.*

Use the web below to name different types of vehicles mentioned in this paragraph.

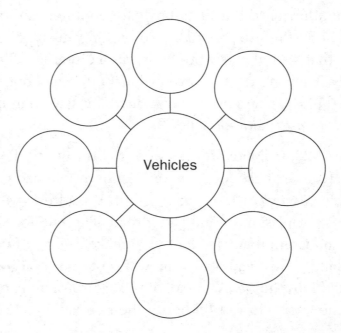

2. Read the paragraph below.

> *All this changed with the dream of one man. His name was John Stevens. He believed that there should be railroads. Here is the story of how one person changed the history of <u>transportation</u> in America. Transportation is a way of moving people or goods from one place to another.*

What words tell you what *transportation* means?

_____

What kind of transportation does your family use to move from one place to another?

_____

3. What is the best clue to the meaning of <u>gigantic</u> in paragraph 1?

  A *huge*

  B *vehicles*

  C *travel*

  D *cars*

4. Look at the sequence chart to the right of paragraphs 3–4. Find the word *propels*. In your own words, tell how steam propels a boat forward. Use another word for *propels* in your answer.

_____

_____

_____

5. Which of these details from paragraph 5 does not help you understand what a <u>monopoly</u> is?

  A *when a company controls something*

  B *built the first steamboat in America*

  C *had all the rights to run steamboats*

  D *No one else could run boats.*

6. Read the sentences below from paragraph 6. Notice that the author provides a definition of *commerce*.

> *Like Fulton, they used the steamboats for commerce. Commerce is the buying and selling goods in order to make money.*

Write three things you might do that are examples of commerce.

_____

_____

Think about what you know about forming new words. What do you think commercial activities are?

_____

7. In which sentence below does <u>survey</u> have the same meaning that it has in paragraph 7?

  A We tallied the results from our survey of the students.

  B The survey showed that more people preferred Choice A to Choice B.

  C She made a survey of the land to decide where to build the house.

  D They passed out a survey at the end of the movie.

Critical Thinking

8. Use your imagination. Brainstorm ideas for what transportation will be like 50 years in the future. Jot them down on a piece of paper. Think about how life will be different because of these different forms of transportation. Then write a science-fiction story that takes place 50 years from now.

Writing	☑
Research	☐
Listening and Speaking	☐
Media Literacy	☐
21st Century Skills: Adaptability	☑
Cross Curriculum Connections: Social Studies	☑

Understand Antonyms, Synonyms, Homographs, Homophones, and Playful Language

Ⓢ 3.4(C)   Identify and use antonyms, synonyms, homographs, and homophones.
3.4(D)   Identify and apply playful uses of language (e.g., tongue twisters, palindromes, riddles).

 Understand the TEKS

Synonyms are words that mean about the same thing. *Pleased* and *delighted* are synonyms. So are *easy* and *simple*.

Often, you can replace a word in a sentence with its synonym without changing its meaning.

Words to Know
antonym
homograph
homophone
pun
riddle
synonym

> Solving the puzzle was <u>easy</u>.
> Solving the puzzle was <u>simple</u>.

Antonyms are words that mean the opposite. *Full* and *empty* are antonyms. So are *easy* and *hard*.

Notice that the sentences below tell something very different from each other.

> Solving the puzzle was <u>simple</u>.
> Solving the puzzle was <u>hard</u>.

- What is another antonym for *simple*?

Homophones are words that sound alike but are spelled differently and have different meanings. It is easy to confuse homophones. For example, read these sentences.

> All the furniture on the porch <u>blew</u> away during the storm.
> The <u>blue</u> cornflowers look beautiful on the table.

In the first sentence, *blew* is the past tense of *blow* and means "were moved by wind." In the second sentence, *blue* names a color.

Homographs are two words that look alike but have different meanings. Homographs can also be pronounced differently. For example, read these sentences.

> Let's stand on the <u>bow</u> of the boat so we can see the dolphins.
> Sally really liked the <u>bow</u> on her new dress.

In the first sentence, *bow* means "front of a boat." It rhymes with *how*. In the second sentence, *bow* means "a knot that is decorative." It rhymes with *low*.

Playful Language

English is rich in synonyms, antonyms, homophones, and homographs. This makes it easy for us to play with language.

A **riddle** is a word puzzle. It asks a question. Often the answer to this question depends on some playful use of language.

> What type of frankfurter is both hot and cold? A chili dog!

This riddle plays with the homophones *chili* (a pepper) and *chilly* (feeling cold).

A **pun** is a play on words that uses words that have more than one meaning.

> Inspector Mendez looked around the fish store where a robbery had just occurred. "Something's <u>fishy</u>," he said.

• Make your own pun using the word *fishy*.

_____

_____

Comprehension Tip
Synonyms and antonyms are good context clues. Use them when you read unfamiliar words.

Measuring Up to the Texas Essential Knowledge and Skills

Guided Instruction

Read the passage below. Then answer the questions in the margin and complete the activities.

Literature Connection

The Little Fish

retold by Dede Mack

1   **A** There was once a poor old couple who lived in a tidy little house at the edge of a deep dark wood. Every day the husband would journey to the sea to catch a fish for dinner. His wife would cook the fish with a little garlic and they would eat it together happily.

2   One day the husband came home empty-handed. "The strangest thing just happened," he said to his wife. **B** "I caught a fish who said that if I threw him back he'd grant me my fondest wish."

3   "My fondest wish is for something to eat," stated the wife. "Go beckon the fish."

4   So the old man went back to the sea to call the fish. Nothing happened. He called again, and still nothing happened. Just then the little fish burst out of the water. "Go back home," the fish said. "Your cupboard is now stocked with delicious food." And sure enough, when the husband came home the cupboard was filled with delicacies from every part of the world.

"The Little Fish" retold by Dede Mack

Guided Questions

Read sentence **A** in paragraph **1**. Highlight the word *tidy*. What are two antonyms for *tidy*?

_____

Highlight the word *threw* in sentence **B** in paragraph **2**. What is a homophone for *threw*? Use the homophone for *threw* in a sentence.

_____

_____

_____

_____

---

5 The next day the wife had an idea. **C** "If that fish of yours can give us all this food, maybe it can give us a big fancy mansion to eat it in! **D** I'm tired of this dirty hovel. Go ask."

6 Dutifully, the husband went back to the sea and again summoned the fish:

> Little fishy in the sea
> My wife asks something more of me
> She says she is not happy yet
> There's other stuff she wants to get
> A fancy house, and we'll be set.

7 **E** To his surprise and amazement, upon his return the old man saw that his tiny house was gone and in its place stood a beautiful mansion. His wife was blissful, but soon enough turned cranky and started to grumble about her poor, tattered dress. Now we need clothes befitting lords and ladies of our rank," she said. "Go ask Fishy."

8 The old man was not eager to go. He was reluctant to ask the fish for too much. But his wife's nagging soon changed his mind. With a heavy heart, he trudged back to the sea and summoned the fish:

> Little fishy in the sea
> My wife asks something more of me
> She says she is not happy yet
> There's other stuff she wants to get
> Some fancy threads, and we'll be set.

9 To his astonishment, the wish was granted. **F** His wife's dress had been transformed into a gown of the finest silk; he himself looked quite smart in a velvet robe studded with jewels.

10 But his wife was still not happy. In fact, she was more miserable than ever. "Look, husband," she said. "We live in a castle and look like royalty. But we're still peasants. We should be King and Queen."

11 "As if," said her husband. **G** But he knew how stubborn and persistent his wife could be, and he left without argument. Once more he summoned the fish.

Guided Questions

Highlight the word *mansion* in sentence **C** is paragraph **5**. What is a *mansion*? Read sentence **D** and highlight an antonym for *mansion*.

_____

_____

Read sentence **E** in paragraph **7**. Highlight the two words in this sentence that are synonyms. Why does the old man react this way?

_____

_____

_____

_____

Read sentence **F** in paragraph **9**. Highlight the word that is a synonym for *changed*.

Read sentence **G** in paragraph **11**. Highlight the two words that are synonyms, or have about the same meaning.

Little fishy in the sea
My wife asks something more of me
She says she is not happy yet
There's *still* more stuff she wants to get
A pair of crowns, and we'll be set.

12   The old man stood there waiting. He promised himself he'd never ask the fish for anything ever again, no matter how unhappy his wife was or how much she nagged. Maybe being Queen would be enough for her. Maybe now she would leave him in peace.

13   Just then, the old man heard something in the wind. If he stood very still, he could just make out the words:

Old man standing by the sea
You WILL NOT get more stuff from me
For happiness cannot be got
It cannot be bartered, sold, or bought—
It's either there, or else it's not.

14   And the fish was true to his word. **H** For it was not a Queen who came to greet him on his return, but a poor peasant woman in a tattered and threadbare dress, her arms open in greeting, her face glowing with the simple pleasure of just being alive.

Guided Questions

Look at the last line of the poem in paragraph **11**. Highlight the word *pair*. What is a homophone for *pair*? What does it mean?

_____

Read sentence **H** in paragraph **14**. Highlight two synonyms that describe the woman's dress.

Answer the following questions based on the passage you just read.

1. Read the sentence below.

> *"If that fish of yours can give us all this food, maybe it can give us a big fancy mansion to eat it in!"*

Fill in the chart below. In the left-hand column, list at least two synonyms for *fancy*. In the right-hand column, list at least two antonyms.

Synonyms and Antonyms for *Fancy*	
Synonyms	**Antonyms**

2. Read the sentence below.

> *Every day the husband would journey to the sea to catch a fish for dinner.*

What is a homophone for *sea* in this sentence? Write a sentence using both words.

_____

_____

 Measuring Up to the Texas Essential Knowledge and Skills

3. The words *wind* and *wind* are homographs. They have different meanings and are pronounced differently. Read the sentence below.

> *Just then, the old man heard something in the* <u>*wind*</u>.

What does *wind* mean in this sentence? Is it pronounced with the /i/ you hear in *win* or the /i/ you hear in *sign*?

_____

_____

Now read this sentence.

> <u>*Wind*</u> *the string around the rope.*

What is the definition of *wind* in this sentence? Is it pronounced with the /i/ you hear in *win* or the /i/ you hear in *sign*?

_____

_____

Critical Thinking

4. Many fairy tales follow a pattern of telling about three magical wishes. Search in the library or on the Internet for one of these tales. Share your tale in a small group. After everyone has had a chance to read his or her story, talk about why this type of tale is so popular. What lesson does it teach?

Writing	☐
Research	☑
Listening and Speaking	☑
Media Literacy	☐
21st Century Skills: Collaboration	☑
Cross Curriculum Connections	☐

Media Connection

5. You can watch at video version of "The Three Wishes" at http://www.youtube.com/watch?feature=player_embedded&v=qGwOMYUhjt4.

On Your Own

Read the selection below. Then answer the questions that follow it.

The Lost Sock

by Jeffrey B. Fuerst

Narrator, Blue Sock, Red Sock 1, Red Sock 2

---

1 **Narrator:** Once upon a time, there were three little socks.

2 **Blue Sock:** Don't you mean once upon a foot?

3 **Narrator:** I guess you could put it that way. . . .

4 **Red Sock 1:** There was a red sock.

5 **Blue Sock:** A blue sock.

6 **Red Sock 2:** And another red sock.

7 **Red Sock 1 and Red Sock 2:** We make a great pair. (*They giggle*.)

8 **Narrator:** The red socks did indeed make a great pair. They went everywhere together. And when they weren't out and about, they nestled in the sock drawer as a sock ball. (*The red socks snore*.) The blue sock, meanwhile, was all alone, which made him feel . . . well, blue.

9 **Blue Sock:** Of course I'm blue! I'm a blue sock.

10 **Narrator:** I mean blue as in sad because the other blue sock is gone.

11 **Blue Sock:** True, I am blue. But I'm not sad. I have a lot of time to myself now that I'm not part of a pair.

---

12   **Red Sock 1 and Red Sock 2:** We like being teammates. Red, red, go red! (*The red socks jump up and down.*)

13   **Blue Sock:** Well, I don't have to worry about being stepped on all day long by smelly feet.

14   **Red Sock 2:** We love being on feet. After a day on smelly feet, we get to go for the best ride around.

15   **Red Sock 1:** And she means around and around and around.

16   **Red Sock 1 and Red Sock 2:** In the washing machine. *Whee!*

17   **Blue Sock:** That is fun. And I do miss the dryer, getting all warm and fluffy. (*Pauses.*) Gee, I guess I am missing out by not being part of a team. (*Sighs, now sad.*) I do miss my brother sock. I don't know where he went. I don't know what happened to him.

18   **Red Sock 2:** Please don't cry, Blue Sock. You might shrink. We don't want you to be sad. Why don't you pair up with me one day?

19   **Red Sock 1:** And you can pair up with me one day, too!

20   **Blue Sock:** You mean it? You're not afraid people will laugh at us?

21   **Red Sock 1 and Red Sock 2:** No! You're our cousin.

22   **Red Sock 1, Red Sock 2, and Blue Sock:** Sock Power!

23   **Narrator:** And so the blue sock paired up with the red socks for a time, but he was still lonely without his brother.

24   **Blue Sock:** I must find him. He is my "sole mate."

25   **Narrator:** So the socks went looking for the missing blue sock.

26   **Red Sock 1:** He's not here under the bed.

27   **Red Sock 2:** He's not here in the bottom of the laundry bag.

28   **Narrator:** They even looked in the sock drawers of the other people in the house.

29   **Blue Sock:** Where could he be? I hope the cat didn't get him.

30   **Narrator:** Then the socks heard the whirr and hum of a sewing machine.

31   **Blue Sock:** The sewing machine. Now I remember! My brother was in an accident and got a hole in his toe. He needed stitches!

32   **Narrator:** And so the socks hurried off to the sewing machine. There they found Blue Sock's brother being mended. The search for the missing sock was a resounding . . .

33   **Red Sock 1, Red Sock 2, and Blue Sock**: Sock-sess!

The End

Answer the following questions based on the passage you just read.

 1. Read the lines below. Think about the different things *pair* can mean.

Red Sock 1 and Red Sock 2: <u>We make a great pair.</u> (They giggle.)

Explain why this dialogue is funny.

_____

_____

2. What is a synonym for <u>giggle</u> in paragraph 7?

A Shout

B Cry

C Say

D Chuckle

 3. Read the sentence below from paragraph 8.

And when they weren't out and about, they <u>nestled</u> in the sock drawer as a sock ball.

What is a good synonym for *nestled*? Rewrite the sentence above with the synonym you chose.

_____

_____

Which sentence do you like better? Why?

_____

_____

4. Read the sentence below.

> *Well, I don't have to worry about being* <u>*stepped on*</u> *all day long by smelly feet.*

What is one meaning of *stepped on* in this sentence?

_____

_____

What is another meaning of *stepped on*?

_____

_____

5. Which sentence below shows a word being used with two different meanings?

   A *The blue sock, meanwhile, was all alone, which made him feel . . . well, blue.*

   B *We like being teammates. Red, red, go red!*

   C *So the socks went looking for the missing blue sock.*

   D *You're not afraid people will laugh at us?*

6. Which sentence uses a homophone correctly?

   A He is the *soul* person left.

   B We had a piece of *soul* for dinner.

   C There is a piece of gum on the *sole* of my shoe.

   D Don't tell my secret to another *sole*.

7. Fill in the chart below. In the left-hand column, write an example of playful language from this story that you particularly liked. In the right-hand column, tell why you liked it.

What I Liked	Why I Liked It

8. Work in a group of four to put on this play. First decide who will play each role. Then talk about what props or costumes are needed. (You might want to perform it using socks as hand puppets.) Decide on sound effects. Work together to practice reading the parts. Then rehearse with costumes, props, and sound effects. Finally, put on the play for your class.

Critical Thinking

Writing	☐
Research	☐
Listening and Speaking	☑
Media Literacy	☑
21st Century Skills: Teamwork	☑
Cross Curriculum Connections	☐

Use a Dictionary or Glossary

3.4(E)   Alphabetize a series of words to the third letter and use a dictionary or a glossary to determine the meanings, syllabication, and pronunciation of unknown words.

⟳ Understand the TEKS

Dictionary

When you read a word that you don't know, you can look up the word in a **dictionary**. A dictionary lists the words of a language in **alphabetical order**. (Alphabetical order is *abc* order.) The information about each word is called an **entry**.

There are **guide words** at the top of a dictionary page. All the entries for words that fall alphabetically between the guide words appear on the page.

> **Words to Know**
> alphabetical order
> dictionary
> entry
> glossary
> guide words
> syllable

• Suppose you see the guide words *hire* and *hobby*. Would the entry for *hive* appear on this page?

_____

How do you know?

_____

An entry tells you many things about a word. It tells:

• how to pronounce it;
• how to divide it into syllables;
• its part of speech;
• its origin or word history;
• its meanings.

Suppose you come across a difficult word in your reading. You decide to look it up in the dictionary. Be sure to check all the meanings for that word. Then choose the definition that best fits the context.

Here is a dictionary entry for the word *tie*.

> **tie** \tí\ *verb* **1.** to fasten together, as with string *noun* **2.** a piece of cloth worn around the neck **3.** a situation where two teams or individuals have equal scores **4.** something that holds people together (from Old English, a rope)

Now read the sentences below.

| The game wound up in a <u>tie</u>. There was no winner. |

- What meaning of *tie* fits this context?

_____

_____

Glossary

Sometimes a book has a **glossary** at the end. This is a listing of words in the book that the author thinks are important for you to know. Often they are special words or terms that deal with that subject matter. For example, in a science book about animals, you might find the word *mammals* in the glossary.

A glossary is unlike a dictionary in these ways:

- It contains only words used in that particular book.
- It contains only the definition of the word that fits the book.
- Which do you think is more likely to have a glossary: a social studies textbook or a novel or fictional chapter book?

_____

Why?

_____

Comprehension Tip
When you alphabetize words, don't stop at the first letter. Look at the first three letters in each word and put the words in order.

Guided Instruction

Read the passage below. Then answer the questions in the margin and complete the activities.

Science
Connection

My Grandmother Talks with Her Hands

by Tara L. Guimont

1   My grandmother talks with her hands. She shows me how to bake peanut butter cookies and how to sew Christmas ornaments. She asks me about my day at school. **A** She listens to my reply with her sharp blue eyes. Grandma notices everything. She can look at my face and tell when something is wrong, even before anyone else can. Maybe because she can't use her ears, she uses her eyes even better.

2   My grandmother tells stories with her hands. She tells me how she got scarlet fever when she was just a baby. When the sickness passed, she couldn't hear anymore. She was deaf.

3   She tells me about growing up far away in Maine with eight brothers and sisters in a big white house. **B** From a shelf, she takes down a small pillow filled with pine needles and she has me smell it. She says that smelling it makes her remember Maine, even though she has lived in Oregon now for a long time.

4   If the afternoon is rainy and long, Grandma will tell me how she had to leave her family when she was only six years old. **C** She went to a school for deaf children in Portland, Maine. She couldn't go home except for Christmas and the summer holidays. She tells me how slowly the train would wind its way through the heavy snow as it carried her home for Christmas. I can almost see her as an excited little girl, sitting with her nose pressed up against the cold train window.

"My Grandmother Talks with Her Hands" by Tara L. Guimont, Reprinted by permission of SPIDER magazine May 2001, text © 2001 by Tara L. Guimont

Guided Questions

Read sentence **A** in paragraph **1**. Highlight the word *sharp*. *Sharp* can mean "having an edge or a point that cuts easily." It can also mean "able to notice things easily." What does it mean in this sentence?

_____

Suppose this article appeared as part of a health textbook. Highlight two words in paragraph **2** you might find in a glossary.
Look at sentence **B** in paragraph **3**. Highlight the word *needles*. A *needle* can be a pointed piece of metal used for sewing. It can also be a thin pointed leaf. What are *needles* in this paragraph?

_____

Highlight *deaf* in sentence **C** in paragraph **4**. *Deaf* can be a noun or an adjective. What part of speech is it here? How do you know?

_____

5   Grandma tells me the teachers were very strict at her school. **D** She had to keep everything orderly and clean. She had to wash and iron her own uniform. Her bed had to be made perfectly—no lumps or creases. She had to eat all the food on her plate—even the breakfast porridge that smelled like wallpaper paste. Students who didn't follow the rules were slapped on the hand with a ruler! Grandma laughs her squeaky laugh when I get angry about that.

Highlight the word *orderly* in sentence **D** in paragraph **5**. Look it up in a dictionary. What does it mean in this sentence? What part of speech is it?

_____

_____

6   But Grandma also has happy memories of her school. **E** She says that the teachers taught her to do many things well. She learned to read, to write letters home, and how to do math. I wrinkle my nose when Grandma tells me that math was her favorite subject.

Highlight the word *taught* in sentence **E** in paragraph **6**. When you look up a verb in the dictionary, you look up its base form, or present-tense form. What word would you look up to find an entry for *taught*?

7   In sewing class she learned to stitch the straightest seams of all. I can picture her at my age beaming as the teacher shows her fine sewing to the rest of the class. Now Grandma sews beautiful tap-dancing costumes for me. The teachers showed Grandma all about cooking, too. On Sundays she teaches me how to whisk the milk and flour into the gravy for the pot roast. Grandma looks far beyond the rain outside the window and nods her head. She is remembering.

_____

Highlight the word *resolute* in sentence **F** in paragraph **8**. Look it up in a dictionary. What does *resolute* mean?

8   Then Grandma turns and looks squarely at me. With her short, determined hands, she tells me that her school taught her to work hard and to be proud of who she is. **F** In signs as resolute as a solider, my grandmother tells me that those were the most important lessons of all.

_____

Answer the following questions based on the passage you just read.

1. Read the sentence below. Pay attention to the underlined word.

> *She tells me how slowly the train would wind its way through the <u>heavy</u> snow as it carried her home for Christmas.*

Now read a dictionary entry for *heavy*.

> **heavy** \he-vē\ *adjective* **1.** weighing a lot **2.** a great amount **3.** difficult to do **4.** hard to digest

Which meaning of *heavy* fits the way it is used in the sentence?

_____

2. Write these words from the story in alphabetical order.

strict	porridge	wallpaper	write	pillow	stitch
whisk	train	straight	teacher	wrinkle	resolute

_____

_____

3. Look up each word in the left-hand column in your dictionary. Show how to divide it into syllables in the right-hand column.

Word	Syllables
ornament	
needle	
remember	
holiday	
uniform	

Critical Thinking

4. Work with a partner. Do some research to find out about sign language. Work together to create an oral presentation. Include charts showing different signs and their meanings.

Writing	☐
Research	☑
Listening and Speaking	☑
Media Literacy	☐
21st Century Skills: Collaboration	☑
Cross-Curriculum Connection: Health	☑

On Your Own

Read the selection below. Then answer the questions that follow it.

Science Connection

Hanging by a Thread

by Sharon T. Pochron, Ph.D.

The caterpillar above is walking normally.
But when a wasp shakes the leaf, the
caterpillar knows it must get away—fast.

1   *Caterpillars have a <u>trick</u> to get out of danger. How do they know when to use it?*

2   A wasp crept toward a caterpillar on a leaf. Dr. Ignacio Castellanos of Mexico watched. He knew the wasp was a caterpillar predator, which meant it ate caterpillars. He wondered what the caterpillar would do. Would it do anything?

3   As the predator walked closer to the caterpillar, the caterpillar spun a silk thread and jumped. It hung from the leaf by its thread. The wasp did not know where the caterpillar went. The caterpillar was safe!

Knowing Without Seeing

4   Caterpillars cannot see, hear, or smell very well. Castellanos wondered how the caterpillar knew the predator was approaching. He and Dr. Pedro Barbosa of Maryland wanted to find out. They thought that maybe the caterpillar could feel the leaf wiggle, or vibrate.

5   Wasps and stinkbugs eat caterpillars. When these insects walk on a leaf to eat a caterpillar, the leaf wiggles. But the wind, falling sticks, and insects that do not eat caterpillars might also wiggle the leaf. Could caterpillars tell the difference between something safe and something dangerous? Or did they hang from a thread every time the leaf wiggled?

6   The scientists wanted to make the leaf vibrate and <u>watch</u> what the caterpillar did. First, they needed to know how to make the leaf vibrate. They used a special machine to record vibrations. The scientists noticed that wasps made one kind of vibration. Insects that do not eat caterpillars made another kind of vibration. Wind, falling twigs, and dropping water each made a different kind of vibration.

Caterpillars Are Wiggle-Wise

7   The scientists put caterpillars on leaves and used another machine to make the leaves vibrate. When the leaves shook the way a predator would shake them, caterpillars behaved as if a real predator were on the leaf. They spun threads and hung.

8   When the leaves shook as if the wind were blowing or rain were falling, caterpillars did nothing. When the leaves shook as if insects that do not eat caterpillars were walking on the leaves, the caterpillars ignored the shaking.

9   The scientists also found that caterpillars could tell the difference between kinds of predators. Both stinkbugs and wasps have to be very close to a caterpillar to see it, but stinkbugs must be even closer.

10   So when stinkbugs were on the leaf, caterpillars could hang from short threads and not be noticed. When wasps were on the leaf, caterpillars spun longer threads to hang farther down—and out of sight.

11   So now we know that caterpillars can tell dangerous wiggles from other kinds of wiggles. People might have to pay attention to what's in front of their nose, but caterpillars have to pay attention to what vibrates under their feet.

Answer the following questions based on the passage you just read.

1. Read the sentence below.

> A *wasp* <u>crept</u> *toward a caterpillar on a leaf.*

When you look up a verb in the dictionary, you look up its base, or "to" form (to *go*). What word would you look up to find the meaning of *crept*?

_____

2. Complete the chart below. Write the form of the verb you would look up.

Word in Article	Look Up
spun	
went	
hung	
knew	
thought	

3. Read the dictionary entry below.

> **trick** \trik\ *verb* **1.** to cheat or fool someone *noun* **2.** a prank or joke
> **3.** a skillful act **4.** an act of magic

Which meaning best fits the way <u>trick</u> is used in paragraph 1?

A Meaning 1

B Meaning 2

C Meaning 3

D Meaning 4

4. Read the sentence below.

> *They used a special machine to <u>record</u> vibrations.*

Look up *record* in the dictionary. What is the meaning of *record* in this sentence?

_____

In this sentence, which syllable in *record* is stressed, or accented—the first or the second?

_____

What is a word that rhymes with *record* when it has this meaning?

_____

Now read the next sentence.

> *They kept a <u>record</u> of their findings.*

Which syllable in *record* is stressed in this sentence?

_____

What meaning does the word have in this sentence?

_____

5. Which word from paragraph 5 would have two different entries in a dictionary because it is a homograph?

A *wind*

B *safe*

C *dangerous*

D *thread*

6. Read the dictionary entry below.

> **watch** \wäch\ *noun* **1.** a small clock that you wear on your wrist **2.** a period of time when someone stands guard *verb* **3.** to observe or pay attention **4.** to be alert

Which meaning best fits the way <u>watch</u> is used in paragraph 6?

A Meaning 1

B Meaning 2

C Meaning 3

D Meaning 4

Critical Thinking

7. Suppose you want to find out more about caterpillars so that you can write a report. Work with a partner. Identity three sources you could use for information.

Writing	☐
Research	☑
Listening and Speaking	☑
Media Literacy	☐
21st Century Skills: Collaboration	☑
Cross-Curriculum Connection: Science	☑

8. In a dictionary, the word *wasp* would come before which of these words?

A Waste

B Washer

C Wart

D Warm

Read the selection. Then choose the best answer to each question.

Willy Wriggler's Wheels

by Kathleen M. Muldoon
from Spider Magazine

1   Willy Wriggler wanted wheels. He was tired of slithering around City Park on his belly.

2   Every day Willy watched people whiz by on wheels—boys and girls on scooters and skateboards, babies in strollers, messengers on bicycles, gardeners riding lawn mowers, children on roller skates.

3   It seemed as if everyone except Willy had wheels.

4   I'll visit Roy D. Rat," Willy said. "He'll help me get wheels."

5   Roy D. Rat lived in a hollow log across from Willy Wriggler's <u>rock</u>. He didn't have wheels, but he could run fast on his four legs. He didn't have to <u>wriggle</u> like Willy.

6   Willy slithered along while Roy skipped beside him. They passed trucks and cars. They passed wheelchairs and carriages and motorcycles. They passed skaters and cyclists.

7   The park was filled with wheels—wheels that were attached to someone or something. There were no loose wheels for Willy.

8   Roy and Willy reached the far corner of the park where workers had recently built new skateboard <u>ramps</u>.

9   *Whiz! Whoosh! WHAM!*

10   Skateboarders raced up and down the concrete slopes. Each wore a brightly colored helmet. Pink helmets and red helmets. Blue helmets and gold helmets. Green helmets and purple helmets.

11   Their heads bobbed like brightly colored balloons as they leaped and dipped on their skateboards.

12   From beneath a nearby bench, Willy and Roy watched the skateboarders until the park closed.

13   Willy sighed.

14   "Just once I'd like to ride a skateboard," he said. "They're the perfect size and shape for me, long and flat."

15   As Willy and Roy D. Rat headed home, the moon peeked out suddenly from behind a cloud and shined on four silver wheels lying by the side of the path. Willy slithered over. Upside down in the grass lay a <u>discarded</u> skateboard.

16   "Wheels!" he exclaimed.

17   Roy D. Rat scurried over to examine the board.

18   "It's cracked," he said. "But it's perfect for you, Willy. Come on. Let's try it out."

19   Roy pushed the skateboard to the top of the concrete ramp. Willy wriggled behind him.

20   "Get on!" Roy ordered.

21   "Wait," Willy said. He searched in the grass until he found what he needed, an acorn cap just his size. It made a perfect helmet. Now he was ready.

22   Carefully, he slithered aboard the skateboard. The crack cradled his body and held it securely in a straight line down the center of the board.

23   "Launch me to the moon!" he cried to Roy.

24   With a gentle push, Roy started Willy rushing down the ramp on his wheels.

25   "COWABUNGA!" Willy shouted to the heavens.

26   WHOOSH! He held his breath as he zoomed to the bottom of the ramp.

27   WHIZZZZZ! Willy shrieked in delight as his board climbed to the top of the opposite ramp, which sat just beneath the moon.

28   "ALLEY OOOOOOOOOOP!" he shouted as the board went backward down one ramp and up another. Immediately the board headed back down. Up and down, backward and forward. Willy wriggled happily as he flew on his wheels.

29   At last he came to a stop in the gully between the ramps. Roy D. Rat scampered down to greet him.

30   "How was it?" he asked.

31   "Awesome," Willy said. "I've been to the moon and back, all in one night."

32   Roy pushed Willy and his wheels back up the ramp. Then together Roy and Willy hid Willy's wheels under a nearby shrub to await his next ride.

33   If you're ever in City Park on a moonlit night, you may get a glimpse of Willy Wriggler whooshing and whamming, leaping and dipping on his very own wheels. Just look for his acorn helmet and his <u>able</u> assistant, Roy D. Rat.

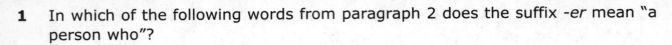
1   In which of the following words from paragraph 2 does the suffix *-er* mean "a person who"?

   A *scooters*

   B *strollers*

   C *messengers*

   D *lawn mowers*

2   In paragraph 5, the word <u>rock</u> means —

   F a stone

   G to move back and forth

   H a type of music

   J to shake

3   In paragraph 5, the word <u>wriggle</u> means —

   A move in a straight line

   B move very quickly

   C move by twisting and turning

   D move slowly and carefully

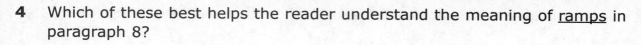

4 Which of these best helps the reader understand the meaning of <u>ramps</u> in paragraph 8?

   F *corner of the park*

   G *workers had recently built*

   H *Whiz! Whoosh! WHAM!*

   J *concrete slopes*

---

5 How does Willy feel in paragraphs 10–13?

   A He envies the skateboarders and wants to be like them.

   B He worries the skateboarders will get hurt.

   C He is happy the skateboarders are having fun.

   D He is angry because the skateboarders have wheels but he doesn't.

---

6 What is the meaning of <u>discarded</u> in paragraph 15?

   F Picked up

   G Thrown away

   H Lost

   J Old and broken

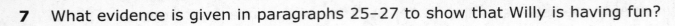

7   What evidence is given in paragraphs 25–27 to show that Willy is having fun?

   A   He shouted to the heavens.

   B   He held his breath.

   C   He zoomed to the bottom of the ramp.

   D   He shrieked in delight.

---

8   A synonym for the word <u>able</u> in paragraph 33 is —

   F   skillful

   G   friendly

   H   slow

   J   tired

Lesson 16

Understand Sensory Language in Literary Text

Ⓢ 3.10(A)	Identify language that creates a graphic visual experience and appeals to the senses.
Ⓢ 3.2(B)	Ask relevant questions, seek clarification, and locate facts and details about stories and other texts and support answers with evidence from text.
Ⓡ/Ⓢ Figure 19(D)	Make inferences about text and use textual evidence to support understanding

Understand the TEKS

Word Pictures

Writers use language to create pictures in the reader's mind. They help you imagine what they are describing.

Word to Know
sensory language

Sensory Language

To do this, writers use sensory language. These are words and phrases that appeal to the senses. Sensory details help you see, hear, taste, touch, and even smell what they are describing.

• Suppose you were describing a garbage dump. What are some words and phrases you would use to create a vivid picture?

_____

_____

Some details appeal mostly to one sense. Some appeal to several senses.

For example, a writer may describe the dew on a flower as "sparkling in the sun." The words "sparkling in the sun" create a strong visual experience. They appeal mostly to your sense of sight.

Another writer might describe a herd of elephants as "pounding on the ground." When you read the words "pounding on the ground," you can almost feel the earth shake and hear the loud noise of the elephants moving.

Read the sentence below.

> The cat's huge, orange, saucer-shaped eyes glowed in the dark.

• This word picture mostly appeals to which of the five senses?

Now read this sentence:

> Joy could hardly wait to bite into one of the sweet, juicy, fat, red strawberries in the bowl.

- This word picture appeals to which senses?

_____

Comprehension Tip

When you read, let yourself form pictures in your mind. These pictures will help you experience what the words are describing.

Guided Instruction

Read the passage below. Then answer the questions in the margin and complete the activities.

Literature Connection

Just Sitting

by Paula B. Terrey

1   My brother has been working on his car in the barn. He comes around the corner of the house, wiping grease from his hands. "What are you doing?" he asks.

2   "Just sitting." I'm sitting on the porch steps. The air is milky warm. Crickets are singing, and fireflies blink under the willow. The lawn is a fuzzy dark blanket stretching to the pond. The pond is a polished black stone.

3   My brother sits next to me.

Guided Questions

Read paragraph **2**. Highlight all the details the author includes to appeal to the senses. Do these details make you feel that you would like to be sitting on the porch steps, too? Why or why not?

_____

_____

_____

"Just Sitting" by Paula B. Terrey, Reprinted by permission of LADYBUG magazine July/August 2009, text © 2009 by Carus Publishing Company

   Measuring Up to the Texas Essential Knowledge and Skills

4　My sister comes out of the house, and the screen door bangs. "What are you doing?" she asks.

5　"Just sitting," my brother and I say. My sister sits next to us. She's brought frozen blueberries in a crockery bowl. The berries make a crunching winter sound as we bite into them. I hold one in my mouth until it's blueberry slush. My brother eats a handful all at one time, and his teeth squeak on the skins.

6　"What are you doing?" my mother asks. She's inside peering through the screen door.

7　"Just sitting," my brother and my sister and I say.

8　My mother opens the door and does not let it bang. Her sigh matches the squeak of the springs as she settles onto the porch swing. She's still wearing her apron, but in a minute she remembers and takes it off.

9　Tonight there is only the barest sliver of a moon. Still, I can see the corn in the dark, much taller than I am—tall enough to hide a man. My daddy is out there, saying good night to the corn. Then he's striding toward us, and I can see the smiling around his eyes and the ears of corn he holds in his arms like a baby.

10　"What are you doing?" Daddy says.

11　My brother, my sister, my mother, and I all say, "Just sitting."

12　My daddy sits beside my mother on the porch swing.

13　The crickets are noisy, but the corn is quiet. My family's just sitting, but my heart is singing.

Guided Questions

The blueberries in paragraph **5** appeal to the sense of taste. Highlight the details about the blueberries that also appeal to the sense of hearing. Did adding these details increase the pleasurable effect? Why or why not?

_____

_____

_____

_____

_____

_____

In addition to sight, the details in paragraph **8** mostly appeal to which sense? Highlight these details.

_____

Highlight the details in paragraph **9** that appeal to the sense of sight.

Read paragraph **13**. What feeling or mood do the details in this story create? Highlight the words that show this.

_____

Answer the following questions based on the passage you just read.

1. For each of the senses, choose a detail from the story you particularly liked. Write it in the chart. Tell why you chose it.

	Sensory Detail	**Reason for Choice**
Sight		
Taste		
Smell		
Touch		
Hearing		

2. Read these sentences from paragraph 9.

> *My daddy is out there, saying good night to the corn. Then he's striding toward us, and I can see the smiling around his eyes and the ears of corn he <u>holds</u> in his arms like a baby.*

How does the author make the corn seem almost as though it were alive?

_____

_____

Notice the verb *holds* in the last sentence. What verb would you replace it with to create a vivid image?

_____

3. Read the last paragraph.

> *The crickets are noisy, but the corn is quiet. My family's just sitting, but my heart is singing.*

Has the narrator really been "just sitting"? Explain your answer.

_____

_____

Critical Thinking

4. Work with a partner. Find a place to sit quietly. Take five minutes to use your senses to observe everything around you. Then write a paragraph or two to describe your surroundings. Try to include details that appeal to at least three of the senses. Read your description aloud to your partner. Compare what each of you observed.

Writing	☑
Research	☐
Listening and Speaking	☑
21st Century Skills: Collaboration	☐
Cross-Curriculum Connection	☐

On Your Own

Read the selection below. Then answer the questions that follow it.

Science Connection

Wind Storm

by Mary Atkinson

1   "Storm coming!" Dad yelled across the water. "Swim back to shore!"

2   We all jumped off the raft and started swimming.

3   Clouds hung low in the sky. Tree-tops whipped back and forth in the wind. Waves splashed against my face, and water got up my nose.

4   "Hurry up, Sammy," cried Tim.

5   "Need a ride?" asked Owen.

"Wind Storm" Reprinted by permission of SPIDER magazine, August 2004, Vol. 11, No. 8, Copyright © 2004 by Mary Atkinson

6   "I'm okay!" I said. I kept my eye on my swimming tree, the tall pine I always kept
in sight, ever since I was little and first learned to swim across the lake. I held it in
my gaze until I reached the other side.

7   From the west, cool air blew in from the mountains. We <u>hugged</u> towels around
our shoulders and raced to the house. Inside, we latched windows, checked
flashlights, and filled jugs with water. I made sandwiches while Tim filled the cooler
and Owen built a fire.

8   That night, the skies howled. The house shook, and the windows rattled.
Branches sharpened their tips against the glass.

9   "Eighty miles an hour!" Dad said. "Those winds sure are blowing." Faster than
driving on the highway. Faster than riding on the train.

10   Huge gusts ripped branches off trees with cracks like lightning. Down the
chimney whooshed a blast of air. It fed the flames and made them roar. Our
dog curled tighter into a ball. We all huddled in front of the fire—my father, my
brothers, and I.

11   Before long, the storm passed. I fell asleep to the sound of a gentle rain.

12   The next morning, all was still. Our dog chased a chipmunk into the woodpile.
A woodpecker tip-tapped on a broken tree. We collected sticks, stacked branches,
and dragged logs aside. I raked up pine cones. Tim fixed the picnic table, and
Owen used the saw.

13   Then, at the water's edge, we all looked out—my father, my brothers, and I.
Trees, like shipwrecks, lay abandoned along the shore.

14   The swimming tree was gone. Only its fallen trunk remained.

15   "Anyone for a swim?" asked Dad.

16   "But my tree . . . ," I said.

17   "Oh, Sammy," said Owen.

18   "Last one in . . . !" called Tim.

19   We all dove off the dock into clear, still water and swam to the raft.

20   Coming back, I stared into the empty space where the swimming tree had been. There, in a spotlight of sun, a small pine, just a puffball of green needles, shook softly in the breeze.

21   I kept my eye on the little pine as I swam back to shore.

22   Then, sitting next to the swimming tree, I cleared away old leaves and broken sticks, just to make sure the little pine would get enough sun.

Answer the following questions based on the passage you just read.

1. Read the sentence below from paragraph 7. Pay attention to the underlined word.

   > We <u>hugged</u> towels around our shoulders and raced to the house.

   When you hug a towel around your shoulders, how are you holding it?

   _____

   _____

   Why might you want to hug a towel tightly?

   _____

   _____

2. Which sentence is the best clue to the fact that trees surround the house?

   A *From the west, cool air blew in from the mountains.*

   B *Tree-tops whipped back and forth in the wind.*

   C *Branches sharpened their tips against the glass.*

   D *Our dog chased a chipmunk into the woodpile.*

3. Read the sentences below.

> *Huge gusts ripped branches off trees with cracks like lightning. Down the chimney whooshed a blast of air. It fed the flames and made them roar.*

Write the effect or result in the chart below.

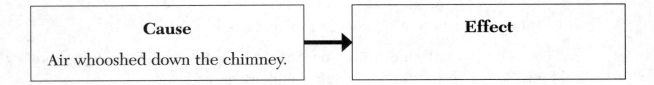

Cause	**Effect**
Air whooshed down the chimney.	

4. Read the paragraph below.

> *That night, the skies howled. The house shook, and the windows rattled. Branches sharpened their tips against the glass.*

The details in this paragraph appeal mostly to the sense of —

A sight

B taste

C smell

D hearing

5. Read the sentence below. Form a picture in your mind of the little pine tree.

> *There, in a spotlight of sun, a small pine, just a puffball of green needles, shook softly in the breeze.*

What color is the pine tree? What size is it?

_____

Do its needles seem fluffy or smooth? How do you know?

_____

How is it moving? Write the words that tell you this.

_____

6. Choose a sentence from this story that you found particularly vivid. Write it on the lines below.

_____

Tell how it makes you feel and why you chose it.

_____

_____

_____

Critical Thinking

7. Work with a partner. Thumb through magazines or use the Internet to find a picture of an animal you would like to describe. Talk about what you see. Create a chart listing the five senses. Jot down words and phrases you could use to describe this animal. Then collaborate to write a description.

Writing	☑
Research	☐
Listening and Speaking	☑
21st Century Skills: Collaboration	☑
Cross Curriculum Connections	☐

Read the selection. Then choose the best answer to each question.

My Magical Maui

by Laura Thomas
from short-story-time.com

1   What I am about to tell you happened many years ago. I was just a young girl, and the Hawaiian Islands were my vacation playground every summer.

2   "Lucy! Please don't go too deep!" my mother shouted from her spot on the beautiful, sun-kissed beach.

3   "Sure, Mom!" I replied. I loved the island of Maui, and the ocean was home to me. When I snorkeled, I pretended I was entering a secret world, filled with mysterious creatures.

4   "A tiny turtle!" I shrieked through my bulky mask. I followed him through the <u>shoals</u> of yellow tangs, and hundreds of other glorious, rainbow-colored fish. As I allowed myself to glide gracefully next to the tiny turtle, I felt his flipper touch my hand. I stayed close, and the two of us swam in a watery waltz.

5   Eventually, I decided to pop my head above the water to clear my mask while Tiny munched on some green stuff. I looked back at the beach.

6   "My mom will be in a panic, Tiny. I have to go. But I'll be back tomorrow, okay?"

7   It's hard to explain, but I believe Tiny smiled at me!

8   I didn't tell anyone about my turtle, and that night, I dreamed a wonderful dream about Tiny showing me the whole ocean. When I woke up, I almost dragged my parents to the beach, and then flip-flopped into the clear blue water.

9   "Be careful, Lucy!" called my mother.

10   "Sure, Mom!" I replied.

11   I swam out to a safe depth, and then waved to my parents. When I reached my usual area at the big, black rocks, Tiny was waiting. My heart flipped as he smiled at me again, and then asked me to follow him. Not with words, of course, but I just knew.

12   Tiny took me on a magical journey; we swam through giant coral reefs, slithered alongside slimy eels, and saw a thousand starfish resting on a rock. But Tiny saved the best until last. Basking in the reflection of the summer sun above us, I discovered a whole family of turtles!

13   Dizzy with excitement, I thought it best to stick my head out of the water and get some fresh air. Then as I plunged back down to join Tiny, I nearly choked. I saw him frantically twisting and turning in a section of fishing net, a silver hook planted firmly in his back left leg.

14   "Wait, Tiny," I cried, "I'll help you, but you have to trust me." Tiny held perfectly still and looked deep into my eyes. My hands were shaky, but I gently pulled the hook free, and the net came away easily.

15   I balled the net up in my fist, as I didn't want any other turtle getting caught. Tiny was safe, and I realized I had been gone for quite some time, so I waved to the turtle family and rose to the surface.

16   To my dismay, my parents were little dots on the beach. Tears pricked my eyes, as I kept my lead-weight limbs in motion. "Tiny," I sniffled, "I simply can't make it back!"

17   But as my heart started pounding, I sensed the biggest turtle beneath me. I gently reached down to hold the edge of her shell, and she started to move, slowly at first. Tiny followed as I held my breath and we propelled through the water with ease. This was a ride I would never forget.

18   I spotted my parents pacing the shore by the time I got close. As soon as it was shallow enough for me to stand, Tiny and the big turtle swerved away. I stood on wobbly legs, and as I looked up, Tiny poked his head out of the water and gave me one final smile.

19   That was the last time I ever saw Tiny, but it was the best day of my life. I told my parents what had happened, and even showed them the net, but they just thought I'd been playing imaginary games.

20   I still have that net today, but never told anyone else my story. I knew nobody would ever believe me.

21   Except maybe you.

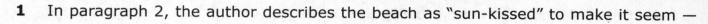

1 In paragraph 2, the author describes the beach as "sun-kissed" to make it seem —

  A unpleasant and too hot

  B bright red, as though burned

  C warm and inviting

  D familiar and unsurprising

---

2 In paragraph 4, the word <u>shoals</u> means —

  F types

  G groups

  H shallow places

  J rocks

---

3 Read the sentence below.

> *I stayed close, and the two of us swam in a watery waltz.*

This sentence creates an image of the girl —

  A dancing through the water with the turtle

  B having trouble keeping up with the turtle

  C being uncomfortable and unsure of herself in the water

  D swimming awkwardly to music heard underwater

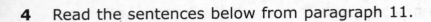

4 Read the sentences below from paragraph 11.

> *Tiny was waiting. My heart flipped as he smiled at me again, and then asked me to follow him.*

The images create a feeling of —

F fear and panic

G mystery

H humor

J excitement and happiness

---

5 Read this sentence from paragraph 12.

> *Tiny took me on a magical journey; we swam through giant coral reefs, slithered alongside slimy eels, and saw a thousand starfish resting on a rock.*

The words "slithered alongside slimy eels" appeal most to the reader's sense of —

A sight

B taste

C touch

D hearing

6 Read the sentence below from paragraph 16.

> *Tears pricked my eyes, as I kept my lead-weight limbs in motion.*

The sensory language in this sentence emphasizes or stresses —

F the fact that the girl weighs too much to swim

G the girl's growing tiredness and fear

H the saltiness of the ocean water

J the idea that the girl has hurt her eyes

Paraphrase Themes in Fables, Legends, Myths, and Stories

⑤ 3.5(A)   Paraphrase the themes and supporting details of fables, legends, myths, or stories.

⑤ 3.2(B)   Ask relevant questions, seek clarification, and locate facts and details about stories and other texts and support answers with evidence from text.

Ⓡ Figure 19(D)   Make inferences about text, maintaining meaning and logical order.

 Understand the TEKS

Theme

Theme is the meaning of the story. It is what the story shows you about life. It is the big idea, or message, the author wants you to understand.

Words to Know
fable
folktale
legend
moral
myth
paraphrase
theme

Read the two sentences below.

> Even though he was hungry, the boy did not take the money.
>
> Honesty pays off in the end.

The first sentence tells what happens in the story. The second sentence tells a big idea based on what happens. This big idea is the theme.

Now look at these two sentences.

> Anita realized that mean old Mr. Grumble really had a kind and loving heart.
>
> You can't always tell what people are like at first glance.

Which sentence tells you a theme?

_____

How do you know?

_____

_____

Traditional Tales

Many traditional tales and stories tell important lessons about life.

• A **fable** is a tale that is told to teach a lesson. Usually, it has animals that talk and act like people. A fable has a **moral** at the end. The moral states the lesson. For example, the moral below comes from Aesop's fable, "The Tortoise and the Hare."

> Moral: Slow and steady wins the race.

• Paraphrase this moral, or put it in your own words.

_____

_____

Write the title of one fable you have read.

_____

• A **myth** is a tale about gods and goddesses and other supernatural beings. Often, myths explain how something in nature came to be. For example, a myth might tell how the stars came to be.

• A **legend** is a story handed down over the ages. Often, legends are based, at least partly, on fact, on the life of someone who actually lived, or on something that actually happened.

• A **folktale** is also a tale passed down over the ages. It is not based on fact.

Comprehension Tip
Myths, fables, and folktales are not realistic, or like life, even though they may teach you something about life. Use your imagination when you read them.

Guided Instruction

Read the passage below. Then answer the questions in the margin and complete the activities.

Literature
Connection

The Hedley Kow
An English Folktale

retold by Marilyn Bolchunos

1 Long ago, near the village of Hedley, there lived a strange and playful trickster. Sometimes it looked like an ordinary object. Sometimes it looked like a donkey or a goat or even a cow. It was known as the Hedley Kow.

2 One evening, an old woman was returning home from helping a neighbor. As she went along the path, she saw an old iron pot lying in the ditch. "Fancy that," she said. "Nobody seems to want this old pot. I will take it home and plant pretty flowers in it."

3 When she tried to lift it, she saw that it was full of gold pieces. "Well, now, if that doesn't beat all," she said. "I'm rich! I can buy a fine house and fancy clothes. I'll never want for a thing."

4 The pot was heavy, so she tied her shawl around it and began to drag it home. After a while, she stopped to rest. When she looked in the pot, she was amazed to see that it was full of silver pieces!

5 "Oh, my!" she said. "Aren't I the lucky one! If it were gold, thieves would have been after me. My friends might have been jealous. But I can hide these silver pieces, take out a few at a time, and live like a queen."

Guided Questions

Trickster characters appear in many folktales. They play tricks on others. What is the name of this trickster? Highlight the sentences that show how this trickster can change shape.

_____

What prediction do you make after reading paragraph **2**?

_____

_____

In paragraph **3**, highlight the sentences that tell the woman's reaction to finding the gold pieces.

What happens to the gold pieces in paragraph **4**?

_____

6 On she went, pulling the pot after her. She was nearing home now. At her gate, she looked into the pot. What a surprise! The silver had changed into a lump of iron. "Iron," she said. "Well, now! No one will be jealous or want to steal this from me. I can use this iron to prop open my door and let in fresh air and sunlight. Lucky me!"

7 As soon as she said that, the pot began to grow. It grew hooves and a tail. It grew a long, cow-like body and a head like a goat's. Then it jumped up and ran off down the road laughing.

8 "Fancy that!" exclaimed the old woman. "I believe I have seen the Hedley Kow! Not many folks can say that, and that's a fact. I'll just sit up by my fire tonight thinking about how lucky I was to see it for myself. I truly must be the luckiest person in the world!"

Guided Questions

Read paragraph **6**. Highlight the words that tell you what happens to the silver.

Read paragraph **7**. What does the pot turn out to be?

_____

_____

In paragraph **8**, highlight the sentence that tells the old woman's reaction to what has just happened to her.

Answer the following questions based on the passage you just read.

1. Read the paragraph below.

> *One evening, an old woman was returning home from helping a neighbor. As she went along the path, she saw an old iron pot lying in the ditch. "Fancy that," she said. "Nobody seems to want this old pot. I will take it home and plant pretty flowers in it."*

What has the old woman been doing?

_____

What does this tell you about her?

_____

2. A good way to identify the theme of a tale is to look at the main character's reaction to what happens.

Complete the chart below. In the right-hand column, tell how the old woman reacts to each event. (The first one is done for you.)

Event	Reaction
The woman finds an old pot.	She's happy because she will take it home and make use of it.
The woman finds the pot is full of gold.	
The gold turns to silver.	
The silver turns to a lump of iron.	
The pot becomes the Hedley Kow.	

 3. Think about what this tale shows about happiness. Circle the sentence below that best tells the theme.

Happiness comes from how you look at the world and your own fortune.

Happiness comes from the things you own.

Put the theme in your own words.

_____

_____

_____

_____

4. Look at the characters and the glasses below.

There is a common saying that some people see the glass as half empty, while others see it as half full.

What do you think this saying means?

_____

_____

How does this saying relate to the old woman in this tale?

_____

Critical Thinking

5. Work in a small group. Talk about what this tale helped you understand about happiness. Tell about other tales you have read or movies you have seen with a similar big idea.

Writing	☐
Research	☐
Listening and Speaking	☑
Media Literacy	☐
21st Century Skills: Collaboration	☑
Cross Curriculum Connection	☐

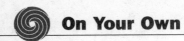

On Your Own

Read the selection below. Then answer the questions that follow it.

Literature
Connection

The Farmer and the Fox

adapted by Neal Levin from a Jewish Folktale

1   Once there lived a very wise fox. He could tell you anything. He could tell you why robins came out in the spring. He could tell you why stars came out at night.

2   But he couldn't tell you why people acted the way that they did. The fox hardly even saw people. He lived in the meadow. People lived on the farm.

3   One day the fox took a trip to the farm. It wasn't that far from the meadow, and he wanted to learn about people.

4   When he got to the farm, he sat down by a field. The field looked like his meadow. It was covered with grass. People must live in meadows, too, he thought. People must live like foxes.

5   He hid in a bush as a farmer came out. And what did the farmer do? He started digging up the field. He started tearing up the grass.

6   "What a foolish man," the fox said. "He ruined the grass. Surely people are not as wise as foxes." The fox went back to the meadow and told everyone how foolish people were.

7   The next day the fox returned to the farm to see what other foolish things people did. Again he hid as the farmer returned. And what did the farmer do? He started sowing grains of wheat in the field.

8   "I can't believe it," the fox said aloud. "He takes good grain and throws it in the dirt. Surely people are not as wise as foxes." He went back to the meadow and told everyone that people were the most foolish creatures on Earth.

9   Many weeks passed. The fox thought the farmer might have grown wiser. He went back to the field, but it had changed. Now it was filled with golden stalks of wheat. The fox wondered if it was a different field.

10   Then he saw the farmer come out. And what did the farmer do? He started cutting down the wheat.

"The Farmer and the Fox" adapted from a Jewish Folktale by Neal Levin Copyright © 2006 by Highlights for Children, Inc., Columbus, Ohio

11   "Foolish, foolish man," the fox cried. "He has all this beautiful wheat, and he cuts it down like weeds. I can't take it anymore." Back to the meadow he went.

12   That evening the fox couldn't sleep. He was thinking of the farmer. Maybe the farmer had reasons for the things that he did.

13   So the fox got up and went back to the farm. The field was empty, but a light glowed from the farmhouse. The fox peered through the window. He saw the farmer grinding the wheat and turning it into flour. He watched as the farmer's wife made the flour into dough and put the dough in the oven. Before long, delicious aromas drifted through the air. Soon the farmer and his wife were enjoying fresh, warm bread.

14   As his mouth watered, the fox finally understood just how wise the farmer really was.

Answer the following questions based on the passage you just read.

1. At the beginning of the story, what is the fox very wise about?

_____

What is he not wise about?

_____

 2. Fill in the chart below. Explain what the farmer is really doing.

What Fox Sees	What Is Really Happening
Farmer digs up field and tears up grass.	
Farmer throws grain in the dirt.	
Field is filled with stalks of wheat.	
Farmer cuts down wheat.	

3. Read the paragraph below.

> *As his mouth watered, the fox finally understood just how wise the farmer really was.*

Think about what the fox has learned. Why does the fox now think the farmer is wise?

_____

_____

4. In paragraph 12, the reader can tell that the fox —

  A is sure that the farmer is foolish

  B really is wise

  C is eager to eat the bread

  D is the one who is foolish

5. Write a sentence that tells the theme of this tale.

_____

_____

Critical Thinking

6. Work with a partner. Brainstorm a list of things people do or make. Each of you should choose one activity. For the activity you chose, make a chart to show the steps in the process. Then write an imaginative tale. Tell it from the point of view of an animal. Make sure the animal misunderstands what is happening. Read your tale over and revise it. Then meet with your partner again. Take turns reading your tales aloud. Give helpful advice for improving each other's writing.

Writing	☑
Research	☐
Listening and Speaking	☑
Media Literacy	☐
21st Century Skills: Collaboration	☑
Cross Curriculum Connection	☐

Compare and Contrast Settings in Myths and Folktales

3.5(B)	Compare and contrast the settings in myths and traditional folktales.
S 3.2(B)	Ask relevant questions, seek clarification, and locate facts and details about stories and other texts and support answers with evidence from text.
R Figure 19(D)	Make inferences about text and use textual evidence to support understanding.

Understand the TEKS

Culture

A **culture** is made up of beliefs and traditions shared by a group of people, such as holidays and other practices.

Every culture has its own myths and folktales. Often, these tales are attempts to understand the world.

> **Words to Know**
> culture
> folktale
> myth
> oral tradition
> setting

Setting

The **setting** of a tale is where and when it takes place. The place of a myth or folktale is where a group of people with a certain culture live. The time is long, long ago when the world was still forming.

Talking animals often appear in folktales. These are the animals that are native to the particular place. In a culture, each animal may represent a certain trait. For example, in African folktales, the spider is often tricky.

- What are two animals you might see in a folktale set long ago in the land that is now Texas?

_____

_____

- What traits might these animals represent?

_____

_____

Oral Tradition

Myths and folktales have been told over and over again. They have been passed down from one generation to another. They are part of the **oral tradition.** This means that most of them started out as stories told orally. Often, the stories changed slightly with each retelling.

• Why do you think a tale gets changed when it is told orally?

_____

_____

Comprehension Tip
Think about how the setting affects the tale. As you read, use sticky notes or highlight details of the setting that you think will turn out to be important.

Guided Instruction

Read the passage below. Then answer the questions in the margin and complete the activities.

Literature Connection

Cheese for Dinner
A Tale from Mexico

retold by Judy Goldman

Guided Questions

1   Coyote was hiding behind a boulder near the lake. He licked his chops and stared at Conejo (ko-NEH-ho). The unwary rabbit was gazing at the full moon that lit the cloudless night.

Highlight the details in paragraphs **1** and **2** that help you picture the setting. Why do you think it is important that there is a full moon?

_____

_____

_____

"Cheese for Dinner" A Tale from Mexico retold by Judy Goldman, Copyright © 2007 by Highlights for Children, Inc., Columbus, Ohio

2   Coyote lunged at Conejo. The rabbit bounded away, leaping over rocks and around bushes, but Coyote stayed right behind him, snapping at his heels.

3   Conejo came to a wall of rock. Desperately, he looked for a way to escape. Finding none, he <u>cowered</u> against the wall, thinking of what to do.

4   Coyote scrambled to a stop and brought his jaws close to Conejo. "Caught you," he said, flashing his pointy white teeth. "I haven't eaten for two days, and I'm hungry."

5   Conejo's mind raced. "You don't want to eat me," he said. "I'm just a scrawny rabbit."

6   "I know you're not much, but you'll do," Coyote said, opening his mouth wide.

7   "Wait!" Conejo yelled. "I have a better idea. I know where you can get something delicious to eat. **A** Just before you started to chase me, I saw an enormous wheel of cheese resting on the bottom of the lake."

8   "Why didn't you get it?" Coyote asked.

9   "I wanted to, but I can't swim. I was thinking about how to fetch it when you surprised me. A big strong coyote like you can probably dive in, pull it out, and eat it all by yourself."

10   Coyote's mouth watered. "Show me the cheese," he said.

11   Conejo led the way to the lake, then pointed, "See?"

12   **B** Coyote saw something round and yellow in the water. "That's a big wheel of cheese," he said. "I'm going to get it right now."

13   Coyote held his breath and dove in. He swam down, down, down. But when he got to the bottom of the lake, he saw no cheese.

14   Where is it? he thought as he struggled to hold his breath. Then he swam up, up, up. Gasping for air, he heaved himself out of the water. To his surprise, Conejo was nowhere to be found.

In paragraph **3**, what prevents Conejo from escaping?

_____

Notice the word *cowered* in paragraph **3**. How is Conejo feeling?

_____

Read sentence **A** in paragraph **7**. Then reread paragraph **1**. Make a prediction. What do you think this wheel of cheese will turn out to be?

_____

_____

_____

_____

Read sentence **B** in paragraph **12**. Highlight the details that describe what Coyote sees in the water.

15   Coyote stared at the cheese in the lake. How can I get it? he wondered. Coyote lifted his head to howl in frustration. At that moment, he saw the full moon. He looked again at the lake and saw the moon's round reflection.

16   "That sly Conejo tricked me!" Coyote snarled.

17   For hours, Coyote searched high and low for Conejo. Not finding him, Coyote went to bed hungry.

18   As for Conejo, he was safe in his cozy burrow.

Guided Questions

Read paragraph **15**. What does Coyote really see in the water?

_____

_____

Read paragraph **16**. What traits describe Conejo? Highlight two words that tell you this.

_____

Answer the following questions based on the passage you just read.

1. Read the first paragraph again.

> *Coyote was hiding behind a boulder near the lake. He licked his chops and stared at Conejo (ko-NEH-ho). The unwary rabbit was gazing at the full moon that lit the cloudless night.*

Look at these details about Coyote.

- hiding behind a boulder
- licks his chops
- stares at Conejo

What is Coyote planning to do?

_____

_____

2. Read the paragraphs below.

> "Why didn't you get it?" Coyote asked.
>
> "I wanted to, but I can't swim. I was thinking about how to fetch it when you surprised me. A big strong coyote like you can probably dive in, pull it out, and eat it all by yourself."

Do you think Conejo is telling the truth? Is he sincere when he compliments Coyote? Explain your answer.

_____

_____

3. Complete the chart below comparing and contrasting Coyote and Conejo.

Coyote	Conejo
• big and strong	
• not very smart	

 4. Short-Answer Response How did the full moon turn out to be more important than you thought it would be? Use details from the tale in your answer.

_____

_____

_____

Critical Thinking

5. Change the setting of this tale. Move it to another place. Choose two animal characters that you would find in this place and that represent traits similar to those of Coyote and Conejo. Using these characters, write your new tale. Then prepare an oral reading of your tale.

Writing	☑
Research	☐
Listening and Speaking	☑
Media Literacy	☐
21st Century Skills: Collaboration	☑
Cross Curriculum Connection	☐

6. If you choose to move your folktale to Texas, visit http://www.tpwd.state.tx.us/ kids/fun_stuff/color/color_texas_animals.phtml. This site will help you learn about Texas animals and illustrate your tale.

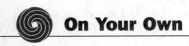 **On Your Own**

Read the selection below. Then answer the questions that follow it.

Multicultural Connection

Fetching Summer
A Mi'kmaq Folktale

retold by Mary Morton Cowan

1   Long ago in the land of the Mi'kmaq, men hunted moose and beaver. Women wove baskets and sewed moccasins. When birch trees turned to autumn gold, women dried fish, lobster, and clams for their families to eat during the dreary months of winter. Children gathered nuts, berries, and wild potatoes.

2   One winter, sadness hovered over a Mi'kmaq wigwam. First Father died, then Mother. Their bodies were covered with beaver skins, wrapped tightly in birchbark, and buried. Five children were left alone. The youngest began to cry.

3   "Do not fear, Little Brother," said his sister, Sweet-flag. "I will take care of you. Mother and Father have crossed the Star Bridge* to the Land of the Souls."

4   Little Brother would not stop crying. Sweet-flag summoned villagers from nearby wigwams, but no one could console the child. Finally Sweet-flag said to her oldest brother, "Brother Blue Jay, you are strong. You must climb the mountain and fetch Bear Woman. She helps sad and lonely children. Perhaps she can make Little Brother stop crying."

5   Snow covered the land of the Mi'kmaq. Icy winds blew strong. Dressed in beaver furs, Brother Blue Jay trudged through the woods on his snowshoes. Up the mountain he climbed, to the village of the Bear People.

---

*The Mi'kmaq people call the Milky Way "the Star Bridge."

6   Bear Woman came with Brother Blue Jay to the wigwam and rocked Little Brother. "Pa-pa-po, pa-pa-po," she sang, until the child fell asleep. But when he awoke, he cried again.

7   Bear Woman thought for a moment. She said to the three older brothers, "Little Brother needs something to play with. Make him a <u>miniature</u> bow and some arrows."

8   Brother Blue Jay shaped a wooden bow and strung it with deer sinew. The other two boys made tiny arrows. But Little Brother did not stop crying.

9   Bear Woman rocked the child again and sang. "Pa-pa-po, pa-pa-po."

10   Still, the boy whimpered.

11   "What is it that would stop your tears?" Bear Woman asked.

12   "I want to be warm," said Little Brother. "I want birds and flowers."

13   Bear Woman thought and thought. Again, she called the three older brothers to her side. "You must fetch Summer," she said. "Take with you three caribou-skin bags. Far to the west, the sky burns and the air is warm. There you will find Sky Spirit. Ask him to help you."

14   At dawn the next day, the three brothers left on their westward journey across the land. On and on they walked—to the River Miramichi, and beyond—until one day they reached the Sky Spirit.

15   "Help us, Sky Spirit," they said. "Our baby brother will not stop crying. Only Summer will make him happy. Please, could we take Summer home with us?"

16   Sky Spirit told them to fill two of their bags with warm air. "Tie the bags tightly, so no air escapes," he said. "Fill your third bag with plants and pairs of birds. These things you must carry back to your home, taking care not to drop them. When you arrive, untie the first two bags. Summer air will melt the snow and ice. It will then be time to plant the flowers and let the little birds fly."

17   The brothers did as they were told. Warm air melted winter away. When the last snow was gone from the woods, they planted a garden and released robins, doves, and song sparrows.

18   Little Brother heard the birds singing and ran out of the wigwam. Yellow and red blossoms nodded in the warm breeze. The child jumped with glee, laughing as he ran among the flowers. Bear Woman smiled. After Summer came to the land of the Mi'kmaq, Little Brother cried no more.

Answer the following questions based on the passage you just read.

1. The Mi'kmaq are native people who live in what is now the northeastern United States and eastern Canada. Read the paragraph below.

> *Long ago in the land of the Mi'kmaq, men hunted moose and beaver. Women wove baskets and sewed moccasins. When birch trees turned to autumn gold, women dried fish, lobster, and clams for their families to eat during the dreary months of winter. Children gathered nuts, berries, and wild potatoes.*

Fill in the chart below. Tell the tasks and responsibilities given to men, women, and children.

	Tasks and Responsibilities
Men	
Women	
Children	

 2. Suppose this tale was moved to the desert in the Southwest. Would all the tasks in the chart above be the same? Explain.

_____

_____

_____

3. In paragraph 3, where is the Land of the Souls?

   A Under the ocean

   B Up in the sky

   C In the meadow

   D On a hill

4. Why does Sweet-flag send Brother Blue Jay to find Bear Woman?

_____

5. What natural event does this tale explain?

_____

_____

6. Before the brothers can release the third bag —

    A they must let out the robins, doves, and song sparrows

    B Little Brother must stop crying

    C the warm air must melt winter away

    D they must plant a garden

Critical Thinking

7. Use the library or the Internet to find other myths and folktales that explain a natural event. Choose one of them. Then share your tale with a small group of students. Tell why you chose it.

Writing	☐
Research	☑
Listening and Speaking	☑
Media Literacy	☐
21st Century Skills: Collaboration	☑
Cross Curriculum Connection	☐

Critical Thinking

8. Write your own tale explaining a natural event. For example, you might explain how bluebonnets got their color. Illustrate your tale. Then form a story circle with four other students and read your tales aloud with expression.

Writing	☑
Research	☐
Listening and Speaking	☑
Media Literacy	☐
21st Century Skills: Collaboration	☑
Cross Curriculum Connection	☐

Read the selection. Then choose the best answer to each question.

Gu Dong Is Coming!

Based on a traditional Chinese folktale

by Xu Li
from Highlights for Children Magazine

1   Rabbit White nibbled grass by the pond where a tall papaya tree stood. A breeze blew through the leaves. Suddenly, Rabbit White heard Gu Dong! He jumped so high his ears brushed the branches of the papaya tree. Such a loud sound must come from a monster!

2   "A monster is coming!" Rabbit White shouted, hopping away as fast as he could. He dared not even look back. "A . . . .a . . . a Gu Dong is coming!"

3   He hopped over rocks and squeezed under fences. He jumped over brooks and logs. He even bounced over Monkey, who was eating a banana on a fallen log.

4   "What's your hurry? Who's Gu Dong? Monkey jumped from the log and <u>dashed</u> after Rabbit White.

5   Rabbit White said, "A monster, big and scary. Together we will be safe. We must call all of our friends."

6   "Gu Dong is coming!" they shouted as they ran. Soon they bumped into Fox.

7   "What's your hurry? Who's Gu Dong?" Fox asked.

8   "I'm sure he is a monster with three big eyes!" Rabbit White said.

9   "With the biggest red eye in his forehead," Monkey added.

10   Fox <u>trembled</u> when he pictured the fearsome Gu Dong.

11   "Stay with us. You will be safe," Rabbit White promised.

12   So Fox and Monkey dashed after Rabbit White.

13   "Gu Dong is coming!" they shouted.

14   Before long, Spotted Deer, Bear, and Tiger had joined them. "Gu Dong is coming!" they shouted together.

15   They ran toward Elephant, who was scratching his side against a tree trunk. "What's your hurry? What's a Gu Dong?" asked Elephant.

16   Elephant trumpeted in alarm when he learned about Gu Dong.

17   Rabbit White said, "Stay with us, and you will be safe."

18   So Elephant, Spotted Deer, Bear Tiger, Fox, and Monkey dashed after Rabbit White.

19   "Gu Dong is coming!" they shouted.

20   Lion walked slowly through the deep grass. "Who's this Gu Dong?" he asked.

21   "He is a monster," said Rabbit White.

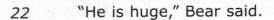

22   "He is huge," Bear said.

23   "He will eat us all," cried Tiger.

24   "He likes deer most," said Spotted Deer.

25   "He has three big red eyes," Monkey chattered.

26   "He can find us anywhere," Fox moaned.

27   "Please hide with us so that you'll be safe, too," said Rabbit White.

28   "Who has seen Gu Dong?" Lion asked, smiling.

29   The animals looked at Rabbit White. He said, "I heard him by the pond."

30   "Let's find out who this Gu Dong is," said Lion. "Rabbit, lead the way."

31   So Rabbit White led Monkey, Fox, Spotted Deer, Bear, Tiger, Elephant, and Lion back to the pond. But no one was there. Only a ripe papaya floated on the water.

32   "I know I heard Gu Dong!" Tears ran down Rabbit White's face. Just then, another ripe papaya fell into the pond. Gu Dong!

33   "Aaaugh!" Rabbit White screamed, then started laughing. "It's only the papaya!" he cried out with joy.

34   Lion picked up a papaya and broke it open. Then they all enjoyed a papaya lunch at the edge of the pond.

             Measuring Up to the Texas Essential Knowledge and Skills

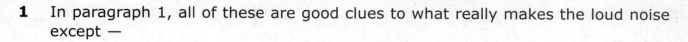

1 In paragraph 1, all of these are good clues to what really makes the loud noise except —

A *nibbled grass*

B *by the pond*

C *tall papaya tree*

D *breeze blew through the leaves*

---

2 In paragraph 4, a synonym for <u>dashed</u> is —

F strolled

G raced

H crawled

J followed

---

3 Each time they tell about Gu Dong, the animals add more details because —

A each new animal adds something based on what it saw

B they become more and more excited and frightened

C the animals are trying to scare each other

D they each saw a different monster and are telling about it

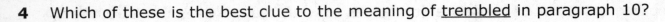
4   Which of these is the best clue to the meaning of <u>trembled</u> in paragraph 10?

   F   *Pictured*

   G   *Fearsome*

   H   *Safe*

   J   *Promised*

---

5   How is Lion different from the other animals?

   A   He stops to find the truth behind the rumor.

   B   He already knows what caused the loud sound.

   C   He is so courageous he is not afraid of monsters.

   D   He is too proud to run away from danger.

---

6   In this folktale, the papaya tree is important because —

   F   the fruit is good to eat

   G   it shows that the tale takes place in a warm climate

   H   it was a falling papaya that first scared Rabbit White

   J   the Lion and the other animals have papaya for lunch

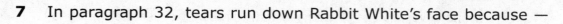

7 In paragraph 32, tears run down Rabbit White's face because —

A he is upset that he cannot prove his story

B he sees Gu Dong at the pond

C he is now frightened of Lion

D a papaya falls on his head

---

8 Which statement best expresses the main message of this folktale?

F Run from terrifying monsters.

G Friends are important and keep you safe.

H Spreading rumors can cause fear and panic.

J Working together can solve problems.

S 3.6(A) Describe the characteristics of various forms of poetry and how they create imagery (e.g., narrative poetry, lyrical poetry, humorous poetry, free verse).

S 3.2(B) Ask relevant questions, seek clarification, and locate facts and details about stories and other texts and support answers with evidence.

S Figure 19(D) Make inferences about text and use textual evidence to support understanding.

3.3 Read aloud grade-level appropriate text with fluency (rate, accuracy, expression, appropriate phrasing) and comprehension.

Understand the TEKS

Poetry

Poetry is language that uses few words to express important ideas. When you read poetry, you experience sound and sense at the same time.

The Look of Poetry

Poetry often looks different from other forms of text. It is written in **lines**. The end of a line is not always the end of a sentence. The lines of a poem are sometimes grouped together. These are called **stanzas**. Stanzas are like paragraphs in a story.

Images

Images are mental pictures. A poet creates images with words and sounds. Images usually appeal to one or more of the five senses (sight, taste, smell, feeling, hearing).

Details that appeal to the senses help you see the pictures the poet wants to create. Images can also stir up feelings. A poem may make you laugh or cry. It may be humorous or just plain silly, or it may be serious or sad.

The Sound of Poetry

Poems are like songs, but you don't need to play an instrument to create the music. The choice and order of the words in lines and stanzas create the musical sounds.

Writers often use **rhyme** and **rhythm** to help express their ideas. **Rhyme** is the repetition of a vowel sound and all the letters that come after it. For example, the words *run* and *fun* rhyme. Rhymes happen when certain sounds are repeated. You may see words that rhyme at the end of lines.

Words to Know
free verse
image
line
lyric poetry
narrative poetry
rhythm
rhyme
stanza

Cooper the cat
Took a long nap.
Then Cooper woke up and sat,
Right in my lap.

- Which words in these lines rhyme?

_____

Rhythm is the pattern of stressed and unstressed sounds you hear as you read. It is created by the order and number of beats in a poem's lines. You can follow the beat of a line of poetry the same way as you do in music—by clapping your hands.

Read aloud the first line of the nursery rhyme below. Clap out the rhythm.

Jack and Jill went up the hill.

- Which words receive the strong beat?

_____

Some poetry does not contain a regular pattern of rhythm and rhyme. It is called **free verse**.

Types of Poetry

Narrative poetry tells a story. There are characters and a plot. There is a narrator, or speaker, telling the story. A narrative poem may even contain dialogue. Many narrative poems have a strong pattern of rhythm and rhyme.

Long ago, narrative poems were told aloud. The rhythm and rhyme made them easy to understand.

Lyric poetry expresses the poet's strong feelings about a topic. It does _not_ tell a story. It is about how the poet feels, not what happens. It contains vivid imagery that creates pictures in the reader's mind. Many lyric poems are short.

Long ago in ancient Greece, these poems were sung while an instrument called a lyre was played. The word _lyre_ gives us the English word _lyric_.

Some lyric poems use rhythm and rhyme. Many are written in free verse.

Comprehension Tip
Use punctuation marks to help you read poetry. A period tells you to stop at the end of a line. A comma tells you to pause. If there is no punctuation mark, read from one line to the next without stopping or pausing.

Guided Instruction

Read the passage below. Then answer the questions in the margin and complete the activities.

from **How doth the Little Busy Bee**

by Issac Watts

How doth the little busy Bee
Improve each shining Hour,
And gather Honey all the day
From every opening Flower!

5   How skilfully she builds her Cell!
How neat she spreads the Wax!
And labours hard to store it well
With the sweet Food she makes.
…

In Books, or Work, or healthful Play
10   Let my first years be past,
That I may give for every Day
Some good Account at last

Guided Questions

Read "How doth the Little Busy Bee." What is the author's purpose for writing this poem?

_____

Is the poem a lyric poem or a narrative poem?

_____

How do you know?

_____

_____

Read aloud the first stanza (lines **1**–**4**). How many beats are in each line?
Line **1**:
Line **2**:
Line **3**:
Line **4**:

Read lines **5**–**8**. Which word in this stanza rhymes with *Cell*?

_____

Read lines **9**–**12**. In what way does the speaker hope he is like the Bee?

_____

_____

Excerpt from "How Doth the Little Busy Bee" by Isaac Watts. Reprinted in Watts, Isaac.
Divine and Moral Songs for Children. New York: Hurd & Houghton, 1866.

How Doth the Little Crocodile

by Lewis Carroll

How doth the little crocodile
Improve his shining tail,
And pour the waters of the Nile
On every golden scale!
5 How cheerfully he seems to grin,
How neatly spreads his claws,
And welcomes little fishes in
With gently smiling jaws!

Guided Questions

Now read "How doth the Crocodile."

How many stanzas are in the poem?

_____

Read lines **1**–**4**. Picture what the crocodile looks like. Which of your five senses does the speaker appeal to in these lines?

_____

_____

What sensory words does the speaker use to help create this image of the crocodile?

_____

_____

Which words rhyme in lines **1**–**4**?

_____

_____

Which words rhyme in lines **5**–**8**?

_____

_____

"How Doth the Little Crocodile" by Lewis Carroll

Answer the following questions based on the two poems you just read.

1. Reread the poem aloud.

   > *How doth the little crocodile*   _____
   >
   > *Improve his shining tail,*   _____
   >
   > *And pour the waters of the Nile*   _____
   >
   > *On every golden scale!*   _____
   >
   > *How cheerfully he seems to grin,*   _____
   >
   > *How neatly spreads his claws,*   _____
   >
   > *And welcomes little fishes in*   _____
   >
   > *With gently smiling jaws!*   _____

   Highlight the words or syllables that get the strong beat.

   Then write *a* in the blank by the word crocodile. Using the letters *a, b, c* and so on, show which words at the end of lines rhyme.

2. What will most likely happen to the little fishes in "How doth the little crocodile"?

   _____

   What feeling does the poem's ending create?

   _____

3. What feeling does the poem "How doth the Little Busy Bee" create?

   _____

4. What lesson does the poem teach you?

   _____

Critical Thinking

5. Work with a partner. Talk about which animal, a bee or a crocodile, you would rather be? Use details from the poems to support your choices. Then list other characteristics that describe the animal you chose. Find a book or magazine article in the media center about your animal. You may want to ask a librarian or media specialist to help you. Use the book or article to add more characteristics to your list. If you don't agree on which animal you want to be, try and convince your partner that it is better to be the animal you chose. Use your list of characteristics to help you.

Writing	☐
Research	☐
Listening and Speaking	☑
Media Literacy	☐
21st Century Skills: Collaboration	☑
Cross Curriculum Connection	☐

Critical Thinking

6. "How doth the Little Crocodile" is an example of a humorous poem, but humor is very individual. What one person finds funny, another may not. Talk to a partner. Talk about what makes something funny. Give examples from your reading or viewing. Then talk about whether you found this poem funny. Explain why. Is it the surpise ending? Is it the images of the crocodile?

Writing	☐
Research	☐
Listening and Speaking	☑
Media Literacy	☐
21st Century Skills: Collaboration	☑
Cross Curriculum Connection	☐

Critical Thinking

7. "How doth the Little Crocodile" is a parody of "How Doth the Little Busy Bee". A parody is a funny imitation of a serious story or poem. Lewis Carroll, the author of "How doth the Little Crocodile" imitated Isaac Watts's poem, "How doth the Little Busy Bee." Carroll made his poem funny. Talk with your partner about how the two poems are the same. Talk about how they are different. Try your hand at writing a parody. Choose another animal. Write a parody of Watt's poem using your animal. Share it with your partner.

Writing	☐
Research	☐
Listening and Speaking	☑
Media Literacy	☐
21st Century Skills: Collaboration	☑
Cross Curriculum Connection	☐

On Your Own

Read the selection below. Then answer the questions that follow it.

Literature
Connection

Purple Snake

by Pat Mora

"It's in there, sleeping,"
Don Luis says and winks.
He knows I want to feel
the animal asleep in a piece of wood,
5   like he does
turning it this way and that,
                listening.

Slowly he strokes the wood,
roughly and wrinkled. Like his hands.
10   He begins to carve his way.
"Mira. Its head, its scales, its tail."
    Don Luis rubs and strokes
    the animal before he paints
        its eyes open.
15   When the paint dries,
    I place the purple snake
    by the green bull and red frog
    that Don Luis found asleep
        in a piece of wood.

Answer the following questions based on the passage you just read.

1. Read the first two lines of the poem.

> *"It's in there, sleeping,"*
> *Don Luis says and winks.*

In your own words, tell what Don Luis means.

_____

2. Circle the items below that describe this poem.

- Narrative poem
- Lyric poem
- Free verse
- Humorous poem

How do you know?

_____

_____

3. How does Don Luis decide where to carve the snake's head, scales, and tail? Write the line that tells you this.

_____

4. When does the snake seem to truly come alive?

_____

5. Read the lines below.

> *Slowly he strokes the wood,*
> *rough and wrinkled. Like his hands.*

The image in these lines appeals mostly to the sense of —

A taste

B touch

C smell

D sight

6. Read the lines below.

> *I place the purple snake*
> *by the green bull and red frog*
> *   that Don Luis found asleep*
> *   in a piece of wood.*

Are the green bull and red frog real animals or something else? Explain.

_____

Critical Thinking

7. Imagine you are a book illustrator. Your company is going to include "Purple Snake" in a collection of poetry. Your job is to illustrate this poem. Use a photograph you find or a drawing you create to capture the ideas and feeling of this poem. Then meet with a partner to share your illustration. Discuss why your illustration would be a good one to accompany the poem in a poetry collection.

Writing	☐
Research	☐
Listening and Speaking	☑
Media Literacy	☑
21st Century Skills: Collaboration	☐
Cross Curriculum Connection	☐

Read the selection. Then choose the best answer to each question.

In the Summer
When I Go to Bed

by Thomas Hood

In the summer when I go to bed
The sun's still streaming overhead
My bed becomes so small and hot
With sheets and pillow in a knot,
5   And then I lie and try to see
The things I'd really like to be.

I think I'd be a glossy cat
A little plump, but not too fat.
I'd never touch a bird or mouse
10   I'm much too busy round the house.

And then a fierce and hungry hound
The king of dogs for miles around;
I'd chase the postman just for fun
To see how quickly he could run.

15   Perhaps I'd be a crocodile
Within the marshes of the Nile
And paddle in the river-bed
With dripping mud-caps on my head.

"In the Summer When I Go to Bed" by Thomas Hood

Or maybe next a mountain goat
20 With shaggy whiskers at my throat,
Leaping streams and jumping rocks
In stripey pink and purple socks.

Or else I'd be a polar bear
And on an iceberg make my lair;
25 I'd keep a shop in Baffin Sound
To sell icebergs by the pound.

And then I'd be a wise old frog
Squatting on a sunken log.
I'd teach the fishes lots of games
30 And how to read and write their names.

An Indian lion then I'd be
And lounge about on my <u>settee</u>;
I'd feed on nothing but bananas
And spend all day in my pajamas.

Measuring Up to the Texas Essential Knowledge and Skills

35   I'd like to be a tall giraffe
making lots of people laugh,
I'd do a tap dance on the street
with little bells upon my feet.

And then I'd be a foxy fox
40   Streaking through the hollyhocks,
Horse or hound would ne'er catch me
I'm a master of disguise, you see.

I think I'd be a chimpanzee
With musical ability,
45   I'd play a silver clarinet
Or form a monkey String Quartet.

And then a snake with scales of gold
Guarding hoards of wealth untold,
No thief would dare to steal a pin—
50   But friends of mind I would let in.

But then before I really know
Just what I'd be or where I'd go
My bed becomes so wide and deep
And all my thoughts are fast asleep.

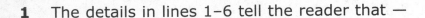
1 The details in lines 1–6 tell the reader that —

   A the boy is taking an afternoon nap

   B the boy's bed is much too small

   C the boy can't sleep

   D the boy needs a blanket because it is chilly

---

2 The details in lines 7–10 tell the reader that the cat the boy wants to be is —

   F pampered

   G ignored

   H wild and fierce

   J unhappy

---

3 All these items describe this poem except —

   A lines grouped into stanzas

   B tells a story

   C strong rhythm

   D has a serious message

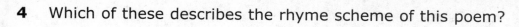

4   Which of these describes the rhyme scheme of this poem?

   F   Every other line rhymes.

   G   The words at the ends of lines do not rhyme.

   H   Each pair of lines rhyme.

   J   Only the first and last line in a stanza rhyme.

---

5   The word <u>settee</u> in line 32 means —

   A   couch

   B   pajamas

   C   house

   D   food

---

6   Read lines 17–18 below.

> *And paddle in the river-bed*
> *With dripping mud-caps on my head.*

The image in the second line appeals most strongly to the reader's sense of —

   F   taste

   G   touch

   H   smell

   J   hearing

7 What happens at the end of the poem?

   A The boy makes up his mind.

   B The boy wakes up.

   C The boy falls asleep.

   D The boy gets lost in his bed.

---

8 Which detail in the picture best creates a sense of humor and imagination?

   F The goat is jumping.

   G The goat is wearing striped socks.

   H The goat has horns.

   J The goat is hairy.

Make Inferences About Plot and Characters from Dialogue in Scripts

3.7	Explain the elements of plot and character as presented through dialogue in scripts that are read, viewed, written, or performed.
Ⓢ 3.2(B)	Ask relevant questions, seek clarification, and locate facts and details about stories and other texts and support answers with evidence from text.
Ⓢ Figure 19(D)	Make inferences about text and use textual evidence to support understanding.

 ## Understand the TEKS

Plays

A **play** is a story that is acted out, or performed for an audience. A written play is called a **script**. A play is often divided into acts. Within each act, there may be scenes.

Characters and Plot

Characters are the people in the story. **Plot** is the pattern of events, or what happens. Plays have characters and plot just like other kinds of fiction. All the characters' names are listed at the beginning of the play. The people who play the characters are called **actors**.

Words to Know
act
character
dialogue
narrator
play
plot
scene
setting
stage directions

In some plays, there is a special character called the **narrator**. The narrator fills in information and tells what is happening. The narrator is not part of the events in the story.

In a play, you learn about the characters and what happens mostly through dialogue. **Dialogue** consists of the words the actors say to each other. Unlike a story, these words are not put in quotation marks. Dialogue is usually set up like this.

---

from The Dance Contest
by Lucy Clark Brown

MERIDITH: Jackson, did you practice that jump last night?

JACKSON: (*Laughing*) Yuh, a little bit!

MERIDITH: What do you mean, "a little bit"? You want to win the dance contest, right?

• What punctuation mark separates the name of the character from the words that character says?

• What is Meridith worried about?

_____

_____

Setting

A play also has a **setting**. This is where and when the events occur. Usually, the setting is described at the beginning of the play.

Stage Directions

Plays often include **stage directions**. Stage directions tell the actors what to do as they say their lines. Stage directions also help readers imagine how the play would look if it were performed. Stage directions are written in _italic_ type.

• Look back at the dialogue on the previous page. What is Jackson doing when he says his line?

_____

Most plays are written to be performed on a stage. They can also be performed on TV or on the radio. Plays are also performed by students in their classrooms or in school auditoriums.

> **Comprehension Tip**
> When you read a script, pay close attention to the stage directions. Use them to picture where the characters move and what they are doing. Stage directions often show how the characters are feeling.

Guided Instruction

Read the passage below. Then answer the questions in the margin and complete the activities.

Literature
Connection

Born to Be Rich

retold by Pat Betteley

1 | **Cast of Characters:** *Narrator, Cobbler, Neighbor, Fisherman's Wife, Wife, Jeweler* |

2   **Narrator:** *Once there was a cobbler who worked very hard but could never fill his purse. Every night as he worked, he sang the same song.*

3   **Cobbler:** *A poor cobbler am I*
Who always needs more.
Why do I work hard,
When I'm born to be poor?

4   **Narrator:** *A rich neighbor heard his song and decided to help. He sent over a cake for the cobbler's family to eat. There were gold pieces hidden inside.*

5   **Cobbler:** Wife, you'll never believe our good fortune. Our neighbor sent over this cake. Take it to the doctor as payment for the last time he took care of little Pedro at no charge.

6   **Narrator:** *When the generous neighbor walked by, he heard the cobbler singing his sad song again.*

7   **Cobbler:** *A poor cobbler am I*
Who always needs more.
Why do I work hard,
When I'm born to be poor?

8   **Neighbor:** What are you singing about? Didn't you and your family eat the cake?

9   **Cobbler:** Why, no. I gave it to the doctor to thank him for his kindness in taking care of little Pedro.

"Born to Be Rich" by Pat Betteley, from FACES January 2008 issue: *Exploring a New World*, Copyright © 2008, Carus Publishing Company, published by Cobblestone Publishing. All Rights Reserved. Reprinted by permission of the publisher

Guided Questions

Read the Cast of Characters. How many actors would you need to put on this play? Which of these characters does not take part in the action of the story?

_____

In paragraph **2**, highlight important information you learn about the cobbler.

What is the cobbler singing about in paragraph **3**? How does he feel?

_____

_____

_____

Read paragraphs **6**–**8**. Why is the neighbor surprised by the cobbler's song?

_____

_____

Read the dialogue in paragraphs **8** and **9**. Highlight what the cobbler did with the cake. What does this tell you about him?

10 **Narrator:** *So the neighbor put together another gift. This time, he hid a purse full of money under a load of pine branches.*

Read paragraph **10**. Highlight what the neighbor did with the money. Why do you think he did this?

_____

_____

_____

11 **Cobbler:** Now, this is good fortune. We can give these pine branches to the baker to burn in his furnace. He has often given us bread even when he had no money.

12 **Narrator:** *The next day, the neighbor heard the cobbler sing his sad song.*

13 **Neighbor:** What's the matter, man? Surely, the pine branches burned brightly.

Read the dialogue in paragraphs **11**–**14**. Why didn't the cobbler find the money?

_____

_____

14 **Cobbler:** You'll have to ask the baker about that. We gave the branches to him to thank him for giving us free bread.

15 **Neighbor:** My dear man, perhaps you are born to be poor, for I have tried to give you money two times now. The first time, I hid coins in the cake. The second, I tucked money under the pine branches. Both times, you gave the fortune away! That is all I can do. I have nothing else to give right now, except this piece of lead I found lying on the street.

Read the neighbor's lines in paragraph **15**. Highlight the conclusion the neighbor reaches about the cobbler. What does the neighbor give him this time?

_____

16 **Cobbler:** Thank you. You are a kind man.

17 **Narrator:** *Since the cobbler had no use for the lead, he placed it high on a shelf. Then he began working into the night, singing his sad song. Later, the fisherman's wife knocked on the door.*

_____

18 **Fisherman's Wife:** Good neighbor, my husband is going to the sea to fish, but he doesn't have enough lead to weight down his fish line. Can you help me?

Read the dialogue in paragraphs **17**–**19**. What does the cobbler do with the lead his neighbor gave him?

19 **Cobbler:** I just happen to have some lead on my shelf. It's yours.

_____

20 **Narrator:** *The catch was good that night, and the fisherman's wife brought the cobbler's family a beautiful, large perch. When the cobbler's wife was cleaning it, she found a shiny stone in its belly.*

21 **Wife:** What's this? It looks like glass. I'll give it to little Pedro and his sisters to play with.

22   **Narrator:** *Just as he blew out the candles before bed, the cobbler caught sight of something shining at his feet.*

23   **Cobbler:** What is that gleaming by our bed?

24   **Wife:** It's a stone I found inside the fish that the fisherman gave to us.

25   **Narrator:** *The next day the cobbler took the stone to a jeweler.*

26   **Jeweler:** This stone is worth a great deal of money. In fact, I can't afford to buy it from you. Only the king can afford such a gem. Would you like me to show it to him at court?

27   **Narrator:** *When the king saw the stone, he wanted it immediately. He bought it from the cobbler for a great deal of money. The cobbler bought a house and farm with the money and lived very well. When the rich neighbor returned home from his travels, he saw the cobbler's fine home.*

28   **Neighbor:** You tricked me. Surely, you kept the money out of the cake and under the pine branches after all. How else could you afford such a home?

29   **Cobbler:** You know that I'm an honest man. I gave away the piece of lead to the fisherman, who caught a wonderful fish with it. The fisherman gave me a fish that contained a shining stone. The king paid a great deal of money for the stone, and I bought the house and farm with it.

30   **Neighbor:** I believe you.

31   **Cobbler:** A thousand thanks, neighbor. Even though I turned my back on good fortune twice, it seems I was not born to be poor, after all.

Guided Questions

Read the narrator's words in paragraph **22**. Based on what you know about this type of tale, what do you infer about the "glass"?

_____

_____

Highlight the important information you learn about the stone in paragraph **26**.

How do you think the neighbor is feeling in paragraph **28**?

_____

_____

_____

In paragraph **29**, highlight the cobbler's summary of the events in this tale.

Answer the following questions based on the passage you just read.

1. Fill in the chart below. Tell what the cobbler had received from each person.

Action	What Cobbler Had Received
Cobbler gives cake to doctor.	
Cobbler gives pine branches to baker.	

2. Why does the cobbler give the fisherman's wife the piece of lead?

_____

What does the fisherman's wife give the cobbler?

_____

3. At the end of the story, how does the cobbler become rich?

_____

What does this tell you about the cobbler? Why?

_____

_____

_____

Critical Thinking

4. Work with a partner. Discuss the meaning of this story. Talk about the title. Tell how the cobbler has really been rich throughout this story. Then collaborate to create a saying that tells what true wealth is. Design a poster displaying your saying.

Writing	☑
Research	☐
Listening and Speaking	☑
Media Literacy	☐
21st Century Skills: Collaboration	☑
Cross Curriculum Connection	☐

5. Write a new song for the cobbler. Make sure this song captures what the cobbler has learned.

Measuring Up to the Texas Essential Knowledge and Skills

On Your Own

Read the selection below. Then answer the questions that follow it.

Literature
Connection

BIG FRIGHT IN THE NIGHT

by Djeema Jansen

1   **CHARACTERS**

Daria
Brady
Skeeter
Samantha
Trees (ten students in tree costumes)
A grizzly bear cub

2   **SETTING**   Around a campfire in the country at night.

Children are sitting around a fire talking and roasting marshmallows. Audience can see a bag of marshmallows, chocolate bars and graham crackers on ground; in background can see trees. Nearby is a small log cabin with windows.

ACT 1

3   **SKEETER:** (*Speaking in an unhappy voice*): Mom says Mr. Allen isn't coming up this summer. What are we going to do without him? He's the coolest person we know.

4   **SAMANTHA:** (*Sadly*): I don't know. What are we going to do? Who's going to climb Bald Peak Mountain with us? Who's going to take us fishing? Who's going to drive us to the General Store for penny candy?

5   **BRADY:** (*Very seriously*): Well, Skeeter, maybe you'll just have to be the leader this summer.

6   **DARIA:** (*Laughing*): Brady! You sound just like Dad. But seriously, who IS going to take us to get penny candy at the General Store? Skeeter can't drive.

7   (*Suddenly, there's a noise. Everyone stops talking. They all turn towards the trees.*)

"Big Fright in the Night" by Djeema Jansen

ACT 2

8   **BRADY:** (*Nervously and quietly*): Did you hear that noise?

9   **SAMANTHA, BRADY and SKEETER:** (*Excitedly but quietly*): YES!

10   **DARIA:** It's nothing! It's just the wind blowing through the trees.

11   **SKEETER:** (*Whispering*): Really? You think so?

12   **BRADY:** (*Pointing to trees*): I don't know, Daria. It sounds like someone's walking. Don't you hear twigs breaking?

13   **DARIA:** C'mon everyone. It's nothing. Let's finish roasting our marshmallows. Then we can make our s'mores.

14   **SAMANTHA:** Daria's right. Let's make our s'mores. It's our first night at the lake. You know we always have s'mores.

15   **SKEETER:** Right!

16   **BRADY:** (*Sighing*): Right, let's forget about the noises. We're at the lake. There are always noises. At least there aren't any bats swooping down on us tonight. (*Everyone laughs.*)

17   (*There is another big noise behind the trees. The children jump up. They all look toward the trees again.*)

ACT 3

18   **SKEETER:** (*Frightened voice*): That's not the wind!

19   **SAMANTHA:** (*Whispers*): That's for sure! What is it?

20   **DARIA:** (*Whispers in very frightened voice*): Skeeter, what do you see?

21   **SKEETER:** Nothing! It's too dark! (*He cups his hands over his eyes to look very closely.*)

22   **BRADY:** (*Pointing toward the trees*): Look! It's a bear cub! (*Enter Bear Cub from behind trees*)

23   (*Everyone stops and stares as a bear cub lumbers toward them very slowly.*)

24   **DARIA:** (*Softly*): Oh, he's so cute!

25   **SAMANTHA:** No, he's not cute right now, Daria. He's dangerous. He'll be cute when we're inside the cabin. (*She starts to back up.*)

26   **SKEETER:** (*Whispering*): Okay, everyone, let's quietly put down our marshmallows. Then we're going to walk very, very slowly to the cabin.

27   **BRADY:** (*Whispering*): That's walk slowly toward the cabin—not run.

28   **SAMANTHA:** (*Whispering*): Right! We don't want to frighten this little guy.

29   **DARIA:** Okay!

30   (*Samantha, Skeeter, Daria, and Brady walk toward cabin.*)

ACT 4

31   (*Children are inside cabin now. Samantha and Brady are looking out window. Skeeter and Daria are sitting at a table playing cards.*)

32   **SAMANTHA:** Wow! Look! He ate all the marshmallows! Now he's eating a chocolate bar.

33   **BRADY:** I bet that he's going to eat everything!

34   **SKEETER:** What an adventure, huh? I can't believe we saw a bear cub.

35   **DARIA:** You know Mr. Allen always said there were bears here! Let's call him tomorrow and tell him we saw a cub. That might convince him to come up to the lake this summer.

36   **CURTAIN**

Answer the following questions based on the passage you just read.

1. Complete the sequence chart below. Tell the most important event in each act.

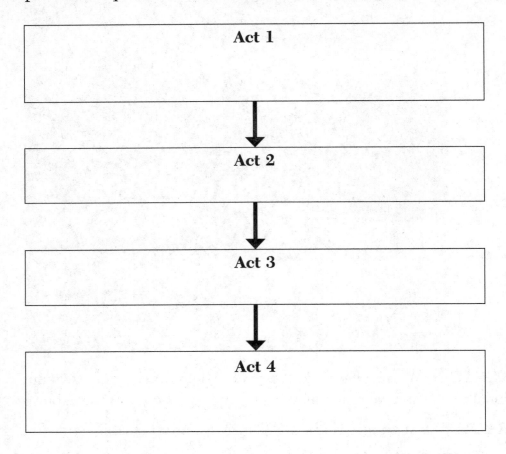

2. From the stage directions in paragraphs 3 and 4, the reader knows that Skeeter and Samantha are —

   A excited

   B disappointed

   C nervous

   D glad

3. What do the children do every summer on the first night they arrive at the lake? Why does this turn out to be important?

   _____

4. Why do the children jump up and look toward the trees again in Act 2?

   _____

5. In Act 2, the character whose words show that she is the calmest is —

    A   Daria

    B   Brady

    C   Skeeter

    D   Samantha

6. Look at the chart below. Complete it to show how Daria and Samantha are different.

Daria	Samantha
Thinks bear cub is cute.	

7. In Act 3, why do the children walk slowly to the cabin instead of running?

_____

_____

8. In Act 4, why do the children now feel excited to have had an adventure?

_____

_____

Critical Thinking

9. Work as a class. Choose a director for this play and assign roles. Design a set and costumes. Then rehearse this play. Give a performance for another class.

Writing	☐
Research	☐
Listening and Speaking	☑
Media Literacy	☑
21st Century Skills: Collaboration	☑
Cross Curriculum Connection	☐

ⓡ 3.8(A)	Sequence and summarize the plot's main events and explain their influence on future events.
ⓢ 3.2(B)	Ask relevant questions, seek clarification, and locate facts and details about stories and other texts and support answers with evidence from text.
ⓡ Figure 19(D)	Make complex inferences about text and use textual evidence to support understanding.
ⓡ Figure 19(E)	Summarize, paraphrase, and synthesize texts in ways that maintain meaning and logical order (within a text and across texts).

⟳ Understand the TEKS

Plot

How many times have you asked your friends, "What was that movie about?" "Was that book exciting?" When you ask questions like these, you are asking about plot.

Plot is the pattern of events in a story. Each important event in the story **affects** what will happen later.

The plot tells about characters and what they do. The **characters** are the people in the story or the animals that act like people. The main character is the most important character.

A story has a beginning, a middle, and an end. Here is how the plot of a story usually unfolds.

- **Beginning** Main character faces a problem.
- **Middle** Character tries to solve the problem.
- **End** Character solves the problem.

> **Words to Know**
> cause
> character
> effect
> event
> plot
> sequence
> summarize

Sequence of Events

What happened first? In what **sequence**, or order, did the events occur? What happened last? Questions like these ask about the sequence of events.

Usually, the plot unfolds in **time order**, or **chronological order**. First one event happens, then the next event happens, until finally the last event occurs. In other words, events occur in the order they would in real life.

Here are some words that help you follow the sequence of events.

first	next	before	soon
second	last	after	until
third	now	later	when
then	once	finally	as

> To everyone's surprise, Mark hit the ball out of the park. **Then** he took off running. **As** he raced around the bases, the crowd cheered.

- Which event happened first?

  _____

- Which two events happened at the same time?

  _____

Cause and Effect

Another way events are connected is through **cause and effect**. A **cause** makes something happen. An **effect** is the outcome or **result**. For example, Mark wouldn't have run around the bases if he hadn't hit the ball. The crowd wouldn't have cheered if he hadn't hit the ball.

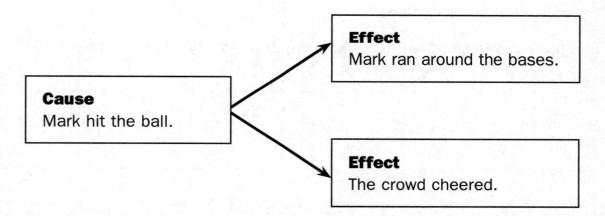

The main events at the beginning of a story **influence** what happens later. You may have to circle back to the beginning to understand why later events happened.

Imagine that at the beginning of a story, a flood destroys Amanda's house and her dog is swept away in it. Since her family now has nowhere to live, they quickly move out of town to stay with relatives. In the middle of the story, Amanda runs away. Why?

When you circle back to the beginning, you find the cause: the flood and the lost dog.

• Why do you think Amanda ran away?

_____

_____

Summary

A **summary** of a story includes only the important events. It leaves out unimportant details and events. It covers the whole story, not just part of it. Usually, it tells the events in time order.

A summary is short. It gives the main idea of the story in the fewest words.

A good summary answers these questions:

• Who has the problem?
• What is the problem?
• What does the character do to solve the problem?
• How is the problem solved?

• Is a summary longer than, the same length as, or shorter than the story?

_____

• How do you know?

_____

Comprehension Tip

As you read, make inferences, or intelligent guesses, about the plot. Look for clues in the story that help you predict what will happen next.

Guided Instruction

Read the passage below. Then answer the questions in the margin and complete the activities.

Literature Connection

Ducktective Max and the Missing Farm Animals

by Donna M. Boock

1   The call came into Headquarters just after I'd quacked—er, I mean, cracked—the case of the stolen golden goose eggs.

2   I answered the phone: "Ducktective Max Quacks. What's the mystery?"

3   "My animals are all gone!" Old MacDonald yelled.

4   "What do you mean?" I asked.

5   "My cow is missing, my three pigs aren't present, and my sheep is lost!" he said.

6   "We're on our way." I hung up the phone and jotted in my notebook:

7   *Old MacDonald's cow, sheep, three pigs—gone! <u>Find them!</u>*

8   Then I explained the situation to Heather Feather, my friend and assistant ducktective.

9   "Let's go!" she said.

10   We went to the pigpen first. We didn't hear an *oink* here or an *oink* there. We didn't hear an *oink-oink* anywhere.

11   "Maybe they flew south for the winter, Max," suggested Heather, picking up a feather from the ground.

12   "Since when have pigs grown wings?" I asked. "This looks like a goose feather, and goose feathers don't belong in pigpens. Our first clue!" I pulled out my notebook and made some notes.

"Ducktective Max and the Missing Farm Animals" by Donna M. Boock, Copyright © 2009 by Highlights for Children, Inc., Columbus, Ohio

---

Guided Questions

Read paragraphs **1**–**7**. Who is the main character? What is unusual about this character?

_____

_____

_____

_____

What event in the opening paragraphs sets the plot in motion?

_____

_____

_____

Highlight the words in paragraph **8** that tell you who Heather Feather is.

Highlight the clue Heather finds in paragraph **11**. What do you think will be the effect of this clue? Read on to see if you are right.

_____

13　"Where would a goose feather come from? Old MacDonald doesn't have any geese," said Heather.

14　I thought for a moment. "But Mother Goose has plenty of feathers! Let's check her out."

15　"Good thinking. What's our plan when we get there?" Heather asked.

16　"Let's just wing it." I took the feather, and we flew south toward Mother Goose's nest.

17　"Mother Goose," I called when we arrived.

18　"Yes," she answered, poking her bill out of her nest. "Who's there?"

19　"Ducktective Max," I answered, flashing my badge. That's my favorite part of the job. "And my assistant, Heather."

20　"We're looking for Old MacDonald's missing animals," Heather added.

21　"How can I help?" Mother Goose asked.

22　"We found a feather in the pigpen. Is it yours?" I asked.

23　"Goodness, no! I haven't visited that farm in ages. I'd have to go the long way, with all that construction on London Bridge."

Read paragraph **14**. Was your prediction correct? Explain. Why did Max reach this conclusion?

_____

_____

_____

_____

_____

_____

Why do you think the author has Mother Goose mention London Bridge in paragraph **23**?

_____

_____

_____

_____

24   Maybe Mother Goose was innocent after all. One thing still bothered me. I reached into my trench coat. "Then where did this goose feather come from?"

25   "Goose feather?" Mother Goose laughed. "Max, that's no goose feather. It's one of your tail feathers!" She pointed to a bald spot.

26   I blushed and stuck my feather in my pocket.

27   "Thanks for your time," I said, flashing my badge again.

28   We were on our way back to Headquarters when we saw Little Boy Blue sleeping by a haystack.

29   "That's it!" Heather cried, her tiny black eyes lighting up.

30   "What?" I asked.

31   "'Little Boy Blue, come blow your horn. The sheep's in the meadow, the cow's in the corn!'"

32   "You're right!" I followed her lead and landed in the field.

33   Heather turned to Blue and shouted, "Blue, wake up! We need your help!" She told him what to do.

34   *Da-da-da-daaah!* went his horn. And the sheep showed up from the meadow.

35   "Play it again, Blue," she said.

36   *Da-da-da-daaah!* he played. And the cow came out of the corn!

37   "One more time," she said.

38   *Da-da-da-daaah!* But no pigs popped out.

39   "Any idea where the pigs are?" I asked.

40   "Sorry, pigs aren't my thing," Blue answered.

41   "Thanks for your help," I said.

42   "What's next, Max?" Heather asked.

43   "Mother Goose Land may still be our answer. Are there any stories about pigs?" I asked.

44   She held up a webbed foot. "'This little piggy went to market. . . .'"

Guided Questions

Read paragraph **25**. How did the feather get into the pigpen?

_____

_____

_____

Read paragraphs **27**–**33**. Highlight the nursery rhyme. What do you think Max and Heather want Little Boy Blue to do? Why?

_____

_____

_____

Circle back and reread paragraph **7**. Then read paragraphs **34**–**41**. What problem still has to be solved?

_____

_____

In paragraph **43**, why does Max ask Heather if there are any more tales about pigs?

_____

_____

_____

45   "You only have three webbed toes. You'll need two more for that rhyme. How many pigs did Old MacDonald say he had?" I flipped through my notebook. "Here it is. He had three pigs."

46   "The Three Pigs—let's go see the Big Bad Wolf!" she said. So we did.

47   When we arrived at Wolf's place, we huffed, and we puffed, and we blew the door in. I flashed my badge. "Wolf, what have you done with the pigs?" I asked.

48   "Nothing," growled the wolf.

49   "Hogwash. We're taking you to the station for questioning," I said.

50   On the way, we saw Jack's Construction School. "That's the house that Jack built," I said, pointing to the tall building.

51   "Max, do you hear that? It sounds like pigs squealing," Heather said.

52   We went in to check it out. "Welcome to Construction 101: How to Build a Stronger House," Jack said. The three pigs were taking notes in the first row.

53   "I told you I didn't do anything," the wolf said.

54   "Maybe you're not such a big bad wolf after all," Heather said.

55   "It seems we've solved another rhyme—er, I mean, crime!" I said, taking out my badge and polishing it on my shirt.

In paragraph **46**, highlight the step Max and Heather take to solve this problem. Based on what you know of the fairy tale, why does Heather suggest this?

_____

_____

_____

Read the rest of the story. What is the solution? How does the solution fit in with the tale of the Three Little Pigs?

_____

_____

_____

_____

Circle back to when Max and Heather talk to Mother Goose. What clue prepares you for the ending?

_____

_____

_____

_____

_____

     Measuring Up to the Texas Essential Knowledge and Skills

Answer the following questions based on the passage you just read.

1. Fill in the sequence chart below. In the boxes, write the five places or people Max and Heather go to. Write them in order.

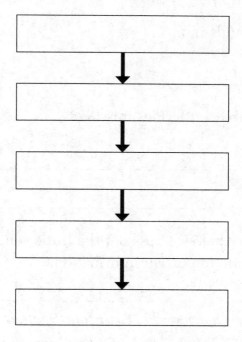

Now use the sequence chart to tell the most important thing that happens at each place. (The first one is done for you.)

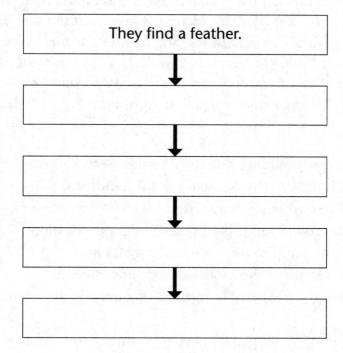

They find a feather.

Elevate

2. In a mystery, you usually find the cause after you learn the effect. Why were the sheep missing?

_____

Why was the cow missing?

_____

Why were the Three Little Pigs missing?

_____

_____

3. Read the summary below. Cross out the three sentences that do not belong. They do not include important information.

> *Ducktective Max Quack and his assistant Heather Feather try to find Old McDonald's missing cow, sheep, and three pigs. First, they go to the pigpen. They don't find the animals there, but they do find a feather. Who does this feather belong to, they wonder. This leads them to Mother Goose. She's a nursery-rhyme character. She tells them the feather came from Max's tail. As they walk back to Headquarters, they see Little Boy Blue. He blows his horn and the cow and sheep return. I wonder where the Three Little Pigs are. Still looking for the Three Little Pigs, they go to see the Big Bad Wolf. He claims he didn't do it, but they take him in for questioning. On the way to the station, they see Jack's Construction School. There they find the Three Little Pigs taking a course in "How to Build a Stronger House."*

Critical Thinking

4. Part of the fun of reading this story comes from knowing the different nursery rhymes and tales it mentions. Work with a small group of students. First identify each nursery rhyme or tale mentioned. If you can, get copies of them and read them aloud in the group. Then talk about how these tales affect the plot. Discuss how knowing them helps make the story humorous or funny. Write a summary of your conclusions.

Writing	☐
Research	☑
Listening and Speaking	☑
Media Literacy	☐
21st Century Skills: Collaboration	☑
Cross Curriculum Connection	☐

Media Connection

5. You can find many fractured fairy tales on the Internet. A good source is http://www.youtube.com. Watch or read a fractured fairy tale. Then tell the class what makes it funny and why.

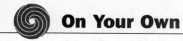

On Your Own

Read the selection below. Then answer the questions that follow it.

Literature
Connection

If Davy Could Yodel

by Bonnie Highsmith Taylor

1   Davy was the smallest cowboy on the Circle S Ranch.

2   But he could ride a horse as well as Slim or Tex or Shorty.

3   He could twirl a rope as well as Buck or Sandy or Will.

4   He could bulldog a steer as well as Charlie or Pecos or Ned.

5   But Davy couldn't yodel.

6   All the other cowboys could yodel. Even Flapjack Pete, the cook, could yodel a little.

7   If Davy could yodel, he could enter the yodeling contest on Saturday and maybe win a hundred dollars and the silver yodeling cup.

8   Davy practiced yodeling all the time.

9   He practiced while he swept out the bunkhouse.

10   He practiced while he pumped water for the cook.

11   He practiced while he pitched hay for the horses.

12   "Keep trying," said Slim, Ned, and Sandy. Davy did.

13   But no matter how hard he tried, he couldn't make it come out right.

14   The night before the contest Davy had a hard time going to sleep. He couldn't stop thinking about the first prize of a hundred dollars and the silver yodeling cup he might win, if only he could yodel.

15   After a while, Davy began to get cold. The fire in the big iron stove in the middle of the bunkhouse had gone out. Davy shivered under the covers. His teeth chattered. Then he heard his dog, Mutt, scratching at the bunkhouse door.

16   "Mutt is cold, too," thought Davy. "He wants to come in." Davy got up and opened the door. Snow covered the ground. Icicles hung from the eaves.

17   Suddenly, an icicle broke loose and fell. It slipped right down the neck of Davy's long-handled underwear.

18   OOOH! It was cold!

19   "Eeeow!" yelled Davy. "Eee—oh—ay—eee—oh!"

20   Slim, Buck, Pecos, and all the other cowboys came running. "What in the world—" cried Shorty.

21   "Why—why, Davy. You're yodeling!" cried Slim.

22   "He is, at that," said Buck. "And right smart, too."

23   "Eee—oh—ay—eee—oh!" yelled Davy as the icicle slid farther down his back. He couldn't believe it. He was yodeling. He sounded as good as Slim, Tex, Shorty, Pecos, Ned, Charlie, Buck, Sandy, or Will. And a whole lot better than Flapjack Pete.

24   Davy opened his mouth wide and threw back his head. Out came "Oh—lee—ay—dee—oh."

25   Again and again and again.

26   On Saturday, cowboys from every part of the county came to yodel in the yodeling contest. They were all very good. But the judges decided that nobody could yodel quite like Davy. All the other cowboys agreed.

27   They whooped and hollered when the judges handed Davy the hundred dollars and the silver yodeling cup.

28   With the hundred dollars Davy opened up his own bank account.

29   The silver yodeling cup is on a shelf in the bunkhouse, right over Davy's bunk. Every night before Davy goes to bed, he takes it down and polishes it on his shirttail—yodeling all the while.

30   "Oh—lee—ay—dee—oh."

31   And all the cowboys holler, "Davy, hush up and go to sleep."

Answer the following questions based on the passage you just read.

1. Reread paragraphs 1–5. What information from these paragraphs would you include in a summary? Why is this information important?

   _____

   _____

2. Why does Davy need to solve his problem?

   A To perform his chores better

   B To stop the other cowboys from laughing at him

   C To keep his job at the ranch

   D To be as good at everything as the other cowboys

3. Read the paragraph below.

   > *If Davy could yodel, he could enter the yodeling contest on Saturday and maybe win a hundred dollars and the silver yodeling cup.*

   Fill in the chart below. Show two things Davy wants to happen.

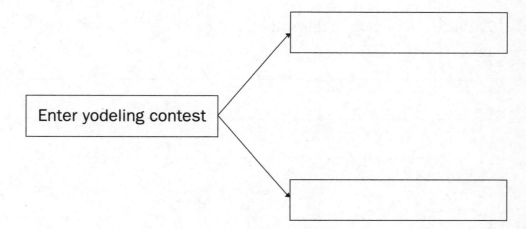

4. Which of these events follows from all the other events?

   A The fire in the big iron stove goes out.

   B An icicle falls right down the neck of Davy's underwear.

   C As Davy yells, he starts to yodel.

   D Davy opens the door to let Mutt in.

5. Suppose Davy had slept well the night before the contest. How would the plot be different?

   _____

   _____

6. Circle back to the beginning of the story. Would this story would have been the same if Davy had been as tall as all the other cowboys? Why or why not?

   _____

   _____

   _____

   _____

7. Write a summary of this story.

   _____

   _____

   _____

8. **Short-Answer Response** When Davy wins the contest, how do the other cowboys feel?

_____

Write two sentences from paragraphs 26–27 that support your response.

Sentence 1

_____

Sentence 2

_____

_____

Critical Thinking

9. Work with a partner. Start by making a list of movies or cartoons you have seen that are based on novels or tales. Then suppose you were to produce this story. Decide on the form it would take. Talk about whether you would make a movie of it, a cartoon, or an animated film. Discuss your reasons. After you have decided on a form, work together to create a storyboard showing the key events.

Writing	☑
Research	☐
Media Literacy	☑
Listening and Speaking	☑
21st Century Skills: Teamwork	☑
Cross Curriculum Connection	☐

Media Connection

10. Use the Internet or the resources in your library to find out how to yodel. Ask your teacher or media center specialist to help you locate videos and books. Write down the steps. Then practice yodeling. Prepare and present a demonstration for your classmates.

Ⓡ **3.8(B)**	Describe the interaction of characters including their relationships and the changes they undergo.	
Ⓢ **3.2(B)**	Ask relevant questions, seek clarification, and locate facts and details about stories and other texts and support answers with evidence from text.	
Ⓡ **Figure 19(D)**	Make inferences about text and use textual evidence to support understanding.	
3.3	Read aloud grade level appropriate text with fluency (rate, accuracy, expression, appropriate phrasing) and comprehension.	

 Understand the TEKS

Characters

Characters are the people in a story. They perform the actions. The events in the story happen to them.

The **main character** is the most important character. This is the character the story is mostly about.

Words to Know
character
dialogue
interact
main character
relationship
trait

Traits

The author describes the characters to help you picture them. You learn how they look and what they are like. These **traits** make the characters seem real. Even fantastic characters, such as animals that talk, have traits that make them seem real.

Sometimes the author tells you exactly what a character is like or feels like.

> Kevin wanted to pet the dog, but he was scared. It looked so big and powerful.

Sometimes the author shows you.

> "Come here," Mrs. Navarro coaxed. "His name is Murphy and he's as sweet as a sugar plum."
>
> Kevin moved toward the dog cautiously.
>
> "That right. Let him smell your hand. That's how he gets to know you.
>
> "Now go slowly, but put your hand gently on his head. Then move it down his back."
>
> Kevin did so with a little more confidence.
>
> "Keep petting him. Doesn't he seem happy now?"
>
> Kevin was smiling now. "Do you think I could come visit him?" he asked.

The author doesn't tell you this, but you probably made the inference that Kevin has gained some confidence.

- Do you think that Mrs. Navarro is kind and understands children? What details support your inference?

_____

_____

_____

Relationships

A character **interacts** with other characters. They talk to each other. They play together. They argue. Two characters may be friends, or they may not like each other at all. How a character gets along with other characters tells you a lot about him or her.

You learn about these relationships through what the characters do. You also learn about them through dialogue, or what they say to each other.

> "Will you help me put this model together?" Doug asked his brother Roger. "I need to take it into school tomorrow and I haven't a clue what to do."
>
> "Sorry," Roger said, "but I have my own homework to do."

- Do Doug and Roger have a close relationship?

_____

How do you know?

_____

- What inference do you make about Roger?

_____

Changes

As a story goes on, a character grows and changes. For example, a character like Roger may learn that it's important to help others. The two brothers may become closer.

When you read, look for relationships that show what the character is like. Pay attention to how the character grows and changes.

Think about how the characters are like people you know. Connecting characters to your own life may help you better understand them.

Comprehension Tip
Keep notes about the characters as you read. Create a T-chart, or two-column chart. Jot the characters' names in the left-hand column. As you read, jot details about each character in the right-hand column. Read over your notes after you finish the story.

Guided Instruction

Read the passage below. Then answer the questions in the margin and complete the activities.

Literature Connection

Best Friends Always

by Mary Kay Morel

Guided Questions

Dear Evie,

I do *not* like our new house. I wish we'd never moved to this town. And I wish I still lived next door to you. What am I supposed to do all summer in this strange place? Just sit around?

Your Best Friend, Kayla

P.S. The moving van doesn't get here until tomorrow. We have to sleep on the floor tonight. Mom says it'll be just like camping, but I doubt that.

Read letter **1**. Why is Kayla unhappy? Highlight the words that describe the relationship between Evie and Kayla.

_____

_____

"Best Friends Always" by Mary Kay Morel, Reprinted by permission of SPIDER magazine, May/June 2009, text © 2009 by Carus Publishing Company

Measuring Up to the Texas Essential Knowledge and Skills

2

Dear Evie,

I loved getting your letter! Now I'll answer your questions. First, do I like my new room? No, I don't! Sure, it's bigger than my old one. But the people who lived here before painted the walls green. I feel like I'm inside a giant celery stalk! Mom says I can choose a new paint color, but I'd rather have my old room back. In fact, I'd rather have my old life back!

Your Seeing-Green Best Friend, Kayla

Look at letter **2**. What do you think has happened between the first letter and the second?

_____

_____

3

Dear Evie,

I forgot to answer the second question. Here goes: no other kids live on my street. At least, I don't see any.

Your Lonely Best Friend, Kayla

Read letter **3**. Why do you think Evie asked about other kids? Highlight Kayla's answer.

_____

_____

_____

4

Dear Evie,

Count me wrong! A girl lives in the blue house next door. Her name is Cordelia. Cordelia's mom brought us chocolate chip muffins yesterday. That's how I met her. She's O.K., but I like you better.

Your Muffin-Eating Best Friend, Kayla

P.S. Don't you think Cordelia is a funny-sounding name?

Read letter **4**. Highlight the words that tell what Kayla thinks about Cordelia's name.

5

Dear Evie,

Mom and I went to the paint store. I picked out a color called Shell Pink. Then we painted all weekend. My room looks much better! Cordelia loves it, too! We sat in here this afternoon, reading books and playing board games.

Your Tickled-Pink Best Friend, Kayla

P.S. Cordelia told me that her name means "sea jewel." Doesn't that sound pretty?

Read letter **5**. Highlight the words that tell what Kayla thinks about Cordelia's name now. Why have her feelings changed?

_____

Dear Evie,

6   No, Cordelia is *not* my new best friend. We just play together. After all, she lives next door. You're still my best friend—and don't forget it!

    Your Very Best Friend Always, Kayla

Dear Evie,

7   You've been riding your bike to the park with Jenna? Wow! I always thought she acted mean. Maybe I was wrong. Maybe she's really nice. Is she your new best friend?

    Your Best (?) Friend, Kayla

Dear Evie,

8   Sorry I forgot to write last week. Cordelia and I bicycle to the park every day. Someone hung an old tire from a big beech tree there. We like to swing on it in the afternoons.

    Your Tire-Swinging Best Friend, Kayla

    P.S. I'm glad you still consider me your best friend.

Dear Evie,

9   I guess it's been ages since I've written. Cordelia and I caught a frog in her backyard yesterday. Just a little one. We put him in an old fruit jar with some leaves. We wanted to keep him there. But he looked really sad, so we let him go. I'm sorry Jenna's family left on vacation. You probably feel bored and lonely without her. I hope they get back soon!

    Your Frog-Freeing Best Friend, Kayla

Guided Questions

Read letters **6** and **7**. Why are the two friends worried?

_____

_____

_____

Read letters **8** and **9**. How have Kayla's feelings about living in the new town changed? Why have they changed?

_____

_____

_____

     Measuring Up to the Texas Essential Knowledge and Skills

10 **Dear Evie,**

I can't believe our old school already started this week! You have to sit next to Troublemaker Hendley? At least Jenna will sit on the other side of you! My new school doesn't begin until the end of this month. I still don't know who the teacher will be. My stomach hurts every time I think about it.

Your Concerned Best Friend, Kayla

Read letter **10**. When Kayla says that her stomach hurts, what do you know?

_____

_____

_____

11 **Dear Evie,**

I'm going camping with Cordelia's family at Yellow Springs State Park. We plan to pitch a tent and sleep out under the stars! We're also going fishing on her family's boat. I can't wait!

Your Excited Best Friend, Kayla

P.S. I hope there aren't any bears in the park . . .

12 **Dear Evie,**

Maybe you're right. Maybe Cordelia is my best friend now. But I count you as my best friend, too. Can't a person have two best friends? Wait a minute! Cordelia can be my new best friend here. And maybe Jenna can be your new best friend there. But we should still be best friends, too. We can be First Best Friends. I think that sounds more important than just being a best friend. What do you think?

Your First Best-Friend, Kayla

Read letter **12**. Highlight the sentences that show what Kayla has learned about being best friends.

13

Dear Evie,

 I'm glad you decided that being a First Best Friend is best of all. I feel that way, too. By the way, my new teacher, Miss Brookston, tells really funny jokes. Yesterday she asked us to write a mystery story. I wrote about some girls who move into an old house and find a green ghost hiding inside. I put Cordelia in my story, and Jenna, too. But you and I were the main characters who solved the mystery. After all, we are First Best Friends!

 Your First and Best Friend Forever, Kayla

 P.S. The green ghost turned out to be a friendly one.

Read the last letter. Why has the green ghost turned out to be friendly?

_____

_____

_____

Answer the following questions based on the passage you just read.

 1. Read the letter below.

> *Dear Evie,*
>
> *I loved getting your letter! Now I'll answer your questions. First, do I like my new room? No, I don't! Sure, it's bigger than my old one. But the people who lived here before painted the walls green. I feel like I'm inside a giant celery stalk! Mom says I can choose a new paint color, but I'd rather have my old room back. In fact, I'd rather have my old life back!*
>
> *Your Seeing-Green Best Friend, Kayla*

Do you think Kayla is funny—that she has a good sense of humor? Why or why not? Write details from the letter that support your answer.

_____

_____

2. Read the letter below.

Dear Evie,

I guess it's been ages since I've written. Cordelia and I caught a frog in her backyard yesterday. Just a little one. We put him in an old fruit jar with some leaves. We wanted to keep him there. But he looked really sad, so we let him go. I'm sorry Jenna's family left on vacation. You probably feel bored and lonely without her. I hope they get back soon!

Your Frog-Freeing Best Friend, Kayla

What does the detail that Kayla hasn't written in a long time tell you?

_____

_____

3. Complete the chart below.

Kayla is unhappy because _____

_____

↓

Kayla misses _____

↓

Kayla meets _____

↓

They _____

↓

Kayla learns that _____

_____

4. Fill in the missing letters. Write Evie's letters to Kayla. Then work with a partner. Evaluate each other's letters and decide which ones to use to fill in the gaps. (You may even decide to combine two letters into a new one.) Then take turns reading Kayla and Evie's letters. Make sure you read them with expression, capturing the way the characters are feeling.

Writing	☑
Research	☐
Listening and Speaking	☑
Media Literacy	☐
21st Century Skills: Collaboration	☑
Cross Curriculum Connection	☐

5. Work with a partner. Write a story together as a series of letters. Decide on who the two main characters will be. Talk about what they are like. Keep a two-column chart to record details. Then decide on the story problem. Each of you should take the part of one character. Then write letters back and forth to each other to tell the story.

Writing	☑
Research	☐
Listening and Speaking	☑
Media Literacy	☐
21st Century Skills: Collaboration	☑
Cross Curriculum Connection	☐

On Your Own

Read the selection below. Then answer the questions that follow it.

Literature Connection

Penguin Hill

by Jill Nogales

1   My little sister was lying in the snow again. "What are you doing?" I asked.

2   "Making snow angels," Kate said.

3   She moved her arms and legs back and forth. "Try it, Pete."

4   I shook my head. I had better things to do than lie in the snow.

5   Behind our cabin is a hill. I had watched some kids riding their sleds down it yesterday. They called it Penguin Hill.

6   This was our first time at the cabin. Kate and I had never had a chance to play in snow before.

"Penguin Hill" by Jill Nogales, Copyright © 2009 by Highlights for Children, Inc., Columbus, Ohio

 Measuring Up to the Texas Essential Knowledge and Skills

7   So far, Kate and I had built a snowman and a snow fort. But now I wanted to go sledding down Penguin Hill like the other kids.

8   Today, I was going to give it a try. Pulling the sled behind me, I headed toward the hill. But before I got there, my hands started hurting from the cold.

9   I looked back at Kate. She was wearing mittens.

10   "That's what I need," I said. "Mittens!"

11   Back at the cabin, I tucked my hands inside my fuzzy blue mittens. Then I headed toward the hill again with my sled.

12   My boots crunched in the snow with each step. Climbing a snow-covered hill isn't easy when you're dragging a sled.

13   I looked down to where Dad was shoveling snow. He waved at me and said, "Have fun, Pete! And remember to hang on with both hands."

14   This morning, I had talked to Dad about sledding down Penguin Hill. He found a sled for me in the shed behind the cabin. Then he showed me where to sit and how to steer.

15   At the time, it had seemed like a good idea. But now I wasn't sure I was brave enough.

16   My foot slipped and I fell facedown in the snow. Then I realized I had let go of the sled. I watched it slide to the bottom of the hill.

17   "What are you doing?" Kate asked as I trudged down the hill.

18   "I'm sledding," I said.

19   "Aren't you supposed to sit on the sled before it goes down the hill?" she asked.

20   I thought maybe I should forget about sledding and make snow angels instead. But then I remembered the other kids laughing and shouting as they slid down the hill.

21   Holding tight to the sled rope, I hiked up the hill again.

22   From the top, the hill looked a lot steeper than it did from the bottom. Did I really want to do this? I sat on the sled to think about it. But then the sled started to slide. I grabbed the rope and held on.

23   "Watch out below!" I yelled as I raced downhill.

24   Before I knew it, the ride was over. I slid to a stop near Kate's snow angels.

25   "Did you see me, Kate?" I asked. "I rode the sled down Penguin Hill!"

26   Kate smiled and clapped for me. I felt so brave, I decided to do it again.

Answer the following questions based on the passage you just read.

1. Read the paragraphs below.

> *My little sister was lying in the snow again. "What are you doing?" I asked.*
>
> *"Making snow angels," Kate said.*
>
> *She moved her arms and legs back and forth. "Try it, Pete."*
>
> *I shook my head. I had better things to do than lie in the snow.*

Does the way Pete acts seem believable? In other words, does it seem like the way an older brother might act toward his younger sister? Explain your answer.

_____

_____

_____

2. Which detail explains why Pete isn't wearing mittens in paragraph 8?

   A   His sister is wearing his mittens.

   B   He didn't realize it was cold out.

   C   The older children do not wear mittens.

   D   He has never played in the snow before.

3. Complete the character chart below to show that you understand the main character.

Who is the main character?	
What do you know about this character?	
What does he want to do?	
Why doesn't he do it at first?	

4. Kate's comment in paragraph 19 shows that she is —

A afraid her brother will hurt himself

B trying to help her brother

C mocking her brother

D confused about how to sled

5. Read the last two paragraphs.

> *"Did you see me, Kate?" I asked. "I rode the sled down Penguin Hill!"*
>
> *Kate smiled and clapped for me. I felt so brave, I decided to do it again.*

How has Pete changed?

_____

_____

Critical Thinking

6. Imagine you are Kate. Write a journal entry telling about your brother learning how to sled. After you are done, read your entry aloud to a partner. Then listen to your partner's entry. Talk about how the entries are the same and different.

Writing	☑
Research	☐
Listening and Speaking	☑
Media Literacy	☐
21st Century Skills: Collaboration	☑
Cross Curriculum Connection	☐

Identify the Narrator or Speaker

3.8(C)	Identify whether the narrator or speaker of a story is first or third person.
Ⓢ 3.2(B)	Ask relevant questions, seek clarification, and locate facts and details about stories and other texts and support answers with evidence from text.
Ⓡ Figure 19(D)	Make inferences about text and use textual evidence to support understanding.

Understand the TEKS

The Narrator

A story has a **narrator**. This is the person who is telling it. The narrator can be a character in the story or an outside storyteller.

> **Words to Know**
> first person
> narrator
> third person

First Person

Some stories are told by a character who identifies himself or herself as *I*. (The pronoun *I* is a first-person pronoun.)

You learn what happens through the "I" character's eyes. You learn what this character thinks and feels.

Read the paragraph below.

> Just at that moment, I saw the boat drifting away from the dock. I tried to get the rope, but it was just out of my reach. I quickly ran up the dock steps to get help. *Skyler would be angry if his boat got away*, I thought. *He would not be happy at all.*

• How do you know this story is told in the first person?

_____

• What is the narrator worried about in the last sentence?

_____

Third Person

In some stories, the narrator is not a character in the story.
The storyteller stands outside the story and tells it. The story is told in the third person. All the characters are identified by the pronouns *he, she,* or *it*. These are third-person pronouns.

The storyteller may focus on one character, telling you what this character thinks and feels. Or the narrator may move from character to character.

> Just at that moment, Elena saw the boat drifting away from the dock. She tried to get the rope, but it was just out of her reach. She quickly ran up the dock steps to get help. She knew that Skyler would be angry if his boat got away. He would not be happy at all.

- How do you know this story is told in the third person?

_____

_____

- On which character does this passage focus?

_____

Comprehension Tip

Words in quotation marks are the words a character says. The pronouns in these words do not help you identify the point of view. Instead, look at the pronoun in the stem.

"I don't want to go," *he* said.

Guided Instruction

Read the passage below. Then answer the questions in the margin and complete the activities.

Literature
Connection

Run-Out Rick
by Ann Treacy

1   I have a problem. I run out of things. My friends even call me Run-Out Rick. Ninety-nine percent of the time, running out is a bad thing. But once, just once, I lucked out.

2   It all started last Thursday morning when the milk ran out and I had to eat cereal with my fingers like it was popcorn. That made me late, but I can get ready for school fast as fleas.

3   However, last Thursday I also ran out of clean socks, clean underwear, and toothpaste. And the bar of soap in the shower was thinner than my favorite pajamas. I could look right through it to see that there were no more clean towels. Just then I ran out of warm water.

4   I was running out of things faster than my allowance runs out in a candy store.

5   The good thing about last Thursday was that it was the last day of school. My teacher, Miss Lange, asked us to write essays about our plans for summer break. My pen ran out of ink, and I had to finish writing with a colored pencil.

6   When we finished, we began taking turns reading our essays. I was eager to tell everyone about my plans to visit Yellowstone before Old Faithful runs out of water. My turn was getting closer and closer when Miss Lange said, "I'm sorry, Rick. We've run out of time."

"Run-Out Rick" by Ann Treacy Copyright © 2007 by Highlights for Children, Inc., Columbus, Ohio

Guided Questions

Read paragraph **1**. Highlight all the pronouns Rick uses to refer to himself. Is this story told in the first person or the third person?

_____

Read paragraphs **2**–**4**. What is Rick's problem?

_____

Highlight the word in paragraph **6** that tells how Rick feels about reading his essay aloud. How do you think he feels when the teacher says they have run out of time?

_____

7   At lunch I ran out of milk money. At home we had run out of peanut butter, so I ate a jelly-only sandwich. At the end-of-school party we ran out of kids, so I had no partner for the three-legged race.

8   I was running out of patience until I remembered that every year my family leaves for a camping trip on the last day of school. I was excited to see that my parents had the packed car waiting when I got home.

9   My whole family goes on the camping trip—aunts, uncles, and cousins. The good thing about a big family is that you never run out of kids to play with! The bad thing is that you run out of everything else, like bug spray, dessert, and tent space.

Read paragraph **9**. Highlight what Rick thinks is the good thing about having a big family. Then highlight what he thinks is the drawback.

10   Did I mention that last Thursday was also my birthday? At the campground, a sign above the mess tent said **Happy Birthday, ick!** because the party store had run out of **R**'s.

11   Uncle Joe, my favorite uncle, is only seventeen. When he saw me, he waved and called, "Rick, my man! Happy birthday. I planned to surprise you with a remote-controlled airplane."

12   "You did?" I said. "Is it here?"

13   "Rick, Rick, Rick. I *planned* to, kid. But the store ran out, so I got you this cool kite instead."

14   I went fishing, but the lake ran out of fish. I juggled oranges until I ran out of hands. I was next in line when the hot dogs ran out. By now you can guess right where I was when the marshmallows ran out.

15   It was the end of a not-so-good day. I had on my mother's socks and my little brother's dinosaur underwear. My teeth felt like they were wearing sweaters. I had a kite instead of a remote-controlled airplane. I ate my empty hot-dog bun and s'more with no marshmallow.

Read paragraph **16**. Why does Rick decide he has to find a cot?

_____

_____

_____

16   I remembered last year's campout—we ran out of sleeping places, and I ended up with no pillow in the backseat of a car with Cousin Molly's smelly dog, Boot. This year I *had* to find a cot to sleep on.

17 I was tired and running out of energy, and daylight was running out, too, so I collected a sleeping bag, a pillow, and a flashlight, and began my search for a cot.

18 As I passed the mess tent, I heard Uncle Joe explaining a card game to some of my cousins. "I'm so good at this game," he bragged, "that I'll give my personal pup tent and deluxe air-filled mattress to any kid who can beat me at it."

19 I kept walking: cards didn't seem like a good idea with my luck. But I skidded to a stop when I heard him say, "the winner is the one who runs out of cards first."

20 I jumped right into the game and that one time my special talent paid off.

21 Last Thursday night I slept well—in a tent, on a wonderful air-filled mattress.

Guided Questions

In paragraph **17**, highlight the words that tell you how Rick feels when he begins his search for a cot.
Read the end of the story. Why does Rick win the card game?

_____

_____

_____

_____

_____

Answer the following questions based on the passage you just read.

1. Because this story is told by Rick, you get to see inside his mind. Read the paragraph below.

> *I was running out of patience until I remembered that every year my family leaves for a camping trip on the last day of school. I was excited to see that my parents had the packed car waiting when I got home.*

In the first sentence, how is Rick feeling? What words tell you this?

_____

What does Rick remember?

_____

_____

How does he feel when he sees the packed car?

2. Read the paragraphs below.

> *Uncle Joe, my favorite uncle, is only seventeen. When he saw me, he waved and called, "Rick, my man! Happy birthday. I planned to surprise you with a remote-controlled airplane."*
>
> *"You did?" I said. "Is it here?"*

Imagine Uncle Joe were telling the story. What might you know at this point that Rick does not know?

_____

_____

3. Use the word web below. In the outer ovals, jot down details that tell about Rick. You may add ovals if you like.

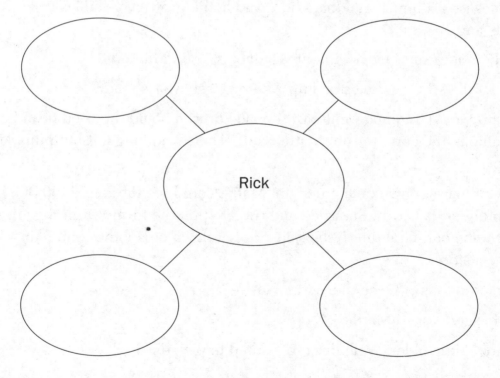

Critical Thinking

4. Part of the fun of this story is that the list of things Rick runs out of goes on and on. Work with a partner. Brainstorm together other things Rick could run out of. Then, working on your own, use the list to create another episode for this story. Meet with your partner again and take turns reading your episodes aloud.

Writing	☑
Research	☐
Listening and Speaking	☑
Media Literacy	☐
21st Century Skills: Collaboration	☑
Cross Curriculum Connection	☐

On Your Own

Read the selection below. Then answer the questions that follow it.

Literature
Connection

The Amazing Turnip

by Frieda Toth

1   On the first day of fall, Mattie sat with Grandma on the steps of the playhouse that used to be a vegetable stand. "Why don't you sell vegetables anymore, Grandma?" Mattie asked.

2   Grandma stretched. "I'm too lazy," she said. "It's a lot of trouble to sell food."

3   "Then why do you have a garden?" said Mattie.

4   "Because it's fun," Grandma said. "And home-grown vegetables make your mouth sing."

5   "My mouth sings even without vegetables," said Mattie.

6   "So it does." Grandma stood up. "Let's go see what's ready."

7   Mattie and Grandma went past the old cornstalks and the tired bean bushes browning in the autumn sun. Mattie said, "There's nothing left but pumpkins and turnips."

8   Grandma sat down on a pumpkin. Mattie could see the round top of a big purple turnip under its leaves. She tried and tried to pull the turnip from the ground. "It won't come out, Grandma," she said. She sat down on another pumpkin. "Will you tell me a story?"

9   Grandma said, "Once there was a girl—"

10   "My age?" asked Mattie.

11   "No, a little older. Well, this girl wanted to pick turnips."

12   Mattie said, "For mashed turnips, right?"

13   "Right," Grandma said. "For mashed turnips, mixed halfway with potatoes. Anyway, she had almost enough for dinner for the whole family when she found one like yours that wouldn't come out. It was one amazing turnip."

14   Mattie said, "Did she give up?"

15   "Nope," said Grandma. "She had a brother, so she went in the house and got him and they both pulled on the turnip."

16   Mattie said, "So the brother pulled her, and she pulled the turnip. But it didn't come out, did it?"

17   "Nope," said Grandma. "It was one amazing turnip. Even with two people pulling, it wouldn't budge."

18   Mattie said, "Well, what then?"

19   Grandma said, "She went and got her mother, and the three of them pulled."

20   "So the mother pulled the brother, the brother pulled her, and she pulled the turnip. Did it come out?"

21   "Nope," said Grandma. "That was one amazing turnip. Even with three people pulling, it wouldn't budge. So she went and got her father, and the four of them pulled."

22   "So the father pulled the mother, the mother pulled the brother, the brother pulled the girl, and she pulled the turnip. Did it come out?"

23   "Nope," said Grandma. "It was one amazing turnip. Even with four people pulling, it wouldn't budge. But there were no more people in the family. It looked as if they were going to have to give up."

24   Mattie said, "Why didn't someone get a shovel and just dig it out?"

25   Grandma stopped talking. She was quiet for a while, then she said, "You know, Mattie, someone should have thought of that. But no one did." She stood up and pointed down the road. "Anyway, just then, the boy who delivered the newspaper rode up on his bicycle, collecting for the month. The girl left the turnip field and went to pay him. Then she asked him to help pull that turnip."

26   "So the paper boy pulled the father, the father pulled the mother, the mother pulled the brother, the brother pulled the girl, and she pulled the turnip. Did it come out?" Mattie asked.

27   "Oh yes!" said Grandma. "They all gave a tremendous pull, and that amazing turnip came out. They pulled so hard that they all fell in the dirt!"

28   "But she finally got her mashed turnips!"

29   "She did. And the one amazing turnip was so big it could have fed half the town. So they invited the paper boy to stay for dinner."

30   Mattie said, "Well, then what happened?"

31   Grandma said, "The paper boy stayed, and he was the nicest boy the girl had ever met, so they grew up and got married, and that was how I met your grandpa."

32   "Grandpa was the paper boy? You were the girl with the turnip?"

33   "Yup!"

34   The sun was going down. Mattie looked at the turnip still in the ground, the turnip that wouldn't budge. She said, "Grandma, nobody else is home right now."

35   Grandma said, "Nope."

36   Mattie said, "And you don't get the newspaper. You read it online."

37   "Yup!"

38   "And I am waaaaay too young for a boyfriend."

39   "Yup!"

40   They looked at each other, and together they said, "We'd better get a shovel."

41   And they went to the shed to find one.

Answer the following questions based on the passage you just read.

1. Sometimes a story has another story inside it. The first story surrounds, or frames, the second story.

    Use the sequence chart below to tell the events in the story about Mattie and her grandmother.

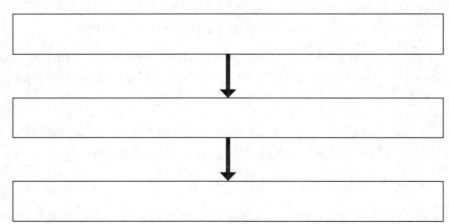

2. Now use the sequence chart to record the events in the story of the amazing turnip. (Two of them have been done for you.)

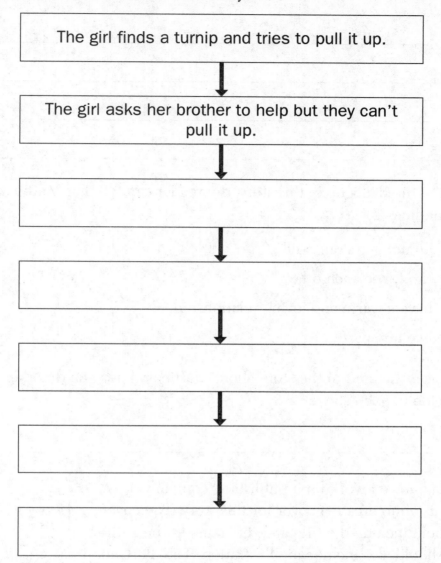

The girl finds a turnip and tries to pull it up.

The girl asks her brother to help but they can't pull it up.

3. Paragraphs 1–8 are told —

  A by an outside narrator in the third person

  B by Mattie in the first person

  C by Grandma in the first person

  D by both Mattie and Grandma in the first person

4. Who tells the story about the amazing turnip that starts in paragraph 9? How do you know?

_____

5. Who does the girl in the story of the amazing turnip turn out to be? Write the line of dialogue that tells you this.

_____

_____

_____

_____

6. From the dialogue in this story, the reader can tell that Mattie and her Grandma —

A do not get along well

B rarely see each other

C have a warm and loving relationship

D live far apart

7. Look at the end of the story about Mattie and her grandmother. Why do they decide to get a shovel?

_____

Critical Thinking

8. Imagine you work for a publishing company. It is your job to create a cover for this story. The cover should include the title and the name of the author. It should also include an illustration. The illustration should give people a sense of what the story is about. It should make people want to buy the book.

Writing	☐
Research	☐
Listening and Speaking	☐
Media Literacy	☑
21st Century Skills: Problem Solving	☑
Cross Curriculum Connection	☐

Read the selection. Then choose the best answer to each question.

The Cat That Could Fly

by Joan Tarcher Durden
from Cricket Magazine

1   I have a cat. A soft and fluffy cat, the color of the smoke that swirls out of the smoke hole when my mother is cooking. A pretty, gray Navajo cat named Suce.

2   Suce has two homes. She lives in my mother's hogan in Chinle, and in my grandmother's hogan a mile away. No one knows when Suce is leaving either of her homes. One moment she's there, and the next she's gone. No one carries Suce from one place to the other. No one sees her walking along the trail.

3   One morning when I crawl out from under my blanket, there is no one to greet me. My mother is not sitting at the fire cooking. My father is not eating across from the fire. Big Sister is not combing her long hair with the hair broom. And Little Boy is not practicing with the bow and arrow that Grandfather gave him.

4   I yawn and stretch and look all around the hogan. I look from the dirt floor that Big Sister sweeps every day, to the rounded wall that my father built of juniper and earth, to the fire where my mother left some fried bread for me. My stomach rumbles, so I eat my breakfast.

5   I pour some goat's milk from the pail into a shallow tin pan and call Suce. But she doesn't come. I call and call. But still Suce doesn't come running for her food. Maybe she is outside hunting for field mice and can't hear me.

6   I stand at the doorway of my mother's hogan. I look out at the yellow sand and the mountains. I look out at my mother's empty sheep corral, and at my father's horses grazing in the distance. But nowhere do I see Suce.

7   Mother sits at her rug loom under the brush shelter. "Have you seen Suce?" I ask. Mother shakes her head. She is busy weaving designs into her rug and watching Big Sister and Little Boy herding the sheep.

8   Father stands at the corral. He is saddling his horse to go to the trading post. "Have you seen Suce?" I ask. But Father shakes his head, too. He is busy fastening the cinch strap around the horse's belly.

9   "I think I will walk to Grandmother's hogan," I say. "She won't know Suce left here without her breakfast." But Mother says the snakes are out and I'm too little to go alone.

10   I start to cry. My father comes and stands beside me. He sings a funny song to make me laugh. He tells me I can sit behind him on the horse and he will take me to Grandmother's hogan.

11   We see no sign of Suce along the winding trail. It is a clear path, not marked by the sharp pointed feet of the sheep, but still we cannot spot her fresh paw prints. All I can see are the hoofprints of Father's horse, showing the way we have come.

     Measuring Up to the Texas Essential Knowledge and Skills

12   When we get to Grandmother's hogan, there is Suce. She is eating breakfast out of a tin plate. Grandfather sits on a wooden box petting her.

13   "Grandfather, did you see Suce coming?" I ask.

14   Grandfather shakes his head. He says he has been sitting and looking at the land since sunrise, but he did not see Suce coming up the trail. He says he just raised his arm to scratch his head, and when he put his arm down, Suce was there.

15   "How did Suce come on the trail unseen?" I ask.

16   Grandfather looks up at the sky, thinking. "Maybe she flies," he says.

17   A few days later Suce comes back to my mother's hogan. I have to know if Suce can fly. So I take Big Sister's green hair ribbon and Little Boy's red headband and my yellow kerchief. I tie them all together and I tie them to Suce's tail. I am sure if she flies back to Grandmother's hogan, someone will see that colorful tail streaking across the sky. Then I will know for sure that Suce can fly.

18   I can hardly wait for Suce to leave my mother's hogan. But this time she stays and stays. And all that time with the funny green, red, and yellow tail tied to her own tail. As annoying as that false tail must be, she never tries to lose it.

19   Today Suce finally left my mother's hogan.

20   And today my uncle is visiting. Uncle says I am silly to think a cat can fly. He offers to take me along the trail and prove to me that Suce walked to Grandmother's hogan.

21   Uncle saddles his horse. He mounts and pulls me up behind him. It is then that we see my yellow kerchief on the roof of the hogan, and Little boy's red headband on the highest pole of the sheep corral.

22   "The wind blew them there," Uncle says.

23   I am not convinced.

24   When we get to Grandmother's hogan, we see Big Sister's green hair ribbon on the roof.

25   "The wind blew it here, too," Uncle says.

26   I am still not convinced.

27   Grandfather comes out of the hogan. He is carrying Suce in his arms. "I found this silly cat on the roof," he says to us. "She was all tangled up in a green ribbon, and meowing."

28   "Grandfather, did Suce fly here?" I asked.

29   Grandfather looks at Uncle. "Did you see any paw prints on the trail?" he asks.

30   Uncle watches Suce slide to the ground and run back into the hogan. He says to Grandfather, "We didn't look closely enough. There have to be paw prints along that trail. Everyone knows cats don't fly."

31   I look up at Grandfather. He gives a little shrug and smiles, so I shrug and smile, too. I know that all cats don't fly. But maybe Suce does.

     Measuring Up to the Texas Essential Knowledge and Skills

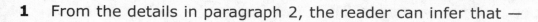
1 From the details in paragraph 2, the reader can infer that —

    A no one cares about Suce's whereabouts

    B Suce prefers grandmother's hogan to mother's hogan

    C Suce can run the mile between the hogans quickly

    D there is something mysterious about Suce

---

2 The details in paragraph 10 show that Father —

    F is warm and loving

    G cannot sing well

    H doesn't take his daughter's worries seriously

    J wants to teach his daughter a lesson

---

3 In paragraph 11, why is it important that there are no sheep footprints?

    A The lack of footprints shows that sheep can fly.

    B This suggests that the winding path is too difficult for animals to walk on.

    C This indicates that the ground is too hard for footprints to show up.

    D Sheep footprints would make it hard to see Suce's paw prints.

4 Read the sentence below from paragraph 31.

> *He gives a little shrug and smiles,*
> *so I shrug and smile, too.*

The reader can infer that —

F neither the girl nor Grandfather likes Uncle

G Grandfather does not want to argue with his granddaughter

H the girl and Grandfather both believe that Uncle is wrong

J the girl thinks that all cats can't fly, but Grandfather disagrees with her

---

5 Which of these words best describes Uncle?

A Imaginative

B Practical

C Stern

D Convincing

6 Which of these best summarizes this story?

F The girl has a pretty cat named Suce who travels from Mother's hogan to Grandmother's hogan. When the girl wakes up late, she cannot find Suce. She wants to go to Grandmother's hogan because she is worried that Suce left without eating breakfast. Father takes her on horseback, but they do not find paw prints along the trail. Suce is there at her grandmother's, eating breakfast while Grandfather sits petting her.

G Suce moves from hogan to hogan, but no one ever sees her coming or going, and they do not see her paw prints along the trail. The girl ties colored clothes to Suce's tail. When Uncle takes the girl to Grandmother's hogan to prove that she can't fly, they find the kerchief on the roof and the headband on a pole. Grandfather finds Suce on the roof tangled up in the ribbon, and he and the girl think they know how Suce got there.

H No one greets the girl when she gets up, and she calls Suce, but Suce does not come running for her food. The girl asks different members of her family if they have seen her, but they have been busy working. The girl wants to see if Suce can fly, so she ties different colored clothes to her tail. Uncle disagrees, and he proves to her that no cats can fly, not even Suce.

J Mother, Big Sister, and Little Boy work at their chores, while the girl searches for Suce. She wants to find out how Suce gets from hogan to hogan without anyone seeing her coming or going. Father takes her to Grandmother's hogan to find Suce, and Grandfather suggests that perhaps she flies. Later Uncle takes her to grandmother's hogan because he wants to prove that Suce cannot fly.

Understand Literary Nonfiction

⑤ 3.9	Understand, make inferences and draw conclusions about the varied structural patterns and features of literary nonfiction and respond by providing evidence from text to support their understanding.
3.9(A)	Explain the difference in point of view between a biography and an autobiography.
⑤ 3.2(B)	Ask relevant questions, seek clarification, and locate facts and details about stories and other texts and support answers with evidence from text.
⑤ Figure 19(D)	Make inferences about text and use textual evidence to support understanding.

Understand the TEKS

Life Stories

The root *bio* means "life." When you see this root in a word, you know the word has something to do with life.

Autobiography

Sometimes people write to tell the story of their own lives. They write an **autobiography.**

An autobiography is the story of a person's life told by that person. (The prefix *auto-* means "self.") The events in an autobiography are true. They really did happen.

When you read an autobiography, the person telling the story is the person that story is about.

Autobiography	
Who Wrote the Story	Who the Story Is About
the author	the author

Point of view refers to the person telling the story. An autobiography is told from the **first-person point of view**. You see the events unfold through the narrator's eyes. You learn what this person thinks and feels.

Just as you use the pronoun *I* to tell about yourself, in an autobiography, the author uses the pronoun *I* to tell about himself or herself.

I was born in Comfort, Texas, on December 15, 1977.

- Suppose you were writing your autobiography. Write a sentence telling where and when you were born.

_____

_____

Words to Know
autobiography
biography
first person
narrator
point of view
third person

Biography

Sometimes people write to tell about another person's life. They write a **biography.**

A biography is the story of a person's life written by someone else. (Notice that the word *biography* does not have the prefix *auto-*, which means "self.")

The author collects information about another person's life. The author has not experienced these events. They happened to someone else.

Biography	
Who Wrote the Story	Who the Story Is About
the author	someone else

A biography is told from the **third-person point of view.**

Because the story is about someone else, the author uses the pronoun *he* or *she* to name this person.

He was born in Comfort, Texas, on December 15, 1977.

- Suppose you grow up to be famous and someone decides to write a biography of your life. Write a sentence about yourself that the author might include in the biography. Use the pronoun *he* or *she*.

_____

_____

_____

Look at the chart below comparing an autobiography and a biography. Both are about Benjamin Franklin.

	Autobiography	Biography
Who the Story Is About	Benjamin Franklin	Benjamin Franklin
Who Wrote the Story	Benjamin Franklin	Dennis Brindell Fradin

Comprehension Tip
Keep a sequence chart as you read an autobiography or a biography. This will help you follow the order of events in the person's life.

Guided Instruction

Read the passage below. Then answer the questions in the margin and complete the activities.

Literature Connection

A Reading Lesson

by Joy Cowley

Guided Questions

> Joy Cowley is the award-winning author of more than three hundred books for children, including *Mrs. Wishy-Washy*, *Red-Eyed Tree Frog*, and *The Rusty, Trusty Tractor*. Her work is loved by children around the world. Joy lives with her husband on a ranch in New Zealand.

1 When I was young, I had a problem learning to read. There were several reasons for this: I changed schools several times, I was not a fast learner, and the way reading was taught in those days didn't have much meaning for me. I was nine before I became a reader. That was when I discovered that reading opened the door to stories, and I really loved stories. I couldn't get enough of them. By the time I was ten, I was reading during every spare moment I had.

2 Now, there weren't a lot of spare moments in my day. My parents were often sick, and we didn't have much money. As the eldest of five children, I needed to work before and after school. But I would walk to school reading a book, read a book under my desk in class, read during the lunch break and again on the way home. Sometimes late at night, I took my father's flashlight to read under the bedcovers.

3 When I was twelve, a neighbor gave me a bicycle. It was very old, but I didn't mind the chipped paint and rattly chain. It was my first bike, and now I could ride to school. Did that keep me from reading? No. I am ashamed to say I rode to school with a book open on the handlebars.

4 In those days, there wasn't a lot of traffic, but even so, my dangerous habit caught up with me. One morning, I rode wham into the back of a parked van.

In this article, Joy Cowley is telling a story about her life. In paragraph **1**, highlight all the pronouns she uses to write about herself.

In paragraph **2**, why can't Joy read as much as she would like to?

_____

_____

Read paragraph **3**. How old is Joy at the time of this event?

_____

In paragraph **3**, highlight the words that tell how she says she feels about reading while riding her bike. Do you think she really felt like this? Why or why not?

_____

_____

_____

       Measuring Up to the Texas Essential Knowledge and Skills

5 The bike was badly crumpled and so was I. My elbows and knee were bleeding, and I had a bump on my head and a broken nose. (That's when I discovered that if you break your nose it doesn't come off in your hand!)

6 If those injuries weren't lesson enough, there was more to follow. The next morning there was a special assembly at school. I had to stand up front between the principal and a traffic officer while all the students heard about my accident and what had caused it. Some kids in my class were quite excited. They thought I was going to prison. When they discovered I wasn't, they lost interest. As for the principal, he said that if he ever caught me reading on my bike again, I would be in very serious trouble.

7 Well, he needn't have worried. My parents couldn't afford to repair the bike, so I had to go back to walking to school—reading a book.

Guided Questions

In paragraph **5**, you learn something funny Joy believed about broken noses. Highlight this information.

Joy doesn't tell how she feels in paragraph **6**, but based on what you have learned, you can probably guess. How do you think she feels?

_____

_____

In paragraph **7**, highlight the reason why Joy now has to walk to school.

Answer the following questions based on the passage you just read.

1. Autobiographies are often told in chronological, or time, order. Read the first paragraph again to follow the sequence of events.

> *When I was young, I had a problem learning to read. There were several reasons for this: I changed schools several times, I was not a fast learner, and the way reading was taught in those days didn't have much meaning for me. I was nine before I became a reader. That was when I discovered that reading opened the door to stories, and I really loved stories. I couldn't get enough of them. By the time I was ten, I was reading during every spare moment I had.*

When did Joy have trouble with reading? When did she become a reader?

_____

_____

What happened when she was ten?

_____

2. Read the paragraph below.

> *Now, there weren't a lot of spare moments in my day. My parents were often sick, and we didn't have much money. As the eldest of five children, I needed to work before and after school. But I would walk to school reading a book, read a book under my desk in class, read during the lunch break and again on the way home. Sometimes late at night, I took my father's flashlight to read under the bedcovers.*

What is Joy's problem?

_____

_____

How does she try to solve her problem?

_____

_____

How could her solution cause a problem?

_____

_____

3. Complete the sequence chart below. Fill in the major events from the episode with the bike.

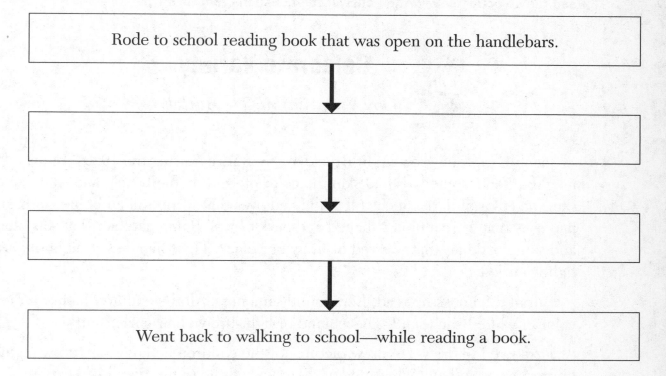

Rode to school reading book that was open on the handlebars.

Went back to walking to school—while reading a book.

4. Because Joy Crowley told her own story, what do you learn about this event in her life that someone else telling the story wouldn't know?

_____

Critical Thinking

5. Think about your life story. Identify a time when you solved a problem. Write about this episode from your life. Use the pronoun *I* for yourself. Arrange the details in chronological order. When you are done, read it aloud to a partner.

Writing	☑
Research	☐
Listening and Speaking	☑
21st Century Skills: Problem Solving	☑
Cross Curriculum Connection	☐

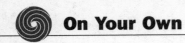

On Your Own

Read the selection below. Then answer the questions that follow it.

Literature
Connection

Celebrate Variety

by Virginia McGee Butler

1   Jacob Ezra Katz grew up in Brooklyn, New York, during the 1920s. In his neighborhood, some kids had skin the color of sand on the beach, and some had skin the color of dark chocolate. Some had eyes that were oval and blue, and some had eyes that were almond-shaped and dark brown. Some had hair that was blond, and some had hair that was red or brown or black. Their hair was straight or wavy or tightly curled.

2   But in the books he read, Ezra found sameness. All the children had skin the color of white beach sand. Their blond or light-brown hair curled softly.

3   Ezra liked to draw. He drew pictures of the children he knew. He drew pictures of grown-ups and animals. None of them looked the same. Ezra liked variety.

Ezra's New Name

4   When Ezra grew up and became an artist, he found out that many people like sameness. It was hard for him to find a job because his name—Jacob Ezra Katz— was a Jewish name. Back then, some places even advertised that jobs were not open to Jews. Ezra was proud of being Jewish, but he felt that he had to change his name to get work. In 1948, he legally became Ezra Jack Keats.

5   Soon Keats was drawing pictures for covers of children's books, and illustrating other writers' stories. In 1960, he coauthored a book with journalist Pat Cherr. As one of the authors, for the first time Keats could choose how to show the story with his illustrations.

Pedro, Peter, and a Lost Dog

6   *My Dog Lost* is about Pedro, a Puerto Rican boy who loses his dog. Keats's story shows the boy looking for his dog in the New York City neighborhoods of Little Italy, Chinatown, Harlem, and Park Avenue. The kids in these neighborhoods don't look alike, but they all want the same thing—to help Pedro find his lost dog.

"Celebrate Variety" by Virginia M. Butler, Copyright 2005 by Highlights for Children, Inc., Columbus, Ohio

7   Ezra Jack Keats created other picture books. His artwork continued to show that all kids don't look the same. He wrote the first American picture book with a black child as the main character. *The Snowy Day* is the story of Peter finding the fun things any boy can do in the snow. Keats modeled Peter on a picture he had found in *Life* magazine in 1940. He had saved the picture for 22 years!

8   In 1963, *The Snowy Day* won the Caldecott Medal. This medal is awarded each year by the American Library Association. The medal is given to the artist of the most distinguished picture book published in the United States.

9   Keats wrote six stories about Peter, showing the boy as he grew up. The stories told about things that happen to most kids—waiting for a present, sending a letter to a friend, having a new baby in the house, or protecting a pair of goggles from a bully.

Kids of All Kinds

10   His books were translated into nineteen languages, including Japanese, Danish, Portuguese, Turkish, Thai, and German. Keats received letters from kids all over the world. He loved to get letters from kids. He kept every one and put many of them on his bulletin board where he worked.

11   In the years since *The Snowy Day* was published, many other writers and illustrators have celebrated variety in their work. Today's books share stories about kids with all types of skin colors, eye shapes, and hair styles. Ezra Jack Keats would have loved seeing the variety.

Answer the following questions based on the passage you just read.

1. Complete the chart below.

Celebrate Variety	
Who is it about?	
Who wrote it?	
Is it an autobiography or a biography?	

2. What can the reader infer from paragraph 4?

    A Jacob was unhappy about changing his name.

    B Jacob's parents had changed their names.

    C Jacob did not like his original name.

    D Ezra Jack Keats was a Jewish name.

 3. Read the paragraph below.

> My Dog Lost *is about Pedro, a Puerto Rican boy who loses his dog. Keats's story shows the boy looking for his dog in the New York City neighborhoods of Little Italy, Chinatown, Harlem, and Park Avenue. The kids in these neighborhoods don't look alike, but they all want the same thing—to help Pedro find his lost dog.*

How are the kids in this book different from each other?

_____

_____

How are they the same?

_____

What does this tell you about the theme, or big idea, of this book?

_____

_____

4. Because this is a biography, what doesn't the reader learn about Ezra Keats?

    A Where he grew up

    B His inner thoughts and feelings

    C What books he wrote

    D Whether or not he was successful

5. Fill in the first column in the chart below.

Children in Jacob's Neighborhood	Children in Books Jacob Read	Children in Illustrations Jacob Drew
	all looked the same	showed a lot of variety

6. Read the last paragraph.

> *In the years since* The Snowy Day *was published, many other writers and illustrators have celebrated variety in their work. Today's books share stories about kids with all types of skin colors, eye shapes, and hair styles. Ezra Jack Keats would have loved seeing the variety.*

How did Keats pave the way for other writers?

_____

_____

_____

Critical Thinking

7. Work in a small group. Go to the library and find some of Keats's books. Each student should select one book to be responsible for. The student should read the book and report on it to the group.

Writing	☐
Research	☑
Listening and Speaking	☑
21st Century Skills: Teamwork	☑
Cross Curriculum Connection	☐

Media Connection

8. You can learn more about Ezra Jack Keats, read some of his books, and play fun games at http://www.ezra-jack-keats.org/.

Read the selection. Then choose the best answer to each question.

Curious Jane

by Nicole Groeneweg
from Appleseeds Magazine

1   The tiny girl huddled in the corner of a henhouse. Waiting for hours, she didn't dare to move. She could hear her family frantically calling her name, but she didn't stir. Valerie Jane Goodall, known as V.J. or Jane, was determined to see exactly how hens laid their eggs. Even as a child (she was 5 years old) Jane had the talent to patiently observe nature.

2   For days, Jane had followed the hens into their coop, but they had only clucked and fluttered away, annoyed with her presence. After several more failed attempts, Jane decided to go into the henhouse before the hens got there. Perhaps then they wouldn't be scared, she thought. So one afternoon when the henhouse was deserted, Jane squeezed in and crouched into a dark corner. For hours, she waited and waited—quietly and patiently.

3   Finally, a hen bustled through the door. Jane barely breathed and did not move a muscle. The hen fussed and clucked, moving straw with her feet, then settled down. Jane watched and waited some more. Her legs were cramped and she ached to move, but she remained still.

4   Finally, the hen raised her rear end and Jane saw what she had waited to see—a white ball hanging between the feathers of the hen's legs. The hen squawked and the white egg plopped into the messy nest. The hen clucked and inspected the egg, arranging it with her beak. Pleased with her accomplishment, the hen rejoined the other feeding chickens.

5   Jane was pleased too as she burst from the chickens' hutch and ran toward the frantic searchers.

6   Jane's grandmother, Danny, was one of the first to notice her granddaughter's love of nature. She watched Jane climb trees and play with her favorite dog, Rusty. One Christmas, Danny gave Jane a tree of her own. Jane named it "Beech."

7   Jane spent countless hours reading her favorite books, including the stories about Tarzan and Dr. Dolittle. She dreamed she would go to Africa as they did. She wanted to live and work with animals just as Dr. Dolittle did.

When Jane was a baby, a chimp named Jubilee was born at the London Zoo. Jane was given a stuffed toy named Jubilee. It was the beginning of a life spent loving animals.

8   As Jane was growing up in England, her interest in nature grew too. At 12 years old, she organized a nature club with two close friends and her younger sister. The girls called themselves the Alligator Club and each had a special name. Jane called herself Red Admiral after the butterflies that flitted through her garden.

9   Red Admiral and the rest of the Alligator Club opened a nature museum in an abandoned greenhouse. They showcased everything from birds' nests to animal bones. Alone with their guinea pigs and many natural artifacts, they displayed a human skeleton. It was left over from an uncle's medical school days. They used the money they earned from the museum's small entrance fee to help save old horses.

10   Jane's childhood dreams came true. She grew up to be the world-famous <u>primatologist</u>, conservationist, and humanitarian, Dr. Jane Goodall. And the curiosity and patience she had as a child helped her to make her groundbreaking discoveries—new knowledge that changed our understanding of both human beings and animals.

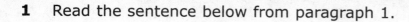

1 Read the sentence below from paragraph 1.

> *She could hear her family frantically calling her name, but she didn't stir.*

Why didn't Jane answer her family?

A She was playing a game with her family.

B She was too excited to speak.

C She didn't care that her family was worried.

D She didn't want to scare the hens.

---

2 Which of these sentences best shows that when Jane was a child, she didn't give up easily?

F *She wanted to live and work with animals just as Dr. Dolittle did.*

G *At 12 years old, she organized a nature club with two close friends and her younger sister.*

H *Jane was pleased too as she burst from the chickens' hutch and ran toward the frantic searchers.*

J *After several more failed attempts, Jane decided to go into the henhouse before the hens got there.*

3 Read this sentence from paragraph 1.

> *Even as a child (she was 5 years old) Jane had the talent to patiently observe nature.*

The author includes this sentence mainly to help the reader understand —

A why patience is important when you are growing up

B why she was successful as a scientist when she grew up

C that Jane was talented when she was 5 years old

D how she became interested in studying animals

---

4 Which sentence from paragraph 9 best supports the idea that Jane was charitable and cared for the welfare of animals?

F *Red Admiral and the rest of the Alligator Club opened a nature museum in an abandoned greenhouse.*

G *They showcased everything from birds' nests to animal bones.*

H *Alone with their guinea pigs and many natural artifacts, they displayed a human skeleton.*

J *They used the money they earned from the museum's small entrance fee to help save old horses.*

---

5 In paragraph 10, the word <u>primatologist</u> means —

A a person who studies chimpanzees, gorillas, and monkeys

B the study of chimpanzees, gorillas, and monkeys

C a group of animals that includes chimpanzees, gorillas, and monkeys

D able to study chimpanzees, gorillas, and monkeys

6 Which of these is the best summary of this selection?

F When she was twelve, Jane Goodall started a nature club. She called herself Red Admiral, and the club was called the Alligator Club. She wanted to study nature when she grew up, and she did.

G When she was five, Jane Goodall showed her love of nature. She also showed her curiosity. She spent days following hens around until she saw one lay an egg. This made her very happy.

H As a young girl, Jane Goodall patiently observed a hen laying an egg. She read many books about nature and put together a nature club. When she grew up, she studied nature and animals and made many new discoveries.

J Jane Goodall grew up to be a famous scientist who studied animals and nature. She showed her love of nature when she was a little girl. Jane's grandmother noticed Jane's love of nature when she played with her dog.

Make Inferences and Draw Conclusions About Author's Purpose

ℝ **3.12**	Identify the topic and locate the author's stated purposes in writing the text.
ℝ **Figure 19(D)**	Make inferences about text and use textual evidence to support understanding.
ℝ **Figure 19(E)**	Summarize information in text, maintaining meaning and logical order.

Understand the TEKS

Topic

The **topic** is what the article is about. The topic can be anything the author wants to write about.

Sample Topics

bears	city life	native American tribes
pizza	clothing styles	life in colonial America
animated movies	holidays in Mexico	

Author's Purpose

The author's **purpose** is why the author is writing. Here are some of the reasons:

> **Words to Know**
> describe
> entertain
> inform
> persuade
> purpose
> topic

• Write to Inform or Explain

The author's purpose is to give information or explain something. For example, textbooks, articles, and how-to instructions are written mainly to inform or explain.

• Write to Persuade

The author's purpose is to persuade you to do something or to believe something. For example, advertisements, TV commercials, and book reviews are written mainly to persuade.

• Write to Describe

The author's purpose is to help you see or experience some place or thing or person. For example, character sketches and travel articles about special places are written mainly to describe.

• Write to Entertain

The author's purpose is for you to enjoy the writing. For example, anecdotes, or little stories about real people, are often written to entertain.

Authors write for different reasons. Two writers can write about the same topic but have different purposes.

For example, imagine the topic is bears. One author might write to give information about bears. Another author might write to tell an entertaining story about bears.

Topic: Bears	
Purpose	**Purpose**
To give information about bears	To tell an entertaining story about bears

• Suppose you wrote about bears. As the author, what would be your purpose?

_____

Authors may have other purposes for writing as well. For example, suppose the author's main purpose is to give information about what bears eat. The author may also want readers to recognize that bears in the wild are just that—wild animals, not pets.

Comprehension Tip
Preview the article before you read. Look at the title. Look at any special graphics. Glance through the article to get an idea of what it is about. This will help you identify the author's purpose.

Guided Instruction

Read the passage below. Then answer the questions in the margin and complete the activities.

Social Studies Connection

The Supreme Court: The Highest Court in Our Land

by Kathy Zahler

1   It is a time of change on the Supreme Court. One member of the Court is stepping down. Now the President must find another member to join the Court. Who can do this important job? People are talking about it. You should know a bit about the Supreme Court. Then you can talk about it, too.

2   Why is the Supreme Court so important? Well, it is the highest court in the United States. Other courts may make decisions. The Supreme Court may decide that those decisions are right. It may decide that the decisions are wrong and overturn them. That may change the way that the laws are understood.

3   The nine men and women on the Court have a lot of power. They can decide which cases are important. They may choose to hear those cases. That means that they listen to the arguments and make a decision. They may also make rules for other, lower courts.

"The Supreme Court: The Highest Court in Our Land" by Kathy Zahler

---

Guided Questions

Read the title. What is the topic of this article?

_____

In paragraph **1**, the author tells her purpose for writing. What is it? Highlight the sentences that tell you.

_____

_____

_____

_____

Read paragraph **2**. What does the author want the reader to learn from this paragraph? Highlight the sentence that states the topic of the paragraph.

_____

_____

_____

Read paragraph **3**. What can the reader learn from this paragraph? Highlight the sentence that tells you the topic.

_____

_____

 Measuring Up to the Texas Essential Knowledge and Skills

4   One person on the Court is named the Chief Justice of the United States. The Chief Justice enters the courtroom first. The Chief Justice casts the first vote in any decision. The Chief Justice decides who will write the Court's opinion. The Chief Justice also swears in the President of the United States. That's an important job!

5   A job on the Supreme Court is a job for life. A justice may retire, or he or she may choose to stay forever. On average, a justice serves for 16 years. Some justices have served for over 30 years! It is a big job, and it can last a long time. For that reason, a President must choose wisely.

Guided Questions

Read paragraph **4**. Why did the author include this paragraph?

_____

_____

_____

Read paragraph **5**. What is the purpose of telling the reader that "a job on the Supreme Court is a job for life"?

_____

_____

_____

Answer the following questions based on the passage you just read.

1. Fill in the chart below. Use your own words. Choose a reason from each paragraph in the selection.

Why is it important to choose a Supreme Court justice wisely?

Paragraph 2: _____

Paragraph 3: _____

Paragraph 4: _____

Paragraph 5: _____

2. Use the chart you just filled in to write a summary of this article.

_____

_____

_____

_____

3. In addition to informing you about the Supreme Court, the author may also wish to persuade you of something. What is it?

_____

_____

Critical Thinking

4. Talk to a partner. Do you think that the author proved to you that the Supreme Court is important? Talk about other jobs in government that you think are important. They might be jobs at the town or city level, at the county or state level, or at the national level. Then write a paragraph about one of those government jobs.

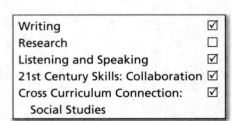

Writing	☑
Research	☐
Listening and Speaking	☑
21st Century Skills: Collaboration	☑
Cross Curriculum Connection: Social Studies	☑

Media Connection

5. You can learn more about the Supreme Court at http://www.congressforkids. net/Judicialbranch_supremecourt.htm.

 **On Your Own**

Read the selection below. Then answer the questions that follow it.

Science Connection

True Blue

by Marsha Getchell

1   There is a mystery in the rain forest in northeastern Australia. To find it, enter the forest at the edge of the grounds at O'Reilly Park. Feel like you're walking into a dark movie theater? Let your eyes adjust to the low light. The thick treetops in the rain forest form a gigantic umbrella called a "canopy." The ground stays damp because sunlight never gets in to dry it out. Notice how quiet it is as you move around? The moist earth and leaves are absorbing the sound of your footsteps.

2   Walk over to the clearing up ahead where more light is coming in. What's this scattered on the ground? Flowers, jewelry, feathers, pebbles . . . and they're all the same shade of blue! Who has left this treasure on the forest floor?

3   Hey, what was that? Up above—did you just see something wing past and skim over the garden of blue? Look! There on that mossy stump—it's a bird no bigger than a pigeon carrying a blue plastic cup. Step back into the shadows and watch what he does next.

4   So, the mystery is solved. This bird, a male satin bowerbird, is the designer of the blue display. Right now he seems very satisfied with it. Just listen to him sing as he struts around!

5   Who's this flying in? A lady satin bowerbird has just arrived. She's the reason for all the male bird's hard work. If his display pleases her, he'll have a wife. The mound of leaves and twigs next to the male's blue treasures is his home or "bower." If the female bird is truly impressed, she'll hop inside and say "I do." Keep your fingers crossed for this little guy.

6   She certainly is taking her time checking out the goods. It looks as if she really goes for all his glass beads. She's making her way toward the door of his bower. It looks like she's going to go inside. Oh, wait a minute—she's turning to take a last look at the bounty.

7   Something catches her eye, and she flits back out to the blue goodies. Oh, too bad. She changes her mind and flies away. Poor satin bowerbird. He'll have to try again.

"True Blue" Reprinted by permission of SPIDER magazine February 2009, text © 2009 by Marsha Getchell

8   There he goes. He's on another mission to find the greatest blue prize ever. Hurry! He's flying out of the forest. See if you can follow him. Look—he's over there at O'Reilly's Guesthouse trying to take a blue jacket off the clothesline!

Answer the following questions based on the passage you just read.

1. Think about the topic of this article. Fill in the chart below.

Where does this bowerbird live?	
What type of bowerbird is the article mainly about?	
Is this article mainly about a male bowerbird or a female bowerbird?	

2. Use the information in the chart to write a sentence telling the topic of this article. Be as specific as you can.

_____

_____

3. The author includes many sensory details mainly in order to —

   A make readers feel as though they are in the rain forest

   B show how humans and birds are different

   C explain how lack of sunlight affects the rainforest

   D persuade readers that bowerbirds can think

4. What is the bowerbird in this article doing? Why is it doing this?

_____

_____

5. Which sentence from paragraph 5 best shows that the author wants the reader to like the male bowerbird?

    A *She's the reason for all the male bird's hard work.*

    B *If his display pleases her, he'll have a wife.*

    C *The mound of leaves and twigs next to the male's blue treasures is his home or "bower."*

    D *Keep your fingers crossed for this little guy.*

Critical Thinking

6. Work with a partner. Choose another animal. Find out how it attracts a mate. Identify sources of information. Divide up the research tasks. After you have both gathered your information, get together to share it and discuss it. Then work together to prepare a report.

Writing	☑
Research	☑
Listening and Speaking	☑
21st Century Skills: Teamwork	☑
Cross-Curriculum Connection: Science	☑

Read the selection. Then choose the best answer to each question.

From Pygg Jars to Piggy Banks

by Marilyn Helmer
from Spider magazine

1   Why are so many coin banks shaped like pigs? Why not dogs or cats or elephants?

2   Coin banks weren't always made to look like pigs. In fact, the name "piggy bank" may have come from a kind of clay and not from the animal at all.

3   The history of the piggy bank goes back to the Middle Ages. At that time in western Europe, metals were expensive to mine. A cheap orange clay known as pygg was used for everyday items such as dishes and jars. In fact, something made from pygg clay was often just called a pygg. The first piggy bank may well have been a pygg in which a thrifty person stashed a few extra pennies to buy a treat on market day.

4   People have always had a penchant for saving pennies. Using a pygg as a coin bank became common practice. Potters began making jars specially for saving coins. These jars took on a piglike shape. Modeling a bank to look like a pig may have come from the name of the clay. Also, people in many parts of the world think the pig

a good luck charm. The earliest Roman coin bank ever found was decorated with a pig. The pig was a valuable farm animal in many countries. It was a symbol of wealth and good fortune.

5   These early clay banks were fragile and easily broken. As time passed, mining became less expensive. Iron, copper, pewter, and silver gradually replaced pygg clay in the production of household items. Although pygg clay lost its popularity, the habit of saving pennies did not. Today people make piggy banks from every material imaginable. These include gold, silver, glass, wood, pottery, and plastic.

6   Do you know the familiar saying, "A penny saved is a penny earned"? It is as old as the early piggy banks. Many a child received his or her first coin bank with this wise advice. The modern-day piggy bank may have changed in size, shape, and spelling. But it saves our pennies just as well as the first pygg did centuries ago.

1 Why does the author begin with two questions?

    A To make the reader think that a coin bank should have a different shape

    B To arouse the reader's curiosity about the shape of piggy banks

    C To introduce the idea that coin banks always looked like pigs

    D To show that the reader already knows a lot about piggy banks

---

2 The main purpose of this article is —

    F to show the difference between pygg jars and piggy banks

    G to give information about the history of piggy banks

    H to encourage readers to save their money

    J to explain how to make a piggy bank

---

3 In which sentence does the author present a possible answer, not something she knows is true?

    A *In fact, the name "piggy bank" may have come from a kind of clay and not from the animal at all.*

    B *The history of the piggy bank goes back to the Middle Ages.*

    C *Modeling a bank to look like a pig may have come from the name of the clay.*

    D *The earliest Roman coin bank ever found was decorated with a pig.*

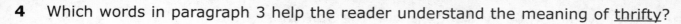

4 Which words in paragraph 3 help the reader understand the meaning of <u>thrifty</u>?

   F *made from pygg clay*

   G *everyday items*

   H *buy a treat on market day*

   J *stashed a few extra pennies*

---

5 Which of these is the best synonym for <u>penchant</u> in paragraph 4?

   A Liking

   B Fear

   C Hatred

   D Luck

---

6 In paragraph 4, the author's main purpose is to —

   F explain why people save their pennies

   G show why people shaped banks in the form of a pig

   H prove that pigs bring good luck

   J tell what potters do

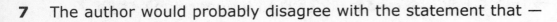

7   The author would probably disagree with the statement that —

   A   saving money is a good habit to develop

   B   piggy banks have an interesting history

   C   today's piggy banks aren't as good as the first pygg banks

   D   a pig is an appropriate form for a coin bank

---

8   The author includes the pictures to show —

   F   how pygg banks have changed over time

   G   that a piggy bank is cute

   H   what the first pygg banks looked like

   J   how many coins a piggy bank holds

Identify Details and Facts That Support Main Idea

R 3.13(A)   Identify the details or facts that support the main idea.
R Figure 19(E)   Summarize information in text, maintaining meaning and logical order.

 Understand the TEKS

Big Idea of Article

Most articles have one **big idea**. This is the main point of the article. It is the big idea the author wants to tell about the topic. The **topic** is what the article is about.

> **Topic:** Music
>
> **Big Idea:** Music plays an important role in our lives.

Words to Know
main idea
paragraph
supporting detail
topic
topic sentence

Main Idea of Paragraphs

Each **paragraph** focuses on one part of the big idea. Usually, each paragraph in an article has its own main idea. The **main idea** is the most important idea.

> **Paragraph Topic:** Music and work
>
> **Main Idea:** Listening to music while you work makes the time pass more quickly.

- What could be another main idea for a paragraph about music and work?

_____

_____

Sometimes a paragraph has a **topic sentence**. This sentence tells the main idea. The topic sentence may be the first sentence of the paragraph. It may also be in the middle of the paragraph or at the end of the paragraph.

Sometimes the author does not state the main idea. You have to state the main idea for yourself. You have to add together the details and tell the main idea in your own words.

Supporting Details

The author includes details to support, or back up, the main idea. Details that support the main idea are called **supporting details**. These details are made up of facts, reasons, and other ideas. These details help to form the main idea.

Paragraph Topic: Music and work

Main Idea: Listening to music while you work makes the time pass more quickly.

Supporting Detail: Some people work more quickly when they hear music with a strong rhythm.

Supporting Detail: Music takes your mind off boring, or repetitive, tasks.

Look at the chart below for an article about celebrating holidays.

Paragraph Main Idea: Celebrating holidays helps us learn about the past.

Supporting Detail: Thanksgiving gives us the chance to learn about the Pilgrims.

Supporting Detail: On Memorial Day, we think about the soldiers who fought in the war.

• What is another supporting detail you could include in this paragraph?

_____

_____

Comprehension Tip

When you read, ask yourself:

• Do I understand the big idea of the article?

• Do I understand the main idea of each paragraph?

• Do I know what details back up the main ideas?

If you can't answer these questions, take time to reread the article or spend a few minutes discussing it with a partner. Be sure to review any words that you do not know or have difficulty pronouncing.

Guided Instruction

Read the passage below. Then answer the questions in the margin and complete the activities.

Science Connection

Home from the Sea

by Kathleen Weidner Zoehfeld

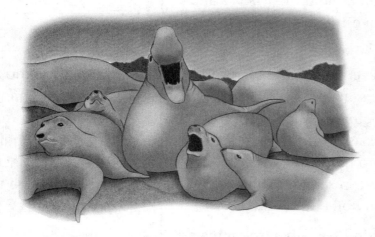

1   In late November the beaches of California's Ano Nuevo Island start getting crowded. But these quiet beaches and others like them are not packed with sunbathers. They are crowded with huge, clumsy blobs of blubber that crawl across the sand like caterpillars the size of hippos.

2   These furry blobs are male elephant seals. Their floppy trunklike noses give you one clue about how elephant seals got their name. The other clue is their size. The biggest males can weigh as much as 5,000 pounds. That's more than a minivan! Every winter they return home to California. They come back from their favorite fishing spots in Western Alaska. It is 3,000 miles away.

3   They look funny on land, as they drag themselves along on their bellies. But they are fast, graceful swimmers. And they can dive deeper than any other type of seal. Some go down almost a mile to get their favorite foods. Their blubber, the thick layer of fat under their skin, helps their bodies withstand the bitter cold and high pressure of the deep, deep sea.

"Home from the Sea" by Kathleen Zoehfeld, from APPLESEEDS October 2005 issue: *Growing Up Before 1492*, Copyright © 2005, Carus Publishing Company, published by Cobblestone Publishing. All Rights Reserved. Reprinted by permission of the publisher

Guided Questions

The topic of this article is elephant seals. Look at the picture and read the first paragraph. Highlight the words in the first paragraph that describe the elephant seals.

Now read paragraph **2**. Highlight the two details the author includes to show how the elephant seal got its name.

Paragraph **3** is mostly about how elephant seals are very good swimmers. What two details does the author include to support this idea?

_____

_____

_____

4   Just like people, seals need to breathe air. But elephant seals can hold their breath underwater for over an hour! They can even sleep underwater! While at sea, they dive almost nonstop. For months, the seals dive and eat fish after fish. They grow as big and as fat as they can.

Highlight the topic sentence in paragraph **4**.

5   Now the male seals have come home to fight. They throw back their heads and roar. They bite and push each other around, protected by the thick skin around their necks and chests. Only the biggest and strongest males will get to mate with the females.

What is paragraph **5** mostly about?

_____

_____

6   Female elephant seals don't have big, long noses. And they are much lighter than the males. Even the biggest females weigh only about 1,600 pounds. While the males were swimming north along the coast for fish, the females swam west. They swam far out into the Pacific Ocean. They zigzagged from place to place in search of a lighter diet of squid. But they, too, return home to breed.

Paragraph **6** is mostly about how female elephant seals are different from male elephant seals. Highlight the detail the author includes to show how they are the same.

7   When they arrive at the beach in December, the females gather together in groups. Within a few days each female gives birth to a little pup. For four weeks the pups drink their mothers' rich milk. They grow fast, gaining up to 10 pounds a day.

8   Once their pups are big and fat, the adult seals mate and then go back to the sea. Elephant seals do not eat when they are on land. So, all of them are very hungry and eager to begin the long journey back to their favorite feeding areas.

In paragraph **8**, highlight the sentence that tells why elephant seals are so hungry when they return to the sea.

9   The pups, now called weaners, stay on shore for two to three more months. They play and paddle around in the water. They slowly are learning how to swim. Soon they will leave the quiet beaches. They will begin their first long migration in search of food.

What is paragraph **9** mostly about?

_____

_____

Answer the following questions based on the passage you just read.

1. Read the paragraph below.

> *Just like people, seals need to breathe air. But elephant seals can hold their breath underwater for over an hour! They can even sleep underwater! While at sea, they dive almost nonstop. For months, the seals dive and eat fish after fish. They grow as big and as fat as they can.*

The author states that both people and seals need to breathe air, but she also includes details that show the differences. How long can elephant seals hold their breath underwater?

_____

What else can they do underwater that humans can't?

_____

2. Read the paragraph below.

> *Female elephant seals don't have big, long noses. And they are much lighter than the males. Even the biggest females weigh only about 1,600 pounds. While the males were swimming north along the coast for fish, the females swam west. They swam far out into the Pacific Ocean. They zigzagged from place to place in search of a lighter diet of squid. But they, too, return home to breed.*

Complete the chart below. Add the details the author includes to support the main idea.

> **Main Idea:** Female elephant seals look and behave differently than male elephant seals.
>
> **Supporting Detail:** _____
>
> **Supporting Detail:** _____
>
> **Supporting Detail:** _____
>
> **Supporting Detail:** _____

3. A summary includes the most important information in an article. Write a summary of the article you just read.

_____

_____

_____

_____

_____

Critical Thinking

4. Articles often include illustrations. Sometimes the main purpose of the illustration is to give information. Sometimes it is to arouse feelings. Look at the illustration with this article. Talk to a partner. Discuss what information this illustration provides. Then talk about the feelings it stirs up. How does it make you feel about the elephant seals? What details in the illustration make you feel this way?

Writing	☐
Research	☐
Listening and Speaking	☑
21st Century Skills: Media Literacy	☑
Cross Curriculum Connection: Science	☑

Media Connection

5. Use the Internet and/or your media center to learn more about elephant seals. A good site to use is http://animals.nationalgeographic.com/animals/mammals/elephant-seal/. Prepare a presentation of your findings. Make an outline of your main ideas and details. Then present your report. Be sure to include photographs to illustration your points.

On Your Own

Read the selection below. Then answer the questions that follow it.

**Social Studies
Connection**

Songs of the Sea

by Catherine Stier

1   You have signed on for months of hard work. You're far from home. The pay is bad. The food is worse. You find rare comfort in the simple songs that you and your work mates sing.

2   This is what a sailor's life was like in the 1800s. The songs sung aboard ships were called *sea shanties* (also spelled *chanteys*). You have probably heard a shanty or two yourself. Many of these songs have lasted through the years. They can often be found in surprising places today.

Sea Shanties Then . . .

3   Sea shanties were valuable friends to sailors. Some shanties, such as "Blow the Man Down," had lively words and melodies. They broke up the boredom of long trips. Other shanties, including one called "Oh, Shenandoah," had a sadder tone. They helped seafarers express longing and loneliness. Still other shanties, such as "Leave Her, Johnny," let sailors grumble about their hard lives.

4   But the first job of the sea shanty was to help the men work as a team. Ships had sails that were controlled by a system of moving ropes. For many jobs, all of the sailors had to tug on the ropes at once.

5   When faced with such a job, the shantyman, or song leader, began a tune. The crew joined in on the chorus, and it might have sounded like a playful sing-along. But when the sailors came to a certain beat, they knew it was the signal to pull together with all of their might.

6   Raising or lowering the anchor called for a rhythm with a slow, steady motion. Then, the shantyman would choose a shanty with a slow, steady beat to match the job. Each duty on the sailing ship had its own rhythm and its own kind of song.

. . . and Sea Shanties Now

7   Sea shanties have been passed down to us in much the same way as folk stories. Long ago, someone came up with a memorable idea and melody. Others repeated the shanty, often adding changes along the way.

---

8   Over time, people saw the sea shanty for the treasure it was. Like any treasure, shanties were collected. Many were written down in books.

9   Where do the old shanties pop up now? Today's musical artists love the fun, beauty, and history of these songs. Many musicians, including Bob Dylan and Harry Belafonte, have their own versions of "Oh, Shenandoah." One group, the Robert Shaw Chorale, recorded a collection of shanties.

10   In Hollywood, shanties serve as a symbol of the sea. A fisherman sings the shanty "Spanish Ladies" in the film *Jaws*. The cartoon character Woody Woodpecker whistles "Blow the Man Down" when he finds himself aboard a pirate's ship.

11   Today, shanties tell us about shipboard life more than one hundred years ago. They help us understand what the working sailor sang and perhaps thought about.

12   So the next time you're doing a boring task, try making up a tune to go along with it. Time may pass more quickly, and your job may seem easier. Also, you may understand why sailors loved those old songs of the sea.

Answer the following questions based on the passage you just read.

1. Read the paragraph below.

> *You have signed on for months of hard work. You're far from home. The pay is bad. The food is worse. You find rare comfort in the simple songs that you and your work mates sing.*

What do the details in this paragraph tell you about a sailor's life at sea in the 1800s?

_____

2. Read the paragraph below. Identify the main idea and supporting details.

> *Sea shanties were valuable friends to sailors. Some shanties, such as "Blow the Man Down," had lively words and melodies. They broke up the boredom of long trips. Other shanties, including one called "Oh, Shenandoah," had a sadder tone. They helped seafarers express longing and loneliness. Still other shanties, such as "Leave Her, Johnny," let sailors grumble about their hard lives.*

Now fill in the chart.

> **Main Idea:** _____
>
> **Supporting Detail:** _____
>
> **Supporting Detail:** _____
>
> **Supporting Detail:** _____

3. The detail about raising and lowering the anchor in paragraph 6 mainly supports the idea that —

　A　a slow and steady rhythm is needed to raise the anchor

　B　this task was a difficult job for sailors

　C　every sailing ship had a heavy anchor

　D　each task had its own type of rhythm and song

 4. What are paragraphs 7 and 8 mainly about?

_____

Write two sentences summarizing the main ideas.

_____

_____

5. Read the paragraph below.

In Hollywood, shanties serve as a symbol of the sea. A fisherman sings the shanty "Spanish Ladies" in the film Jaws. *The cartoon character Woody Woodpecker whistles "Blow the Man Down" when he finds himself aboard a pirate's ship.*

Which sentence in this paragraph is the topic sentence?

_____

_____

6. The main idea of paragraph 9 is that —

A it is fun to listen to sea shanties

B sea shanties are part of the music we hear today

C "Oh, Shenandoah" is a sea shanty

D Harry Belafonte sings sea shanties

Critical Thinking

7. Work in a small group. Identify movies and cartoons in which you have heard sea shanties. Think about pirate movies. Think of animated movies with sea creatures. Talk about how hearing the songs affected your viewing of the movie.

Writing	☐
Research	☐
Listening and Speaking	☑
21st Century Skills: Media Literacy	☑
Cross Curriculum Connection: Social Studies	☑

Elevate

8. Imagine you are living in the 1800s and have signed on to a ship. Write an imaginary journal entry about a day at sea. Be sure to include singing sea shanties.

Measuring Up to the Texas Essential Knowledge and Skills

Lesson 27

Draw Conclusions and Support Assertions

ⓡ **3.13(B)**   Draw conclusions from the facts presented in text and support those assertions with textual evidence.

ⓡ **Figure 19(D)**   Make inferences about text and use textual evidence to support understanding.

Understand the TEKS

Informational articles contain many details and facts. Details are the individual bits of information. For example:

> The seal weighed 28 pounds. It had a shiny coat.

Facts are information that can be proved. For example:

> Independent Day falls on July 4.

Sometimes the author tells you what is important about these details and facts.

Often, the writer doesn't tell you everything. You have to draw your own conclusions.

Words to Know

assertion
conclusion
detail
fact

Drawing Conclusions

Drawing conclusions is putting information together. You add up the details and facts to figure out what they mean.

Detail or Fact	+	Detail or Fact	+	Detail or Fact	=	Conclusion

You draw conclusions all the time. For example, suppose you go to a store that has just opened in your neighborhood. Inside, you see an aisle full of different jars of paints. There is a shelf with different sizes and types of brushes. Two rows are filled with different types of paper. In one section of the store, there are easels. In another, there are frames you can use for paintings.

Before you went into the store, you didn't know what type of store it was. After you looked around, you drew a conclusion. Based on all the details, you concluded that this is an art-supply story.

Now look at the details below.

> **Details:** caw caw sounds are coming from a tree
>
> **Details:** leaves are shaking
>
> **Details:** sound of the fluttering of wings
>
> **Details:** feathers at base of tree

• Draw a conclusion. What animals are living in the tree?

_____

When you state your conclusion, you make an **assertion**. You use details and facts to back up this statement.

Read the passage below.

> Lamar was awakened early on the morning of July 4. His bedroom window faced the main street of town. Normally, the street was very quiet at this time of day, but now it was filled with the noise of bustle and activity. He was about to go back to bed and try to get some more sleep when a drum roll forced him out of bed.

• Draw a conclusion. What is happening outside Lamar's window?

_____

• What facts and details support your conclusion, or assertion?

_____

_____

_____

Read the paragraph below.

> The giraffe was eating leaves. Its head was over the top of the tall tree. Its legs and neck were very long.

• What conclusion do you draw about the giraffe's height?

_____

• What facts or details support your conclusion?

_____

_____

Guided Instruction

Read the passage below. Then answer the questions in the margin and complete the activities.

Science/Health Connection

Doctor Dog

by Jennifer Mattox

Guided Questions

Look at the title. Then read the first paragraph. Who or what is Dr. Dog? Is Dr. Dog really a doctor? Explain.

_____

_____

_____

_____

1 The sun is not up yet, but a three-year-old dog named Ansley is on his way to work. He works at Nationwide Children's Hospital helping children who need therapy. The therapy helps kids learn skills again after they've been sick or injured.

2 Ansley's owner is Jenny Lundine. She is a speech therapist. Jenny brings Ansley to see six kids twice every day.

"Doctor Dog" by Jennifer Mattox, Copyright © 2008 by Highlights for Children, Inc., Columbus, Ohio

3 Ansley plays fetch with kids who need to make their arms or legs stronger. Kids who have lost speech skills learn how to talk again. They give Ansley commands such as "sit," "stand," and "roll over." Kids who have trouble remembering can learn by giving Ansley commands in a certain order.

A Friendly Furry Face

4 Part of Ansley's job is to make kids feel happier. One patient, a two-year-old girl, often wakes up cranky because of her illness. When Jenny says, "Up," Ansley puts his front paws on the little girl's bed. The girl rolls over to see Ansley's friendly furry face. She smiles.

5 During group therapy, the kids do a cheer to encourage one another. Ansley wears big sunglasses and holds a pompom in his mouth. "Ansley adds an exciting layer to what we are already doing," says Jenny.

6 When someone gives Ansley the command "lap," he gently places his paws on the child's lap. Most children love it when Ansley is told to "jump" on their beds so they can pet him. He can also walk backward, turn off lights, and shut doors. He knows forty commands in all. He learned them when he spent six months at a special dog school called Canine Companions for Independence.

Healing Fun

7 Ansley can't give medicine or take X-rays. But he can help kids get better. When the kids don't feel like doing their therapy, Ansley makes it more fun. Having fun helps the kids work harder and heal faster.

8 After a long day at the hospital, Ansley and Jenny are ready to return home. Tomorrow, Doctor Dog will rise early and do it all again.

9 Ansley's job may sound like a lot for a dog. But smart, energetic dogs like Ansley seem to enjoy working. And for the kids at Nationwide Children's Hospital, he's the perfect medicine.

Guided Questions

Read paragraph **3**. Highlight the problems the different children have. Why do you think Ansley can help these children?

_____

Read paragraph **4**. Is Ansley a fierce dog or a gentle dog? Highlight details that support your conclusion.

_____

Read paragraph **6**. Is Ansley the only dog who works with children like this or are there others? Highlight evidence in paragraph **6** that supports your conclusion. Tell how you reached your conclusion.

_____

Read paragraph **9**. Highlight the author's conclusion about how Ansley feels about his job.

Answer the following questions based on the passage you just read.

1. Read the paragraph below.

> *Ansley's owner is Jenny Lundine. She is a speech therapist. Jenny brings Ansley to see six kids twice every day.*

A speech therapist is someone who helps people who have problems speaking. What does this tell you about the type of children Ansley works with?

_____

 2. Find two sentences from the article that support the conclusion you drew for question 1. Then fill out the chart below.

> **Conclusion:** _____
>
> **Detail:** _____
>
> **Detail:** _____
>
> _____

 3. Read the paragraph below.

> *Part of Ansley's job is to make kids feel happier. One patient, a two-year-old girl, often wakes up cranky because of her illness. When Jenny says, "Up," Ansley puts his front paws on the little girl's bed. The girl rolls over to see Ansley's friendly furry face. She smiles.*

Why is part of Ansley's job to make kids feel happier?

_____

_____

Find a sentence from later in the article that backs up your conclusion. Write it on the lines below.

_____

_____

Critical Thinking

4. Talk to a partner about these questions. Do you think Dr. Dog plays an important role in the lives of the children at this hospital? Why or why not? Would they miss him if he didn't visit anymore? As you discuss these questions, use evidence from the article to support your conclusion. Then tell whether or not more hospitals should have programs like this one.

Writing	☐
Research	☐
Listening and Speaking	☑
21st Century Skills: Collaboration	☑
Cross Curriculum Connection: Health	☑

Elevate

5. Another way people are trying to help children in hospitals recover is by sending in clowns. Use your school media center or the Internet to find out more about this program. Then talk to a partner. With the information you learned from the article "Doctor Dog," draw conclusions about caring for ill children.

On Your Own

Read the selection below. Then answer the questions that follow it.

Science Connection

The Black-Capped Wonder

by Constance Brochet

1   It feeds hanging upside down and it weights less than four pennies. It can brave temperatures of minus 60°F, yet it's so tiny and tame, it will come eat right out of your hand. Can you guess what it is?

2   It's the black-capped chickadee, a small grey bird with black feathers atop its head and under its chin. Unlike many other birds, the chickadee doesn't fly south for the winter. It stays—even in places as far north as Alaska. To help it stay warm during the chilly months, the chickadees grow a winter coat of thick feathers that makes it 25 percent heavier than during the summer.

3   In warmer weather, chickadees eat lots of insects—hundreds a day. The little birds will hang upside down on tree branches and look for eggs or larvae hidden on the undersides of leaves. In the fall, chickadees will hide seeds for the colder months—up to 100,000 a year! They'll stuff seeds under bark or in cracks and never hide two in the same place. Amazingly, they have a good enough memory to remember where their stores are throughout the winter.

4   How does the chickadee stay so tiny if it eats so much? The answer to this question has to do with how quickly chickadees burn energy. For humans, chickadees, and all other animals, food fuels the body. It helps it create energy to keep warm. As small as it is, the chickadee needs to eat a lot, especially during the cold months. In fact, chickadees eat 20 times as much in winter as they do in summer. Their normal body temperature drops 10 degrees lower so that they don't have to eat even more. Having a good memory for where they've hidden seeds helps, too. If they spend too much time looking for food, they would burn up more energy.

5   Hunger and cold aren't the only enemies the chickadee faces. Hawks, owls, raccoons, and house cats are among the animals that will prey on chickadees, if given the chance. Other birds, including crows and starlings, will steal and eat its eggs, too.

6   How does the tiny creature protect itself? One way it scares intruders away or warns of danger is with its voice. The chickadee can make 15 different sounds, including a frightening hiss.

"The Black-Capped Wonder" by Constance Brochet, Reprinted by permission of SPIDER magazine February 2010, text © 2010 by Carus Publishing Company

7   Researcher Chris Templeton at the University of Washington has discovered that the different sounds a chickadee makes communicate different messages to its friends. For instance, if a chickadee spots a predator sitting still, it will call out "Chick-a-dee!" Depending on how frightened it is, the chickadee will add "dees" to the end of its call. Each additional "dee" means it is all the more worried.

8   "Chick-a-dee-dee-dee" might mean "Beware! A house cat is around!" while "Chick-a-dee-dee-dee-dee-dee-dee-dee-dee-dee-dee-dee-dee-dee-dee-dee-dee-dee-dee-dee-dee-dee-dee" could mean a more fearsome pygmy owl is lurking.

9   What happens when a chickadee sounds the alarm? Mustering strength in numbers, a group of its friends gathers and mobs the owl until it goes away.

10   This little black-capped wonder may be tiny, but it sure is a tough little survivor— and pretty smart, as well, don't you think?

Answer the following questions based on the passage you just read.

1. Read the paragraph below.

> *It's the black-capped chickadee, a small grey bird with black feathers atop its head and under its chin. Unlike many other birds, the chickadee doesn't fly south for the winter. It says—even in places as far north as Alaska. To help it stay warm during the chilly months, the chickadees grow a winter coat of thick feathers that makes it 25 percent heavier than during the summer.*

What fact do you learn about the chickadee's winter coat?

_____

Think about birds that fly south for the winter. What conclusion do you draw about their coats? Why?

_____

_____

2. All these details from paragraph 3 support the conclusion that chickadees are smart except —

   A they eat lots of insects—hundreds a day

   B they look for eggs hidden on the undersides of leaves

   C they hide seeds for the colder months

   D they remember their hiding places

 3. Read the paragraph below.

> *How does the chickadee stay so tiny if it eats so much? The answer to this question has to do with how quickly chickadees burn energy. For humans, chickadees, and all other animals, food fuels the body and helps it create energy to keep warm. As small as it is, the chickadee needs to eat a lot, especially during the cold months. In fact, chickadees eat 20 times as much in winter as they do in summer. Their normal body temperature drops 10 degrees lower so that they don't have to eat even more. Having a good memory for where they've hidden seeds helps, too. If they spend too much time looking for food, they would burn up more energy.*

Complete the chart below.

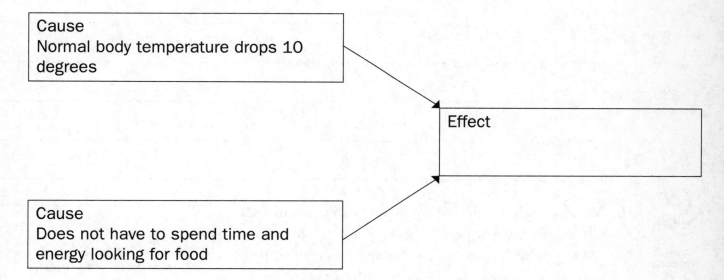

4. Based on the information in paragraphs 7–9, the reader can conclude that chickadees —

   A cooperate with each other

   B battle their enemies

   C are weak animals

   D fight with each other

5. Read the last paragraph.

This little black-capped wonder may be tiny, but it sure is a tough little survivor—and pretty smart, as well, don't you think?

Write an answer to the question at the end of the paragraph. Use facts and details from the article to support your answer.

_____

_____

_____

_____

_____

_____

Critical Thinking

6. Many people think that their pets can communicate. Choose an animal people have as a pet. Then do some research to answer these questions: Can this animal communicate? If so, how does this animal communicate with others of its kind? Prepare a multimedia presentation to present your findings.

Writing	☑
Research	☑
Listening and Speaking	☐
21st Century Skills: Media Literacy	☑
Cross Curriculum Connection: Science	☑

 Measuring Up to the Texas Essential Knowledge and Skills

Identify Cause and Effect Relationships

ℝ 3.13(C)   Identify explicit cause and effect relationships among ideas in texts.
ℝ Figure 19(D)   Make inferences about text and use textual evidence to support understanding.
ℝ Figure 19(E)   Locate and use specific information in graphic features of text.

Understand the TEKS

Cause and Effect

Writers connect ideas to help you follow them. They show how the ideas are related. One way ideas are related is through cause and effect.

> **Words to Know**
> cause
> effect
> reason
> result

The **cause** is why something happens or why something is a certain way. The **effect** is what happens as a result of the cause.

When you tell the cause of something, you give the reason. Read this sentence.

> The veterinarian put the cat on a diet because it was too fat.

Why did the veterinarian put the cat on a diet? The cause or reason is that she was too fat.

The effect is the result. What did the veterinarian do because the cat was too fat? The veterinarian put the cat on a diet.

You can use a graphic organizer to show cause and effect.

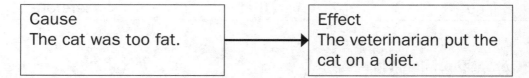

Cause
The cat was too fat.   →   Effect
The veterinarian put the cat on a diet.

Read the sentence below to find cause and effect.

> Rolling in the mud helps the pig stay cool.

• Why does the pig roll in the mud? (This is the reason or cause.)

• What does the pig do in order to stay cool? (This is the effect or result.)

_____

Different Sentences

Sometimes the cause and the effect are in different sentences.

> Washing your hands often is a good tip to follow, especially during flu season. It helps remove harmful germs.

• Why is it a good idea to wash your hands often?

_____

> Polar bears have a thick layer of fat or blubber. It may be as thick as 4 inches. It helps them survive in cold regions.

• What is the effect of polar bears having a thick layer of fat?

_____

Signal Words

Here are some words that signal cause and effect.

as a result	because	in order to
since	so that	therefore

Comprehension Tip

When you read, look for signal words. They can help you identify causes and effects.

To find the cause, ask yourself, "Why did this happen?"

To find the effect, ask yourself, "What happened as a result of this?"

Guided Instruction

Read the passage below. Then answer the questions in the margin and complete the activities.

Science Connection

The Night Shift

from Click Magazine

1   Most people work and play when it's light out. At night, when it's too dark to see well, we sleep. Many animals do the same. But some animals are busiest at night. Why?

2   It's too hot and dry during the day.

3   A frog can die if the hot sun dries out its skin. The night air is cooler and moister.

4   The fennec fox rests in a shady spot to escape the heat of the day. Like most animals living in the hot desert, it waits until night falls to hunt for food.

5   The dark makes it easier for some animals to hide—and for others to be found.

6   Leopards hunt at night, silently sneaking up on their prey. If they're seen, then dinner might get away.

7   A mouse scurrying across a bright, sunny field would soon be seen and eaten. It's harder for enemies to find the mouse in the dark.

8   Fireflies flash their bright lights to tell other fireflies where they are. Would a mate spot the light in the daytime?

9   The skunk's bold white stripes are easily seen in the dark. They warn enemies to stay far away from the skunk's stinky spray.

"The Night Shift" Reprinted by permission of CLICK magazine October 2008, text © 2008 by Carus Publishing Company

---

Guided Questions

Read paragraph **1**. In your own words, tell what question this article answers. Begin your question with the word *why*.

_____

_____

Highlight the cause. This answers the question above.

Highlight the words in paragraph **3** that tell what can happen if the sun dries out the frog's skin. Is this a cause or an effect?

_____

Read paragraph **6**. Why do leopards hunt at night?

_____

_____

10   How do night animals find their way in the dark? They have supersharp senses.

11   Big eyes let in more light and help animals see in the dark. The little tarsier's eyes are huge, even bigger than its brain.

12   The back of a cat's eye acts like a mirror. Light that enters the eye is reflected back, making the eye seem to glow—and giving the cat extra light to see by.

13   The kiwi doesn't need to see to hunt. It uses the nostrils at the tip of its long beak to sniff out worms underground. It's one of the few birds with a good sense of smell.

14   You can see an owl's big eyes but not its ears. Those tuffs of feathers on its head have nothing to do with hearing. The owl's keen ears are hidden behind the feathers on its face. Owls hunt mainly by sound and can find a mouse just by listening to its rustle in the grass.

15   Raccoons have good eyes, ears, and noses. But most important are their nimble fingers. A raccoon can tell if something's good to eat just by touching it.

16   How do you get around in the dark?

Guided Questions

Read paragraph **11**. Highlight the words that explain why the tarsier has such big eyes.

Read paragraph **14**. What is the reason why owls can hunt mainly by sound?

Answer the following questions based on the passage you just read.

1. What three reasons does the article give to explain why some animals hunt at night? Fill in the chart to show your answers.

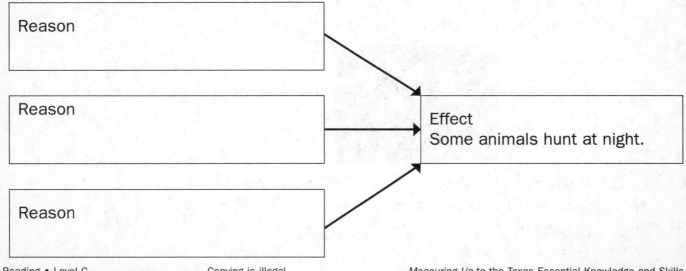

Reason

Reason

Reason

Effect
Some animals hunt at night.

2. Look at the first reason in your chart. Name one area of the country where this would be a reason why animals hunt at night.

_____

Name one area where this wouldn't be a reason.

_____

_____

 3. Reread the paragraph below from the article. Think about cause and effect.

> *Fireflies flash their bright lights to tell other fireflies where they are. Would a mate spot the light in the daytime?*

Answer the question in the paragraph above.

_____

Explain why.

_____

_____

4. Which animal does the article include to show how a good sense of smell can help in the dark?

_____

Which animal shows how animals can use their sense of touch to "see" in the dark?

_____

_____

Critical Thinking

5. Look at the question at the end of this article: *How do you get around in the dark?* Meet with a partner. Share your thoughts about this question. Then, on a separate piece of paper, write a paragraph giving your answer. Include information about how you use your senses other than sight (smell, hearing, touch, and maybe even taste). Be sure to arrange your ideas to show causes and effects.

Writing	☑
Research	☐
Listening and Speaking	☑
21st Century Skills: Collaboration	☑
Cross Curriculum Connection: Science	☑

On Your Own

Read the selection below. Then answer the questions that follow it.

Science Connection

Where in the World Does Wind Come From?

by Dana Nourie

1   Wind scatters leaves around your yard. It carries plant seeds to new places. It cools you down after a kickball game. It seems to blow in every direction at once. But where does wind come from?

2   It comes from everywhere! But how could that be? To understand what causes wind, you first need to know that air expands and rises as it gets warmer. To prove this, try these simple demonstrations.

Magic Power

1. Set a lamp on a table and ask an adult to remove the shade, or use a lamp with a bulb that points downward.

2. Sprinkle talcum powder onto a cloth and wait until all the powder settles.

3. Turn on the lamp and wait a minute or so until the bulb is hot.

4. Gently pick up the cloth and hold the powder a few inches from the hot bulb. Watch as talcum particles magically rise from the cloth.

"Where in the World Does Wind Come From?" by Dana Nourie, Reprinted by permission of SPIDER magazine April 2009, text © 2009 by Carus Publishing Company

3   This is not magic, of course. This light bulb warms the air around it. The air rises, taking the light powder with it. The same thing happens to indoor dust on warm summer days. Have you ever seen dust swirling in a sunbeam shining through a window? You may have noticed that this doesn't happen in winter. That's because winter air is too cool and dense to lift dust particles.

Hot-Air Balloon

1. Ask an adult to heat a pan of water.

2. While the water heats, stretch the mouth of a balloon over the opening of an empty glass bottle.

3. When the water begins to boil, have your adult helper remove it from the heat. Place the bottle in the hot water.

4. Watch as the balloon slowly swells. The air in the bottle is warming, expanding, and rising into the balloon.

---

4   What do these tricks have to do with the wind? Well, the sun heats the earth's surface unevenly. The heated patches of ground warm the air above, making it expand and rise. Then cool air nearby rushes in to replace the warm air. A similar thing happens when you suck air up through a straw and more air rushes in behind it.

5   Because the sun warms the earth in regular patterns, we have regular wind patterns. At the equator, the air constantly heats and rises, so there is little or no wind. The calm zone is called the doldrums. But north and south of the equator, cooler air rushes in to replace the belt of rising warm air, creating two belts of steady wind. Merchants once relied on these winds to help sail their cargo ships from Europe and Africa to the Americas, so they are called trade winds. Other areas of the earth have predictable winds, too.

6   You may have noticed that certain parts of your home region are often windy, while other parts are not. Even small areas have regular heating patterns, and these create local winds. If you live near a mountain in the western United States, you've probably enjoyed the warm chinook that sometimes blows in winter.

7   No matter where you live, you'll welcome a wind into your neighborhood. And now you'll know where it comes from!

Answer the following questions based on the passage you just read.

1. What is the purpose of the demonstration titled "Magic Powder"?

   _____

   Why do you need to use talcum powder?

   _____

2. Look at paragraph 3. Fill in the chart below. Show what happens to dust particles when the air is cold.

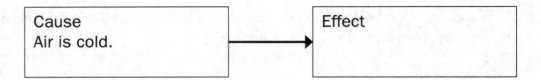

   | Cause
Air is cold. | → | Effect |

3. What is the purpose of the demonstration titled "Hot-Air Balloon"?

   _____

   Why do you need to use a balloon?

   _____

4. There is little wind at the equator because —

   A there is too much rain

   B the air is too cold

   C the air is always warm

   D there is an equal amount of warm and cold air

5. Complete the chart below.

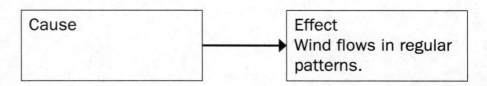

   | Cause | → | Effect
Wind flows in regular patterns. |

6. In "Hot-Air Balloon," which of these does not happen when you place the bottle in the boiling water?

   A The air in the bottle warms up.

   B The air in the bottle expands.

   C The air in the bottle turns colors.

   D The air in the bottle rises.

Critical Thinking

7. Work in a small team. First talk about what you learned from this article. Then design another demonstration. Show the effect of heating air. Using the examples from this article, write the instructions for your demonstration. Create illustrations to show what happens at each step. Present your instructions and illustrations to your class.

Writing	☑
Research	☐
Listening and Speaking	☑
21st Century Skills: Problem Solving	☑
Cross Curriculum Connection: Science	☑

Use Text Features to Locate Information and Verify Predictions

Ⓡ 3.13(D)	Use text features (e.g., bold print, captions, key words, italics) to locate information and verify predictions about contents of text.
Ⓡ Figure 19(D)	Make inferences about text and use textual evidence to support understanding.
Ⓡ Figure 19(E)	Summarize information in text, maintaining meaning and logical order.

Understand the TEKS

The purpose of informational articles is to inform. Informational articles give details and facts about a topic.

These articles often contain special **text features**. These features:

- help you make predictions about the article,
- help organize the information;
- make important information easier to find;
- make the information easier to follow.

Words to Know
boldface
caption
heading
headnote
illustration
italic
key word
list
prediction
section
title

Titles and Headings

The **title** is the words that name the article. A **heading** is a title for a section of an article. A **section** is a group of paragraphs that all deal with the same big idea. An article may have several sections, each with its own heading.

When you preview an article, you look at the title and headings. They give you a general idea about the content of the article. You use them to make **predictions**. As you read, you verify, or check your predictions.

Headings also help you **locate information**. For example, suppose you are reading an article about pirates. You want to find information about the pirate Captain Kidd. When you see the heading **Famous Pirates**, you know you should search for information about Captain Kidd in this section.

Type Treatment

An article may highlight information by using different **type treatments**—the way the type looks.

Boldface type makes information stand out. Headings for sections are often put in boldface type. Important words in paragraphs, called **key words**, may appear in boldface type, too.

Italic type also says, "notice me." But text in italics is often less important than text in boldface type.

Look at the headings below.

      Fruit Juice Smoothies
        What They Are Made of
        Why People Like Them

- Which heading is the most important?

_____

- How do you know?

_____

Words used in special ways may be put in *italic* type or in quotation marks. Words that the author will define may appear in *italics* or **boldface**.

Noticing **boldface** and *italic* type can help you when you skim an article to find specific information.

Headnotes
Sometimes an article starts with a note at the top of the page. It captures the reader's interest or gives important information. Reading the headnote helps you make predictions about the article. The headnote may be set in *italic* type. It may appear in a box.

Illustrations
Informational articles may contain **illustrations**. The purpose of including illustrations is to provide important information.

Illustrations can be drawings or photographs. They can be diagrams that show the parts of something or how to put something together.

Captions tell about the illustrations. Sometimes they are simply a title. Sometimes they provide an explanation of what the illustration shows.

Lists
Important facts and other information may be set off in a list. Usually, the list has a bullet (•) or number by each point.

Comprehension Tip
When you want to find specific information, let your eyes help you. Look for headings and words in boldface type. Try to match them with the fact or detail you want to locate.

Guided Instruction

Read the passage below. Then answer the questions in the margin and complete the activities.

Science Connection

Time to Change Clothes

by Marilyn Kratz

1 Isn't it fun to take off your sweaters and change into T-shirts every spring?

2 Some birds change their "clothes" in spring, too. They do it by *molting*. Molting means losing old feathers and getting new feathers to replace them. New feathers push the old, worn feathers out of the bird's skin.

3 Birds that live in harsh deserts and grasslands usually molt twice a year, in spring and in autumn. Their feathers wear out faster than those of other birds. Most other birds molt mainly in the fall.

| **Guided Questions** |

Preview this article. Look at the title, the headings, and the illustrations. What do you think this article is about? Read on to see if you are right.

_____

_____

_____

Find the word *molting* in paragraph **2** and highlight it. How did the author make this word easy to find? What does *molting* mean? Highlight the definition.

_____

_____

Hiding from the Enemy

4 Molting may take five to twelve weeks to complete. Ducks lose their feathers quickly. They are not able to fly until the new wing feathers grow in. They have dull feathers until then to help them hide.

5 Some birds become a different color when they molt. Ptarmigans can hide more easily all year long.

Looking for a Mate

6 Often male birds wear more colorful feathers after their spring molt. That is when they are trying to attract a mate. Egrets grow long, flowing plumes during spring courtship season. They shed the plumes soon after.

Getting New Colors

7 Some birds get a new color when the faded edges of their old feathers wear down. The inner part of the feather is a different color, and it begins to show. In spring, the male house sparrow gets his black "bib" in just that way.

8 Keep an eye on the birds you see around your yard. Maybe you'll catch them "changing clothes."

Answer the following questions based on the passage you just read.

1. What are the headings in this article? Write them in the chart.

   A _____

   B _____

   C _____

   What type treatment helps you identify the headings at a glance?

   _____

 2. Use the headings above as a guide in order to write a summary of this article.

   _____

   _____

 3. Under which heading do you think you would find the answer to this question: *Why do birds hide when they are molting?*

   _____

   Read that section to verify or check your prediction. Then answer the question: *Why do birds hide when they are molting?*

   _____

   _____

Critical Thinking

4. Work on a team. Imagine your team is in charge of a Web site about birds. Your project is to put this article up on your Web site. To do this, you want to add illustrations. Talk about what illustrations you would like to include. Make a list.

Writing	☑
Research	☑
Listening and Speaking	☑
21st Century Skills: Media Literacy	☑
Cross Curriculum Connection: Science	☑

Then divide up the tasks of searching for illustrations. You may use the library, magazines and books around the classroom, and the Internet. Once your team has found the illustrations, write captions for each one.

 Measuring Up to the Texas Essential Knowledge and Skills

On Your Own

Read the selection below. Then answer the questions that follow it.

A Prickly Adventure

by Barbra Hesson

Ouch! A porcupine's quills are as sharp as needles. They protect the porcupine from its enemies. The name *porcupine* comes from a Latin word that means "thorn pig."

1 | *A baby porcupine is lost in the woods. How does he stay safe?*

2   It is a warm day. A baby porcupine, or *porcupette*, sleeps in the hollow of a tree. Porcupines are awake at night and asleep during the day.

3   The porcupette's mother loves to climb trees. She is sleeping many feet above him. The porcupette could climb when he was just two days old, but he can't yet go as high as his mother.

4   When a beetle tickles the porcupette's toe, he wakes up. He follows it out of the tree. But his eyes cannot see far, and he soon loses track of the beetle.

Out on His Own

5   The porcupette waddles on short legs through the forest. He munches on bark, twigs, and leaves. His favorite things to eat are dandelions and apples. When he comes across an old deer antler, he chomps on that. This helps wear down his growing teeth and provides his body with important minerals.

6   The long shadows turn to darkness. The porcupette is not sure which tree his mother is in, but she will wake up soon. With his long whiskers, the porcupette feels the bottom of a tree. There he curls up and waits for her to find him.

7   The porcupette has keen ears. He hears a snap and the soft padding of footsteps. Is this his mother? He stands on his hind legs and sniffs the air. He has a good sense of smell and knows right away it isn't his mother. He makes a sound like a human baby's cry. Something moves closer. The *something* is a wolf.

Stay Back, Wolf!

8   When the porcupette was born, his quills were soft. But within one hour they hardened into stiff, hollow hairs. Normally his quills lie flat, but now he is scared. His muscles tighten. This raises his quills. If the wolf touches the porcupette, the sharp quills will stick into the wolf's skin.

9   The wolf approaches, and the baby porcupine gives two warnings. First, he makes a clacking noise with his teeth. Second, he gives off a strong smell from a small patch of skin on his lower back.

10   The wolf steps back. He has come across quills before and didn't like them. He turns and runs into the forest.

11   *Sniff, sniff.* A new smell floats toward the porcupette. This time it is his mother. They touch nose to nose, and his mother grunts to him.

12   The baby porcupine makes a soft *mmmmm* sound.

13   Tired but safe, the porcupette follows his mother. They move through the forest in search of more tasty things to eat.

---

14   **Porcupine Points**

- A porcupine does not hibernate during the winter. It finds things to eat, such as twigs or bark, close to home.

- For gripping and climbing trees, porcupines' feet have sharp curved claws and bumpy rough pads.

- A mother porcupine has only one baby at a time. The baby drinks the mother's milk for about a month.

- An adult porcupine is three feet long and weighs up to 25 pounds. Adult porcupines have about 30,000 quills.

Answer the following questions based on the passage you just read.

1. The headnote in italic type helps the reader predict that this article is mostly about —

    A how porcupines care for their young

    B how baby porcupines can get lost

    C what porcupines eat

    D how baby porcupines protect themselves

2. Read the paragraph below.

    > It is a warm day. A baby porcupine, or *porcupette*, sleeps in the hollow of a tree. Porcupines are awake at night and asleep during the day.

    What type feature helps readers locate the word *porcupette*?

    _____

    What is the definition of *porcupette*?

    _____

 3. Reread paragraphs 5–7. What would be another good heading for this section?

    _____

4. Read the paragraph below.

> *The wolf approaches, and the baby porcupine gives two warnings. First, he makes a clacking noise with his teeth. Second, he gives off a strong smell from a small patch of skin on his lower back.*

Use details from the paragraph to complete the chart.

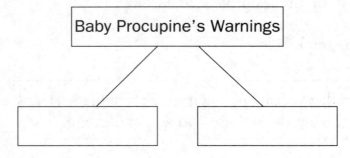

Baby Procupine's Warnings

 5. Look at the list. What type feature makes it easy to identify each of the points?

_____

Why do you think the author used this type feature instead of numbers?

_____

6. Where can the reader find information about the origin of the word *porcupine*?

   A In the caption under the illustration

   B In the section under the heading **Out on His Own**

   C In the section under the heading **Stay Back, Wolf!**

   D In the list under the heading **Porcupine Points**

Critical Thinking

7. Talk to a partner. Discuss how the type features made this article easier to read. How did they make it easy to locate information? Draw up a summary of your discussion.

Writing	☑
Research	☐
Listening and Speaking	☑
21st Century Skills: Teamwork	☑
Cross-Curriculum Connection	☐

Read the selection. Then choose the best answer to each question.

Big Red Roo!

by Kathy Kranking
from Ranger Rick Magazine

1   It leaps like a rabbit. It kicks like a horse. It has the head of a deer. And its babies look like gummy bears. Yep—with a red kangaroo, we get the whole zoo.

2   A *red kangaroo* may look like a blend of different animals, but it's a kangaroo, through and through. This hopper is the largest of all roos, standing about as tall as a human grownup. Its hops are big, too. With long, strong legs like pogo sticks, a red roo can travel 25 feet in a single leap. That's about as far as six 10-year-old kids lying head to toe along the ground. And it travels at speeds of up to 30 miles per hour.

3   A red roo's thick tail is almost as long as its body. The roo uses it for balance when hopping. When not hopping, it uses the tail to support itself, kind of as a third leg.

4   Kangaroos can't move their legs separately. They always either hop or "crawl" by putting their weight on their front paws and tail while lifting their feet forward.

5   Red kangaroos live in the grasslands and deserts of Australia. The weather there is hot and dry, but these kangaroos have no problem keeping their cool.

6   To keep cool in their warm home, red roos do a weird thing: they wet their arms with saliva. And check out that big-clawed paw. A roo's front paws are good for digging out a shallow resting spot in the dirt. They also come in handy when the roo is defending itself.

7   As the sun begins to go down, roos get up. They search for food while the air is cool. They may even find a waterhole for a group slurp.

STAYING COOL

8   Red kangaroos live in areas that get hot during the day and have little rain. But these hoppers have ways of beating the dry heat. Remember how a red roo is like a combination of a lot of animals? Add "camel" to the list. Just as camels can go for long periods without drinking, roos can, too. The roos do it by getting their water from the foods they eat—mostly grasses and other plants.

9   Red roos also keep cool by "chilling out." If they were active all day while the sun was out, they'd just get hotter. Instead, they dig shallow beds to lie in and wait out the heat. If they're lucky, they can find a shady shrub and dig a bed next to it. Then, after the sun goes down and things cool off, they spend the night looking for food.

10   You might say that red kangaroos have this next trick "up their sleeves." They lick their arms until the fur and skin there are sopping wet. When air blows across the wet areas, the saliva underlineevaporates. That carries away body heat and helps cool off the roos.

11   And the last thing red roos do to stay cool? They pant. Guess we can add "dog" to the list, too!

       Measuring Up to the Texas Essential Knowledge and Skills

12   Supporting themselves with their strong tails, two male kangaroos "duke it out" (**see photo right**). Roo fights include scratching, pawing, wrestling, and kicking. Extra-thick skin on the stomach and neck helps prevent serious injuries.

PUT 'EM UP!

13   Red kangaroos may look peaceful, but they can get rough and tough. Males "box" with each other using their arms. They also lean back on their tails and kick each other with their powerful back legs. Their fights are usually to decide who will mate with a female.

14   Like all kangaroos, red roos are *marsupials* (mar-SOO-pee-uls), which means they raise their young in pouches. A baby roo, called a *joey*, is born "not quite done." It's pink, hairless, and blind. But it has strong legs and tiny claws.

15   Right after a joey is born, it crawls across its mother's belly to her pouch. Inside the pouch, the baby finds a nipple and grabs on to it with its tiny mouth. There it stays, drinking its mother's rich milk and growing, week after week after week.

OUT OF THE POUCH

16   Finally, after about four to five months, the joey pokes its head out of the pouch for the first time. After a few more weeks, it begins crawling out of the pouch to explore. But at any signs of danger—such as wild dogs called *dingoes*—it hops back into the pouch.

17   After spending months growing inside its mother's pouch, a joey begins peeking out at the world. Even after it has moved out of the pouch, it still helps itself to a quick drink once in a while.

18   The joey soon begins spending more and more time out of the pouch, still poking its head back in for drinks of milk. It also begins eating grasses and other food. And eventually it is able to take care of itself, leaping like a rabbit, kicking like a horse . . . well, you know—being a whole zoo in one kangaroo.

    Measuring Up to the Texas Essential Knowledge and Skills

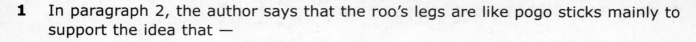

1 In paragraph 2, the author says that the roo's legs are like pogo sticks mainly to support the idea that —

   A its legs are very strong

   B roos are good at leaping

   C roos can travel up to 30 miles an hour

   D red roos are about as tall as human adults

---

2 What is the main reason the author includes headings in bold type?

   F To help the reader know what information is in each section

   G To tell the main idea of the whole article

   H To show why there are pictures with this article

   J To make the article more interesting

---

3 The author includes the first picture mainly to show —

   A how the roo slurps water

   B how the roo digs a hole

   C that the roo has large claws on its front paws

   D how the roo keeps cool

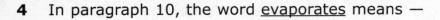

4   In paragraph 10, the word <u>evaporates</u> means —

   F   vanishes into the air

   G   gets wetter

   H   cools off

   J   dries off

---

5   Which of these is the best summary of the information in paragraphs 8–11?

   A   Red kangaroos are like dogs because they pant. They are like camels because they can go for long periods of time without drinking. They are like a lot of other animals. Kangaroos aren't active during the day.

   B   Red kangaroos are active during the night. This is when they search for food. They eat mostly plants because this gives them the water they need. Red kangaroos are not active during the day.

   C   Like dogs, red kangaroos pant when they get too hot. They also get water from the plants they eat. They have other ways of staying cool, too, and they need to stay cool because they live in a hot place.

   D   Red kangaroos have several ways of staying cool. They get a lot of water by eating mostly grasses and other plants. They are active mostly at night when it is cool. They cool off by licking their fur and panting.

---

6   In paragraph 14, the author says that a joey is born "not quite done" because —

   F   it has strong legs and tiny claws

   G   its mother takes care of it after it is born

   H   it has to develop inside its mother's pouch

   J   it hides in its mother's pouch when there is danger

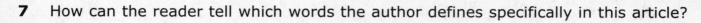
7 How can the reader tell which words the author defines specifically in this article?

   A   They are in italic type.

   B   They are in bold type.

   C   They are inside quotation marks.

   D   They are in all capital letters.

3.14	Identify what the author is trying to persuade the reader to think or do.
Ⓡ Figure 19(D)	Make inferences about text and use textual evidence to support understanding.
Ⓡ Figure 19(E)	Summarize information in text, maintaining meaning and logical order.

 ## Understand the TEKS

Writer's Purpose

Sometimes the writer's **purpose** is to **persuade**. The writer wants readers to do something or believe something. For example, the writer may want readers to volunteer to help others. Or the writer may want readers to adopt a pet from a shelter.

> **Words to Know**
> connotation
> evidence
> persuade
> position
> purpose

Position

The **position** is what the author wants to happen. It may be stated in the beginning of the text.

> Why buy a pet from a pet store when you can save a life by adopting a stray from a shelter?

Evidence

In the main part of the article, the author provides **evidence** to support the position. The evidence might be facts, details, examples, or stories. For example, the author might provide facts about the number of stray animals in shelters and what their lives are like.

• What evidence would you use to support the position that people should adopt pets from shelters?

_____

_____

Connotation

Some words have strong **connotations**. This means that they arouse strong feelings. A writer may use adjectives, adverbs, nouns, and even verbs with strong connotations to support a position.

> These *sad-eyed, homeless* creatures are *hungry* for love.

- How do the words *sad-eyed*, *homeless*, and *hungry* make you feel about the animals in shelters?

  _____

- What adjectives might you use to arouse sympathy for animals in shelters?

  _____

Structure

The author organizes the evidence to match the purpose. An author might show causes and effects. An author might organize the evidence from *least important idea* to *most important*. This way the reader is left thinking about the strongest point.

Conclusion

At the end, the author may summarize the main points. The writer may end with a call to action. This is what the writer wants readers to do.

Comprehension Tip

When you read persuasive text, ask yourself:

- What does the author want me to believe?

- What does the author want me to do?

- Has the author convinced me? Why or why not?

Guided Instruction

Read the passage below. Then answer the questions in the margin and complete the activities.

Music/Arts Connection

Why Athletes Should Take Ballet Lessons

by Sherie Garton

1   Picture a group of athletes. What comes to mind? Do you see rough-and-tumble activities? Do you think of touch football and wrestling? Probably, you don't think of ballet. But athletes can be helped by taking ballet lessons.

2   Ballet develops strength. Have you ever watched one dancer lift another dancer in the air? Have you seen one dancer catch another dancer? This takes strength. You need strength when you are slugging a baseball. You need it when you are serving in tennis. You need it when you are tackling another player in football or wrestling.

3   Ballet develops coordination. Picture the tricky steps dancers do. They look so graceful. Dancers make the steps looks so easy. Ballet can help athletes train their muscles to perform difficult moves.

"Why Athletes Should Take Ballet Lessons" by Sherie Garton

Guided Questions

Read the title. What is the author's purpose?

_____

_____

_____

_____

Read paragraph **1**. Highlight the sentence that tells the author's position.

What is the main point the author makes in paragraph **2**? Highlight the topic sentence.

_____

_____

_____

Read paragraph **3**. Highlight the topic sentence. How does the author support the idea that ballet develops coordination?

_____

_____

 Measuring Up to the Texas Essential Knowledge and Skills

4   Ballet develops balance. Try standing on one foot for thirty seconds. Then move your raised leg around in a circle. Do this five times. Did you lose your balance? Ballet dancers can do this and many even more difficult moves. They may twirl on their toes. They may walk on point. Practicing ballet helps everyone develop balance.

5   Today, some football teams practice ballet to help them in the field. Some tennis players take lessons to improve their game. Some skiers study ballet to help them on the slope. Ballet is one of the best ways for athletes to develop strength, coordination, and balance. So if you want to do well at sports, don't forget to take a ballet class.

Guided Questions

Read paragraph **4**. Highlight the topic sentence. Do the details in this paragraph convince you that ballet develops balance? Explain.

_____

_____

_____

_____

Read paragraph **5**. Find the sentence in which the author summarizes her three main points. Highlight it. Which three words tell what ballet develops?

_____

_____

Answer the following questions based on the passage you just read.

1. Read the sentences below from paragraph 5.

> *Today, some football teams practice ballet to help them in the field. Some tennis players take ballet lessons to improve their game. Some skiers study ballet to help them on the slope.*

What sources do you think the author may have used to find this information?

_____

_____

Elevate 2. Complete the outline below.

> Position: _____
>
> Point 1: _____
>
> Point 2: _____
>
> Point 3: _____

3. Did the writer convince you that athletes should take ballet classes? Provide reasons to back up your response.

_____

_____

_____

_____

Critical Thinking

4. *Should school vending machines sell candy, ice cream, and potato chips? Should they sell only healthy foods? These are foods like apples and bananas.* Take a stand on this issue. Then write a persuasive composition supporting your position. When you are done, meet with a partner. Read your persuasive composition aloud. Listen to your partner read aloud. Talk about how to make each composition even stronger.

Writing	☑
Research	☐
Listening and Speaking	☑
21st Century Skills: Teamwork	☑
Cross Curriculum Connection: Health	☑

On Your Own

Read the selection below. Then answer the questions that follow it.

Social Studies Connection

Make a Difference at Your School!

by Christy Gilbert

1   Don't believe anyone who tells you that your school can't make a difference in your community. You can. Here's how. Your school can recycle.

2   Look around your classroom right now. Here's what you might see: books, notebooks, papers, pencils and pens, computers. When you go to lunch, look around the lunchroom. Here's what you might see: glass bottles, plastic bottles, plastic trays, and a lot of left-over food. When you go home, look around your house. Here's what you might see: more glass or plastic bottles, a stove, a refrigerator, a computer, telephones, newspapers, and clothes. You might also see a car and a few bicycles.

3   Think about this. You're in the school lunchroom. You've just finished drinking a small bottle of grape juice. What do you do now? Do you throw the bottle in a recycle box? Or, do you just throw the bottle in a wastebasket? If your answer is the wastebasket, it's time to make a change! It's time to think about making a difference in your school. Here's what you and your friends can do.

Start a Recycling Program

4   You can get together with your classmates and make a recycling plan. Make it simple. Make it fun. Make it happen. Here are a few ideas to get you started.

5   Put together a team of students, teachers, and parents to oversee the program. Have a meeting. Discuss the school's goals. Talk about how you want to get everyone involved. Think of ways to get started.

Promote Recycling

6   Here are some ways to get your whole school involved in recycling.

- Start a recycling campaign. Put up posters around the school. On some posters, show what to recycle. On other posters, write recycling facts. Put cardboard boxes in every classroom. Students and teachers can recycle paper. Put boxes in the lunchroom to recycle aluminum cans and plastic bottles. Put a suggestion box in a convenient place where students can write other ideas for recycling.

"Make a Difference at Your School!" by Christy Gilbert

- Plan a Zero Garbage Day Challenge. Challenge students to wear a plastic bag around their waists. Whatever garbage they have, they MUST put in plastic bag. At the end of the day, see who has the least garbage! See who has the most!

- Here's another idea! Have a Detective Day! Appoint several detectives from each class. Have volunteers design garbage tickets. Whenever the detectives see students throwing away garbage, they can write them a garbage ticket. On the garbage tickets, write different "fines." The fines tell how the person must reduce garbage for one day or one week.

- Organize a field trip to a local recycling center so students can see just how much garbage communities are recycling.

- Get together a clothing drive. Encourage students to bring in clothes that they've outgrown but that are still in good condition. Students may also want to bring in toys or books they no longer want. Find a new home for all items by calling a local shelter, children's hospital, or library.

7   Okay, you've gotten your classmates involved. Now it's time for the hard work. You've got to keep the program going. Think of other projects that can grow out of your recycling program. You want to keep everyone interested! For example, do a science project. Build a school yard compost. A compost is an outside area where you throw left-over food from school lunches. You can also make a compost inside using a big bin. Eventually, you'll have rich soil and a lot of worms. Then plant a beautiful butterfly garden.

8   These are just a few suggestions. You probably can think of many more. Just remember this. The world is truly full of too much garbage. Every school must find ways to recycle. Schools can make a difference. The more schools that recycle, the more students and teachers will learn. Then they can pass along the recycling message to other schools. It is so important for human beings to protect this beautiful earth. This is our home. We need to take care of it. That means keeping wherever our little corner of the world is beautiful. If everyone does, the world will be a more beautiful place.

Answer the following questions based on the passage you just read.

1. Which of these tells the author's main purpose for writing this article?

    A To tell an entertaining story about recycling

    B To explain how to recycle

    C To give information about schools that recycle

    D To persuade students to make a difference by recycling

2. Read the paragraph below. Pay attention to all the details the author includes.

> *Look around your classroom right now. Here's what you might see: books, notebooks, papers, pencils and pens, computers. When you go to lunch, look around the lunchroom. Here's what you might see: glass bottles, plastic bottles, plastic trays, and a lot of left-over food. When you go home, look around your house. Here's what you might see: more glass or plastic bottles, a stove, a refrigerator, a computer, telephones, newspapers, and clothes. You might also see a car and a few bicycles.*

Now complete this chart. Put the things you might see in the correct category.

Classroom	Lunchroom	Home

3. What do all the items in the chart above have in common?

_____

4. Which of the following statements does not support the author's position in this article?

A Make sure you put your cans in the recycle bin.

B Let's keep the Earth a beautiful place.

C No one really cares what happens to the Earth.

D Recycle your clothes, toys, and bicycles.

 5. How does the author feel about the ability of students to make a difference? Support your answer with evidence from the article.

_____

_____

_____

Critical Thinking

6. Work as part of a problem-solving team. Identify a problem you think students in your school can help solve. Then develop a plan for solving this problem. Create a poster announcing the project that encourages students to get involved.

Writing	☑
Research	☐
Listening and Speaking	☑
21st Century Skills: Problem Solving	☑
Cross Curriculum Connection: Social Studies	☑

 Measuring Up to the Texas Essential Knowledge and Skills

Locate and Use Specific Information in Graphic Features

3.15(A) Follow and explain a set of written multi-step directions.
Ⓢ **3.15(B)** Locate and use specific information in graphic features of text.

Understand the TEKS

Instructions

Instructions tell you how to do something. They may tell how to put something together, how to play a game, or how to build a pet's home.

There are usually several parts to multiple-step instructions.

Introduction This part usually tells you something about the item you are going to put together. It might give you background information or tell you why you are going to enjoy something.

What You Will Need This part tells you what you will need to put together the item. This information is usually in a bulleted list. (Bullets look like this: •.)

What to Do This part tells you what you will need to do to put together the product. It may show you a diagram or it may show how to do something through pictures. The information in this part of the instructions is usually in steps.

• How do you think the author organizes these steps?

It is important to follow the steps in order. The steps may be numbered (1, 2, 3, 4, etc.).

After You Finish Often the instructions will include information about what to do after you have completed the steps. This part can include how to use the product or what you can do with the product when you are finished.

Graphic Features

Illustrations help you visualize what you are reading. They may be drawings or photographs.

Diagrams show in detail what something looks like. They may provide the parts of something. They may show how something works. Diagrams usually have labels pointing to specific parts.

> **Words to Know**
> caption
> diagram
> graph
> instructions
> introduction

Captions are the words by the illustration or diagram. The caption may be a simple title or it may provide an explanation.

A **graph** displays important data. It shows the relationship between two or more sets of numerals. This data can be shown in different ways. It can be a bar graph, a line graph, or a circle graph.

- Suppose the author used a bar graph to show how many skateboards were sold each month over a six-month period. What would the tallest or longest bar show?

_____

Comprehension Tip
Use both words and pictures when you read instructions. The illustrations help you visualize what to do.

 Guided Instruction

Read the passage below. Then answer the questions in the margin and complete the activities.

Science Connection

The Sands of Time

by Julienne Marlaire

When you visit the beach this summer, bring home some of that sand . . . then create your own minute timer!

What You'll Need:

- pattern
- scissors*
- sand
- glue or tape
- tall glass
- metal strainer
- wristwatch with a second hand or stopwatch

Guided Questions

Read the first paragraph. What can you use beach sand to make?

_____

"The Sands of Time" Published by SPIDER magazine, June 2004, Vol. 11, No 6, Copyright © 2004 by Julienne Marlaire

What to Do:

1   Cut out the pattern along the solid lines (including the center hole).

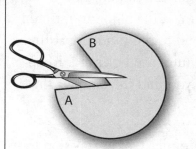

How are the pictures of the steps helpful?

_____

_____

2   Shape the circle into a funnel, overlapping section B on top of section A, and glue.

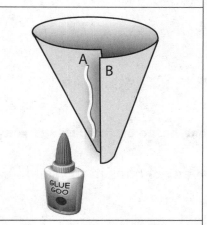

3   Run the sand through the strainer to get rid of any clumps.

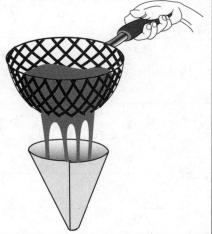

4   Set the funnel in the glass so that the funnel's hole is not more than 1/3 of the distance from the glass's rim to the bottom of the glass.

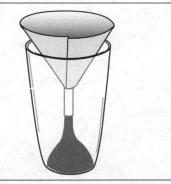

Read step **4**. Highlight how far the funnel's hole should be from the glass's rim. Then look at the illustration. Draw an arrow by the part that shows this.

5   Now experiment! Pour sand into the funnel. With your wristwatch, time how long it takes for the sand to flow through the funnel and into the cup. If the amount of time is less than one minute, add more sand to the funnel next time. Try again. If it's more than one minute, use less sand. Keep experimenting with the sand until you find the amount that exactly equals one minute.

*Scissors are sharp! Use them carefully. Get permission to use scissors from a parent or teacher.

Guided Questions

Read step **5**. What should you do if the sand runs through in less than one minute? Highlight this information.

Look at the footnote. What does the writer advise about scissors?

_____

_____

Answer the following questions based on the passage you just read.

1. How do you get rid of any clumps in the sand? Where is this information?

_____

_____

2. Fill in the chart below. Tell when you would first use each item.

What You'll Need	Step When You First Use It
• pattern	
• scissors	
• sand	
• glue or tape	
• tall glass	
• metal strainer	
• wristwatch with a second hand or stopwatch	

Elevate How could you reorder the list of what you'll need to make it easier to follow?

_____

_____

Elevate **3.** Which step will most likely take the longest? Explain why.

_____

_____

Critical Thinking

4. Work with a partner. Think about something you made for which you needed instructions. In sequence, tell your partner what you did. Then listen to your partner tell about something he or she made. Write up each other's instructions. Then review them for accuracy.

Writing	☑
Research	☐
Listening and Speaking	☑
Media Literacy	☐
21st Century Skills: Teamwork	☑
Cross Curriculum Connection	☐

 On Your Own

Read the selection below. Then answer the questions that follow it.

Science Connection

Fiddler Crab Pets

by Dora Gilbert

Male   Female

Fiddler crabs live along ocean beaches and salt-water marshes.

"Fiddler Crab Pets" by Dora Gilbert

1   Ever think about having a fiddler crab for a pet? Even though they are shy and may
not seem very friendly, they are really interesting to watch. They're also funny and
very cute, especially when they move sideways! The males have one oversized claw.
The large claw is used to fight off enemies. The smaller claw is used to eat food. The
females have two tiny claws, and they use both claws to stuff food into their mouths.
It's quite a sight! Some people say that when a fiddler crab uses its small claw to eat, it
looks like a bow moving across a fiddle! That's how it got its name!

2   You might think it's ridiculous to have a fiddler crab for a pet! No way you say!
Kids don't have fiddler crabs for pets, but look at this graph. It shows how many pets
were sold last year at Leaping Lizards Pet Store. Fiddler crabs were quite popular!

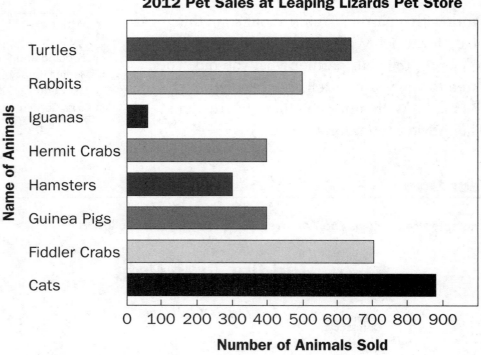

2012 Pet Sales at Leaping Lizards Pet Store

3   The nice part about having fiddler crabs for pets is that they are small. They only
grow to about 2 inches. Another interesting fact about fiddler crabs is that they molt.
That means they ease themselves out of their old shells when the shells have grown
too small. When they do this, you'll be able to see their two claws, along with their
eight legs curled up inside a new shell. Now that's cool!

4   It's not good to get only one fiddler crab though. They really like company so get
at least two. That way you'll be able to see two fiddler crabs molt instead of one.
Okay, I've convinced you, right? Now you want to know where to get them and how
to care for them. Here's what to do. Make a plan for buying your new pet. It might
look like this.

1. Research fiddler crabs on the Internet or at library. Learn everything that I can.
2. Find out how to set up aquarium. Draw a diagram.
3. Buy supplies—one 10-gallon aquarium, aquarium salt, sand, hair grass, shells, and long-handled net and scraper for cleaning aquarium. Find glow-in-the dark plants! DON'T FORGET SHRIMP PELLETS!
4. Set up aquarium before buying fiddler crabs.
5. Buy two fiddler crabs—one male and one female. Give them names!

5   Okay, you have a plan. You've researched fiddler crabs. You even found an article on having fiddler crabs as pets. That really convinced you. Now you're ready to buy two fiddler crabs, but first you need to draw a diagram for how to put your aquarium together. You can use the information that you researched to help you. The diagram might look like this:

Diagram of a Fiddler Crab Aquarium

6   The day before you get your fiddler crabs, mix together a salt-water solution. Use a one-gallon carton. Fill it with water. Add two and one-half teaspoons of aquarium salt, or sea salt, and mix. Let the mixture sit overnight. This is the water that crabs like best. They don't like fresh water. In fact, your fiddler crabs won't live long if you put them in tap water.

7   Okay, it's store time! Make a list of the supplies you need. Go to a pet store in the area where you live. Buy everything you need. When you choose the fiddler crabs, watch them for a few minutes to make sure they are active and alert.* Also, make sure they each have eight legs and two claws! Find a male and a female. Remember, the male has one claw that is bigger.

8   Now go home and make a home for your pets. Use your diagram to help you. First put in the sand. Be sure to make one side higher than the other. Build one side up to about 6 inches. You don't want to make the sand any higher because the crabs could climb out! Then slope the sand down to 1 inch. Next, slowly add the salt-water solution you made. Leave at least 3 to 4 inches of sand for the beach. Fiddler crabs don't like to spend all their time in water. They like beaches, and they like to dig in sand. Plant hair grass, and add shells. Now you can gently put your pets in their new home.

9   Remember to change the water, and clean the aquarium about every two weeks. Fiddler crabs do very well in aquariums. If they lose a leg or a claw, don't worry. Legs and claws grow back. Also, when they molt, don't take their old shells out of the aquarium because they will eat them. The old shells provide the fiddler crabs with a lot of calcium.

10   Feed them regularly but not too much! Besides shrimp pellets, they like fresh fish and sliced zucchini. Be sure to take some time to watch them. You can find out how they dig tunnels, and move sideways! If you get near a male fiddler crab, it will even wave at you with its oversized claw. Remember to wave back!

*NOTE: If you live in a coastal area, you may be able to find your own fiddler crabs along a beach or marsh at low tide. Be sure to always have an adult family member with you to help.

Answer the following questions based on the passage you just read.

1. Where do fiddler crabs live?

_____

In what two places can you find information about where fiddler crabs live?

_____

_____

(Elevate) 2. Look at the first illustration. What do you notice about the female and male fiddler crabs? How are they different?

_____

_____

3. From the graph, the reader can tell that the animals the pet store sold the fewest of in 2012 were —

    A turtles

    B iguanas

    C cats

    D guinea pigs

4. According to the list, what is the very first thing someone should do before buying a fiddler crab? Why is this so important?

_____

_____

_____

5. Which sentence from the article best helps explain why fiddler crabs are one of the pet store's better-selling products?

    A *They really like company so get at least two.*

    B *The nice part about having fiddler crabs for pets is that they are small.*

    C *Another interesting fact about fiddler crabs is that they molt.*

    D *The females have two tiny claws and they use both claws to stuff food into their mouths.*

6. Read the paragraph below.

> *Now go home and make a home for your pets. Use your diagram to help you. First put in the sand. Be sure to make one side higher than the other. Build one side up to about 6 inches. You don't want to make the sand any higher because the crabs could climb out! Then slope the sand down to 1 inch. Next, slowly add the salt-water solution you made. Leave at least 3 to 4 inches of sand for the beach. Fiddler crabs don't like to spend all their time in water. They like beaches, and they like to dig in sand. Plant hair grass, and add shells. Now you can gently put your pets in their new home.*

Complete the chart. Fill in the steps for making an aquarium in order.

Step 1: Put in the sand.

Step 2: _____

Step 3: _____

Step 4: Slowly add salt-water solution.

Step 5: _____

Step 6: _____

Step 7: Put the fiddler crabs in their new home.

Critical Thinking

7. Work with a partner. Prepare a demonstration showing how to make an aquarium. First decide what equipment you will need. Then divide up the responsibility of demonstrating the steps. Write the text for your steps. Then rehearse. Make sure each of you speaks clearly and audibly. When you are satisfied, present your demonstration to the class.

Writing	☑
Research	☐
Listening and Speaking	☑
21st Century Skills: Teamwork	☑
Cross Curriculum Connection: Science	☑

Read the selection. Then choose the best answer to each question.

Presto Change-O!
A Butterfly Appears

by Chris Dietel
from Highlights magazine

1   I found a caterpillar and put it in a cage. I gave it plenty of food—the same kind of plant that it was eating when I found it. Then I watched it closely. Maybe the caterpillar would change into a butterfly right before my eyes. I even had a special camera to photograph it.

One day the caterpillar stopped eating.

2   It searched for a new place to form a protective shell. It is called a <u>chrysalis</u>. The caterpillar climbed up to a high spot on a stick. Then, using special glands in its mouth, it made thin strands of silk. The caterpillar made a silk loop and attached it to the stick. It slipped into the loop. Later, the caterpillar's upper body hung out from the stick. Its lower end was attached by a silk pad.

The caterpillar slowly changed shape.

3   During the next two days, the caterpillar's organs and tissues were changing inside its body. On the outside, it still looked like a caterpillar. Then it began to twitch a lot. I waited patiently with my camera.

4   Finally the caterpillar stretched its body. Its skin split down the middle behind its head. The caterpillar wiggled back and forth. Its skin split some more. Shedding its old skin, the caterpillar had a new form. It was a green chrysalis.

The chrysalis wriggled like a worm.

5   Its old skin bunched up at the bottom. Then it fell to the ground. The new chrysalis had appeared in only a few minutes. In the next few hours the chrysalis hardened into its final shape and turned a darker color.

"Presto Change-O! A Butterfly Appears" by Chris Dietel, Copyright © 2004 by Highlights for Children, Inc., Columbus, Ohio

6   After two weeks the chrysalis suddenly changed to almost black. When the morning sun shone on the chrysalis, it began to twist back and forth. Then the top half split open. I could see the bright yellow of a new creature.

In seconds the butterfly popped out.

7   It used its new long, thin legs to walk up the stick. At first, its wings were crumpled. They quickly expanded as the butterfly pumped blood into the veins of each wing. In a few minutes, the wings were full, revealing their bright colors. I was happy to see the butterfly fly off.

8   The butterfly will use its bright colors to attract a mate. Together they will produce eggs. The eggs will hatch into more caterpillars. And those caterpillars will eat, grow, and then—presto-chang-o— more butterflies will appear.

Stage	Picture	Time to Change into Next Form
Egg		5–10 days
Larva (Caterpillar)		3 weeks
Pupa (Chrysalis)		2–3 weeks
Adult (Butterfly)		

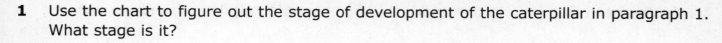

1 Use the chart to figure out the stage of development of the caterpillar in paragraph 1. What stage is it?

  A Egg

  B Larva

  C Pupa

  D Adult

---

2 The main purpose of paragraphs 2–4 is to —

  F give information about caterpillars

  G tell why a caterpillar splits its skin

  H show how a caterpillar makes silk

  J explain how a caterpillar turns into a chrysalis

---

3 The headings tell the reader that this article is organized —

  A to show the sequence of events in the life cycle of a butterfly

  B to compare and contrast a butterfly and a caterpillar

  C to give the reasons a caterpillar turns into a butterfly

  D to move from the most important event in a butterfly's life to the least important

4 The reader can conclude that the first signal that a caterpillar is ready to change form is —

F it grows wings

G it stops eating

H it makes silk

J it hangs upside down

5 Which of these phrases is the best clue to the meaning of <u>chrysalis</u> in paragraph 2?

A *protective shell*

B *new place*

C *special glands*

D *strands of silk*

6 The different colors of a chrysalis indicate —

F how far along it is in its development

G what color the butterfly developing inside it is

H how much sun it gets

J how many butterflies are inside it

Image Acknowledgments

Mastery Education (formerly Peoples Education) has made every effort to obtain permission for the reprinting of all selections contained herein. If any owner of copyrighted material is not acknowledged herein, please contact the publisher for proper acknowledgement in all future editions and reprinting of this book.

pp. 4–5, photos, © Unteroffizier/Dreamstime.com; p. 7, illustration, Shutterstock.com, © Maria Bell; p. 38, photo, courtesy of Shutterstock.com, © AISPIX by Image Source; p. 50, photo, Shutterstock.com, © João Encarnacão; p. 200, photo, Shutterstock.com, © idreamphoto; p. 211, illustration, Shutterstock.com, © Johnny Sajem; p. 233, illustration, Shutterstock.com, © djapart; p. 293, photo, Shutterstock.com, © George Burba; p. 311, photo, Courtesy of the Jane Goodall Institute; p. 324 (top), photos.com, a division of Getty Images. All rights reserved; p. 324 (bottom), Shutterstock.com, © Phil Kestell; p. 325, Shutterstock.com, © Anna Ts; p. 360, photos.com, a division of Getty Images. All rights reserved; p. 368, photo, © 2012 by Meike Marks/Photos.com, a division of Getty Images. All rights reserved; p. 369, photo, Shutterstock.com, © Katarina Christenson.

Scoring Rubrics for Written Responses

These generic scoring rubrics can be used in the evaluation of many types of written responses.

2-Point Rubric

2 Points	A 2-point response is accurate and complete, and fulfills all the requirements of the task. Necessary support and/or examples are included, and the information given is clearly text-based. Any extensions beyond the text are relevant to the task.
1 Point	A 1-point response includes some correct information, but may be too general or overly specific. Some of the support and/or examples may be incomplete or omitted.
0 Points	A 0-point response is inaccurate, confused, and/or irrelevant, or the student failed to respond to the task.

4-Point Rubric

4 Points	A 4-point response demonstrates an understanding of the task, completes all requirements, and provides an insightful or creative response to the prompt. Language and organization are sophisticated. Few or no errors in grammar or mechanics exist.
3 Points	A 3-point response demonstrates an understanding of the task, completes all requirements, and provides an adequate and comprehensive response to the prompt. Language is appropriate, and organization is logical. Few errors in grammar and mechanics exist, and those do not interfere with meaning.
2 Points	A 2-point response demonstrates a partial understanding of the task, completes some of the requirements, and provides an unfinished, inconsistent, or otherwise flawed response to the prompt. Language is simplistic, and organization may be hard to follow. Errors in grammar and mechanics exist.
1 Point	A 1-point response demonstrates minimal understanding of the task, fails to complete all requirements, and only tangentially refers to the prompt. Language is simplistic or inappropriate, and organization is illogical. Multiple errors in grammar and mechanics interfere with meaning.
0 Points	A 0-point response is irrelevant, illegible, incomprehensible, or not in English.

Copying is permitted..   *Measuring Up* to the Texas Essential Knowledge and Skills